Praise for *Animal Voices*

Dawn Brunke takes us along on her incredible journey as she learns how to communicate with animals. She teaches us that animals are our teachers—they teach us to trust ourselves, and as a result of that trust we find out who we are. Whether you are a skeptic or a believer, *Animal Voices* will give you valuable new insight into the world of telepathic animal communication.

Carol Gurney,
animal communicator and author of *The Language of Animals*

Powerful! Moving! A compelling journey reminding us that the wisdom of the animal kingdom offers a window to our own inner mysteries. Through personal experience and intimate case histories, Dawn Brunke has masterfully crafted a "must read" for skeptics and animal lovers, alike.

Gregg Braden,
author of *Awakening to Zero Point, Walking Between the Worlds,* and
The Isaiah Effect: Decoding Our Future through the Lost Science of Prophecy

Animal Voices cuts through the shadow of our projections and beliefs about animals with both warmth and wit. These loving and wise messages from our feathered, furred, and exoskeleton-clad kin will move hearts and minds in new directions, inspiring even the most skeptical reader. Provocative, healing, and a must read for anyone who has opened his or her heart to another species.

Joanne Lauck,
author of *The Voice of the Infinite in the Small:
Re-visioning the Insect-Human Connection*

This is an important and amazing book! With grace and eloquence, Dawn Brunke takes the reader on a wondrous journey into the rich potential of the human-animal connection. Packed with profound insights and joyful surprises, *Animal Voices* is educational, entertaining, and extremely pertinent to the urgent need on our planet for a deeper understanding of all life.

Steve Johnson,
flower essence therapist and author of *The Essence of Healing*

Animal Voices

Telepathic Communication in the Web of Life

Dawn Baumann Brunke

Bear & Company
Rochester, Vermont

Bear & Company
One Park Street
Rochester, Vermont 05767
www.InnerTraditions.com

Bear & Company is a division of Inner Traditions International

Library of Congress Cataloging-in-Publication Data

Brunke, Dawn Baumann.
  Animal voices : telepathic communication in the web of life / by Dawn
Baumann Brunke.
      p. cm.
Includes bibliographical references.
  ISBN 1-879181-91-6
  1. Human-animal communication. 2. Telepathy. I. Title.
  QL776 .B78 2002
  133.8'9—dc21
                              2002004407

Printed and bound in the United States at Lake Book Manufacturing, Inc.

10 9 8 7 6 5 4

Text design and layout by Rachel Goldenberg
This book was typeset in Adobe Garamond with Pablo as the display typeface

For more information about animal communication please visit the author's Web site at www.animalvoices.net.

Contents

Part Three

A Question of Perspective

Part Four

The Call for Transformation

Part Five

Into the Shadow

Part Six

Shadow and Beyond

Part Seven

Remembering the Sacred Web

Giraffe in Africa. Photo by Dawn Brunke.

Acknowledgments

This is a book of many voices. My heartfelt appreciation goes to all who have contributed, whether their names appear within these pages or not.

Thanks to communicators and friends: Chrys Long-Ago, Carole Devereux, Jane Hallander, Sam Louie, Penelope Smith, Raphaela Pope, Mary Getten, Teresa Wagner, Marta Williams, Ilizabeth Fortune, Joan Ocean, Carol Gurney, Morgine Jurdan, Nedda Wittels, Nancie LaPier, Marcia Ramsland, Diana Roth, Toraya Ayres, Anita Curtis, Jeri Ryan, Sharon Callahan, Jim Worsley, Laura Simpson, and Jude White Bear.

Thanks to manuscript readers who offered valuable feedback, suggestions, and support through various revisions: Sam Louie, Nancie LaPier, Toraya Ayres, Jackie Rahm, Charlie Renideo, Delisa Renideo, Joanne Lauck, A.B., and my mother, Carol Edler Baumann.

Thanks for written words of inspiration and reassurance: J. Allen Boone and Strongheart, Penelope Smith, Brugh Joy, Walt Whitman, and Michael Roads.

Thanks to all the good people at Inner Traditions/Bear & Company, in particular to my editor Laura Schlivek, to Peri Champine for a great cover, and to Jon Graham in Acquisitions, who endured my persistence. Thanks to my copy editor, Victoria Sant'Ambrogio. Thanks also to Jackie Kosednar, publisher of *Alaska Wellness,* for faith and trust.

Thanks to my parents for lifelong support. And to family and friends for sharing the excitement. Thanks to my husband, Bob, for unwavering encouragement, and to my daughter, Alyeska, for irrepressible joy, laughter, and love of animals.

A deep and profound thanks to all of the animal beings and spirits who started this. This book never would have happened without you—the many individual animals and animal groups who so generously contributed insight, wisdom, eloquence, and humor. Thanks to the birds on the bush, the goldfish, moths, mosquitoes, and spiders, who presented challenging information just when I needed it most.

Finally, an extra special thanks to my very good pals, Barney, Max, and Zak, who sat with me daily during the writing of this book, who nudged me on to awakening with an encouraging soft paw, and who continue to remind me that life, and death, are grand adventures indeed.

Spider web. Photo by Dawn Brunke.

Introduction
The Web

I don't understand it. But for that matter I don't understand how a spider learned to spin a web in the first place. When the words appeared, everyone said they were a miracle. But nobody pointed out that the web itself is a miracle.

E. B. White, Charlotte's Web

As a child, one of my favorite books was *Charlotte's Web* by E. B. White. I especially loved Charlotte, a quick-witted gray spider, who spun words into her web in an attempt to save her friend Wilbur the pig from an untimely death. "Some pig!" boldly exclaimed the words in Charlotte's web. "Radiant" and "Humble" were other adjectives Charlotte used to describe Wilbur. Most of the farmers and townspeople believed the words were miracles, supernaturally inspired messages that could not be explained. They looked to the pig, certain that he was the one behind the mystery. Charlotte smiled, delighted that her trick had worked.

As Charlotte explained to Wilbur, spiders have been weaving webs for generation upon generation. "I don't know how the first spider in the early days of the world happened to think up this fancy idea of spinning a web, but she did, and it was clever of her, too," said Charlotte. I thought it was equally clever of Charlotte to be a spider who understood how words could so greatly influence humans.

There are some who believe that spiders spin webs not merely from instinct, but with the collective memory of all spiders who have ever spun webs since that first spider in the early days. As each spider spins a web, the idea goes, it becomes easier for all spiders to create webs, spinning with less effort and the potential for greater intricacy.

Some believe that human evolution follows a similar path. As a new talent is discovered by one individual, others may simultaneously or soon thereafter find the talent within themselves. As more individuals engage in the new behavior, it becomes easier for others. Call it the hundredth monkey, the hundredth spider, or even the hundredth human; it is all a variation of the same pattern in the grand Web.

The Web of Life reminds us that every thought and action affects everyone and everything. An idea comes to one of us and a thread on the invisible web quivers as circumstances conspire to bring events, ideas, people, animals, and countless other forms of assistance into our lives.

Although this book began with a simple interest in animal communication, it has become a widespread collaboration. More than two dozen communicators and one hundred animals have shared their energy, wisdom, humor, and blessings for the completed work to unfold.

Just as the barnyard animals brought Charlotte word suggestions to display on her web, just as E. B. White collaborated with the subtle energy of a wonderful gray spider he called Charlotte, we are all, consciously or unconsciously, working together to create something quite spectacular, something that propels us into a new creation of Being.

How do we begin our journey? Often, it is not where we are going but what we find along the way that holds the key to our true adventure. It is frequently the diversions and strange circumstances that lead us to the most extraordinary places—heartfelt, humorous, amazing, sometimes barely believable.

In 1995, my husband and I moved to Alaska. We had no definite plans, neither one of us had jobs, but away we went, toting our young daughter, two dogs, and a 20-foot trailer. Not long after arriving, I picked up a copy of *Alaska Wellness*, a magazine focused on alternative healing and the connection of mind, body, and spirit. A tiny notice in the back advertised for an editor. Though I had never done any professional editing, I applied and, to my surprise, was hired.

One of my first duties involved sorting through a box of articles not yet published. One in particular caught my eye. It was written by Chrys Long-Ago, a woman who claimed to talk with animals. Not only that, the animals talked back to her! I was fascinated by the story, which detailed Chrys's conversations with a guinea pig named Geisha.

When I later interviewed Chrys, she told me about J. Allen Boone, a writer whose primary teacher in animal communication had been an award-winning German shepherd war dog and film star named Strongheart. I found two of Boone's books and read them with a growing sense of wonder, amazement, and deep respect.

Questions about human-animal communication filled my mind. Was it really possible to have an intelligent conversation with an animal? Did animals truly have a capacity to understand the world beyond themselves? Did they have a sense of spirituality? Did they know something we didn't? What would animals tell us, both about themselves and about us, if we approached them with serious intent? Was a deeper, more vital relationship between humans and animals—and all of life—something we had forgotten about, something we had left behind in the course of our evolution?

Through the Internet, I found Buddy, a horse who works with communicator Carole Devereux. Buddy was the first animal who agreed to an interview with me. It was a curious set-up: I posed my questions to Carole, who connected with Buddy, asked my questions, wrote down his responses, and read them back to me. A part of me couldn't help but wonder if the whole thing wasn't one quick step away from farce, though another part of me was exhilarated, feeling as if I had just entered a new world. Carole put me in touch with other animals and communicators, who gave me more names, and so the web grew.

It soon became apparent that what I was involved in was something much greater than myself. As I thought about it, meditated on it, dreamed about it, I realized with growing surprise that not only was this something I had chosen; it was something that had also chosen me.

Ask for something with the deepest part of your being and the universe responds. This is a thrilling realization, though you often discover that the universe may respond in a way that is not exactly in line with what you had in mind.

My central focus had been asking communicators to be the medium through which animals might answer the basic question, "What would you most like humans to know?"

It was all going quite well until Marta Williams, a communicator I had been interviewing over the phone, stopped me short. "If you're going to write a book about this, maybe you should try it too," Marta suggested gently. A deep sense of unease shuddered through me. Surely I would not be asked to do *that!* It was one thing to interview animals through professional communicators, but certainly I would never be talking directly with animals myself!

A few weeks later, I experienced my first direct communication with a flock of birds. It was an exceptional event for me, one that changed the focus of this book dramatically and brought me to a deeper place of understanding how this thing called animal communication really works.

From my initial opening with the birds, there was no stopping the flow of communications I received, though I sometimes considered trying. Most often it happened spontaneously, when I was least expecting it.

Deeper and deeper the process unfolds. Are we ever really in control? I no longer believe that I was the one who had the idea to write this book. There was mystery afoot, and the plan was presented to me through a series of challenges. Was I willing to let go of an old worldview in order to learn something new? Was I ready to begin living with a sense of wonder? Was I willing to trust my experiences as so many others seemed to trust me?

My heart has been touched by all who speak in this book as well as by those who have offered feedback, help, and support. It reminds me of the web, of Charlotte, and how all manner of extraordinary events conspire to create a world in which a pig and a spider can become best of friends. Are we ready to see that we, too, are capable of creating such a world? As so many animals remind us time and again, we are all more intimately connected than we can imagine. Perhaps more than anything, this book is about trusting that connection, trusting the flow of life as we open to and feel the deeper union between each one of us and All That Is.

A special group of animals remarked, "It is essential that humans begin to awaken to their connection with all of life. As you open to animals, you will also open deeper to yourselves. This is one of the roots of your return home."

May we open to this journey. May we trust ourselves and the unfolding of our paths just a little bit more. And may we all remember, ourselves and each other, human and animal alike, within the sacred web of life.

Part One

Through the Unknown, Remembered Gate

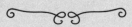

For You

Briana (horse) ~ Anita Curtis

Animal communication is very important now and in the upcoming years. The lives of humans must expand by communication with all life or they cannot grow spiritually. It is not for the animals—we already communicate. It is for you.

1

The Journey Home

In the very earliest time,
when both people and animals lived on earth,
a person could become an animal if he wanted to
and an animal could become a human being.
Sometimes they were people
and sometimes animals
and there was no difference.
All spoke the same language.

Netsilik Eskimo Song

In the larger expanse of human history, communicating with animals is really nothing new. Our ancestors did it. Though, of course, the world was different then; humans had not yet forgotten. We were still connected to all—land and sky and water, wolf and buffalo, raven and sea turtle and spider and all other living things, which was everything because everything was alive. There was a single language. Do you remember? It was a language of being, where the smallest was joined to the largest, all things not apart, but a part of the All.

"Life to these ancients was an all-inclusive kinship in which nothing was meaningless, nothing unimportant, and from which nothing could be excluded," wrote J. Allen Boone. "Every living thing was seen as a partner in a universal enterprise. Each had an individual contribution to make to the general good which it, and it alone, could supply."[1] By means of this commonly shared language, all beings were able to share their thoughts, feelings, and unique perspectives of the world.

This was a long time ago. It was way before Once Upon a Time, though even then a little bit of the connection remained. Animals continued to act as divine messengers throughout the ages. Showing up as friends, tricksters, and supernatural guides in our fairy tales, myths, stories, and dreams, they urged us onward, calling our attention to that essential piece of the puzzle that finally led us to shout, *Aha!* It was the animals who kept trying to bring us home.

Things are different now. We've come so far, though in the grand scheme of things,

7

perhaps we're not so far from where we started. Some would say our journey of evolution hasn't necessarily been for the better; others point out that change, no matter where it takes us, is all a learning experience.

"We shall not cease from exploration," wrote T. S. Eliot,

And the end of all our exploring
Will be to arrive where we started
And know the place for the first time.
Through the unknown, remembered gate
When the last of the earth left to discover
Is that which was the beginning . . . [2]

There is no denying that in today's world the idea of literally talking with animals seems a bit strange. The notion feels new and different because it's been so long since we consciously did such a thing. We have separated ourselves so far from the web of life that some might wonder why, even if we could communicate with animals, would we want to? For we have generally been taught that most animals are incapable of thought and intelligence. What could anyone possibly learn from talking with an animal?

"Whenever I was properly humble and willing to let something besides a human be my instructor, these various four-legged, six-legged, and no-legged fellows shared priceless wisdom with me," wrote Boone. "They taught me that perfect understanding and perfect co-operation between the human and all other forms of life is unfailing whenever the human really does his required part.[3]

Boone did his part, not only learning from animals but also helping humans to learn. Even now, nearly fifty years since his book *Kinship with All Life* was printed, many in the field quote this distinguished man, citing his writing as a source of both inspiration and validation.

Boone was a direct descendent of Daniel Boone and an acquaintance of Houdini— one of the few, in fact, who ever got the magician to reveal some of his illusions. For many years he worked as a reporter and Washington correspondent.

It was only after Boone moved to California and became involved in the film industry that he started talking with animals. Blame it on Hollywood. Boone never called himself a communicator, nor did he take lessons from a human. Rather, his teacher came in the form of a remarkable dog named Strongheart.

Strongheart was a German shepherd who became a leading Hollywood film star in the 1920s, a forerunner to other canine stars such as Rin Tin Tin and Lassie. Strongheart came from a long line of blue-ribboned shepherd dogs in Germany, known for their physical strength and expertise as police and war dogs. Strongheart had been trained as a war dog during World War I.

Two of Boone's friends, a playwright and a Hollywood animal trainer, were responsible for bringing Strongheart to America. When both needed to leave on business, it was Boone who accepted the job of caring for Strongheart. The day Strongheart arrived at his doorstep, Boone was given explicit instructions never to talk down to the dog. This was a million-dollar movie star, after all.

The first lesson between man and dog took place that evening, when Strongheart decided to sleep on the bed with his rear end facing Boone's face, a position Boone didn't favor. After a few sharp words and several minor battles over position, ending with

Strongheart. Photo courtesy of Bianca Leonardo.

Boone being knocked out of bed, Strongheart pulled open the curtains that covered the French windows in the room. It was a deliberate action that startled Boone into realizing that Strongheart, with his military training, desired to face the direction of most possible danger.

Boone wrote that there was no sleep for him that night. What he found most astonishing was that while he had spoken to Strongheart in a human language of thoughts and feelings expressed through verbal sound symbols, the dog had been able to understand perfectly. Not only that, but Strongheart had answered in his kind of language and, with keenly penetrating dog wisdom, made it possible for Boone to understand him, too.

Thus began Boone's adventure to find out more about Strongheart as an individual and "try in all possible ways to discover how we were related as individual expressions of life in a highly intelligent universe."[4] No small feat.

Boone went on to write several books about his relationship with Strongheart and other animal acquaintances. Along the way, what he discovered about humanity was this: "We are living too much on the fringe of ourselves, floundering about, fractured and frustrated, in mere superficialities, instead of being at home *inside* first."[5]

Again and again we find it is all a journey home.

"My focus has been on helping people come home to realize who they are and to commune with all life," says Penelope Smith, one of the leading teachers in the animal communication field today. "The thrust is to restore this communion, this ability to be at one with all life, whether it's animals, plants, rocks, the earth, the air, all the elements, and to realize that everything is alive and we are all in kinship."

Among those who communicate with animals—which entails not only talking, but listening too—is the agreement that once you begin, you can't turn back. It may seem like a small step at first, a short chat with a dog, an exchange of greetings with some birds; but, inevitably, the ramifications—and rewards—are enormous.

Like Boone, many communicators have discovered that the path begins unexpectedly. Not only that, the road is frequently bumpy, meandering, and unfamiliar. Early on, one must trespass the boundaries of conventional, polite society, because we all know that normal people do not hold conversations with animals. Further on are other roadblocks: chasms of incredulity and mirages of self-doubt. But so too are there vistas of wonder, moments when everything is real and true and singing brightly within one's soul.

So, how does the journey begin? And how does the human reconnection with animals reflect the larger picture of who we are? In the following pages, six professional animal communicators share their stories of how the adventure began.

Nedda Wittels has an M.A. in American history and an M.S. in teaching. She was a high school teacher for ten years and spent another ten years in the computer industry. Like many communicators, Nedda felt connected to animals all her life. She remembers talking with animals as a child, though told by adults that she must have been imagining these conversations. This didn't stop Nedda from conversing with animals; but she stopped telling others about it. As time went on, she hid her talent from herself, accepting the idea that the conversations were just pretend.

When Nedda first read Penelope Smith's *Animal Talk*, she thought she would learn to communicate with animals by following the guidelines in the book. Instead, to her astonishment, she realized that she was already receiving animal communications and had been doing so all her life. "Most importantly," Nedda said, "I was reminded that animals are sentient beings capable of the full range of emotions and spiritual qualities, such as loyalty, honesty, patience, and joy."

Sam Louie is an attorney with a law degree from Columbia University. Early in his career, Sam became very close to his dog, Heathcliff. One morning on the way to work, Sam heard Heathcliff say, "Don't leave me." Sam thought he was working too hard. But he soon heard additional messages from Heathcliff as well as from others.

"I started to become hypersensitive," said Sam. "For example, while I had never noticed dead animals on the road before, I started to see them. When I saw a road kill, I could actually see the animal getting hit, the whole traumatic scene."

Searching for teachers to help him learn to filter what he was seeing, Sam studied animal communication techniques with Jeri Ryan and Penelope Smith.

"I was a public defender for ten years in a pretty rough county with high volume crime, lots of murder," Sam told me. "Much of why I decided to work with animals rather than humans was to get away from all the ugliness of human life. But what I ended up learning is

Sam Louie. Photo by Stacey Shulman.

that while I was helping animals to some extent, it's really humans I work with. I'm helping humans find peace of mind and helping them to connect."

Sam found that in order to work with animals, he needed to confront his own prejudices and fears. "My belief is that all creatures are made of the same thing," said Sam. "If one type of dog, like my dog, is worthy of love, then all dogs are worthy of love. And if humans and animals are made of the same soul essence, then that leads to the conclusion that all humans are worthy of love. That's a lesson we might all learn from our animals—that each one of us is worthy of ultimate, unconditional love. This work is teaching me about accepting humans for who they are."

Teresa Wagner has a master's degree in counseling psychology and worked as a manager at a Fortune 500 company for ten years. Like many communicators, she talked to animals as a child and never thought it strange.

Wanting to fit in as a teenager and be like everyone else, however, Teresa squelched her abilities. It wasn't until much later, while reading Machaelle Small Wright's *Behaving as if the God in All Life Mattered,* that Teresa reconnected to the animal kingdom. "It was a glorious remembering, as if I had awoken from amnesia."

While on a whale-watching trip off Cape Cod, Teresa was ecstatic when a humpback whale came to the boat and stayed for nearly an hour. "I felt a great love going back and forth between us," said Teresa. "I was changed. I kept telling the whale,

'Thank you for coming' and 'I love you.' And all of a sudden I heard the whale talking back, with great love and great wisdom."

Thus began a journey of conscious remembering that wasn't always easy. When she lost her job and identity as a successful career professional, Teresa was pushed to focus inward. She recalls,

> One of my guides, a mountain lion, kept telling me, "Your energy in this life-time is very much like mine, to be a mountain lion, to be strong and travel far. But right now you need to heal and be more like an iris." He told me this as I was walking in the forest, right as I came across some iris flowers. I almost fainted, because I heard it and there were the irises! He said, "Don't think you are being inactive or useless because it seems like life is standing still. You need to trust that you will get all you need to nurture and help you grow, just as an iris bulb does." So, for that time, I was an iris.
>
> It was during those iris years that I met people who were called animal com-municators. I didn't know such a thing existed. I thought I was just this weirdo who talked to animals. I started taking courses. What was fun for me, and also a little surprising, was that it was like breathing. The courses confirmed what I was already doing.
>
> I believe that we choose our basic life circumstances when we choose an incar-nation. I think my soul knew that painful healing opportunities were going to be here for me this time, so the support of all of nature was here for me also. The silver lining in this one little lifetime for me is, how can I not talk to animals? How can I not trust nature and use nature and tap into its healing power? Be-cause it was there for me; it was the first thing I learned.

Mary Getten is a naturalist and coordinator of a marine mammal stranding alert net-work. Though she had always loved animals, dreaming of sitting with Jane Goodall in the jungle, Mary's involvement with animals began as an adult volunteer at a marine mammal center.

Working with stranded seals, sea lions, and other cetaceans, Mary found it frus-trating not to know what was wrong with an animal. After taking a class in animal communication, Mary felt a new frustration when she found that people weren't ready to listen to her. "I dropped the communication at that point because it was too upset-ting to have information I couldn't use."

Later moving to the San Juan Islands in Washington, Mary immersed herself in the world of animals. She volunteered at a whale museum and wildlife rehab center. As a naturalist on a whale watch boat, Mary came to know certain whales quite well.

Still, she wanted to know them even better and once again felt that if she could talk to animals, it would make a difference. "As the universe would have it, I received a flyer about animal communication," Mary said. This time, people were ready to listen. After taking classes and refining her abilities, Mary opened a practice as an animal consultant and began her own investigation into the world of orcas.

Mary Getten.

Nancie LaPier was first taught to communicate with animals by the world of nature. Before that, she was a legal secretary and the manager of an accounting firm. As did so many communicators, Nancie felt connected to animals since childhood. Her attempts to communicate with them, however, began later in life. Nancie told me it started when one of her parrots began denuding himself. Although she tried traditional veterinary procedures and behavioral approaches, none were successful.

One day while in a relaxed, meditative state, Nancie sensed that the parrot's problem was spiritual in nature. She felt motivated to draw upon skills she had learned about the auric field twenty years before but had not practiced since. Approaching the parrot, she could indeed feel "knots" in his auric field. Even more interesting, Nancie found she could clear the knots.

The experience stimulated Nancie to look deeper into nature and the animal kingdom. At the time, she was living on seven acres of land in a state forest and was often outdoors in a meditative frame of mind. "I began to question many of the things I saw," Nancie told me. "For instance, one time I saw a woodpecker slam into a sliding glass door. He immediately flew to a tree and hung onto the trunk. I watched and asked in my mind, 'What's the purpose of that?' Very clearly, I heard that he was drawing healing energy from the tree in an attempt to regenerate himself."

Finding that experience intriguing—"intriguing that I got the answer, and also intriguing that the animal kingdom apparently has innate intelligence on how to survive in nature that human beings have lost touch with"—Nancie experienced an awakening.

"I began to see faces in the woods looking back at me," said Nancie. "The faces were varied: anything from Mark Twain to religious figures to Native Americans to half-human, half-animal faces. They were huge, not the size of a human being, but huge faces looking out at me. They were not saying anything really, just looking, making themselves available."

Nancie became a student of nature and spent three years alone learning from animals, nature spirits, and other guides. "I had no confirmation on any of this. I talked to my guides about wanting to find a teacher to work with, and kept hearing, 'You can't. You need to keep going inside. This is something that you need to learn for yourself.'

"I now know it was a very important thing to have happen, on different levels, for different reasons. One day, attempting to follow the threads of various metaphysical ideas, I threw up my hands and said, 'My God, I feel like a jack of all trades and master of none.' I then heard my guides say to me, 'No, you're the master of one.' I said, 'What?' And they said, 'One! O-N-E!' I understood that to be not one, singular, but oneness, as in unity.

"So, that was my path," Nancie sighed. "It has been an interesting path, something that I had to walk with a lot of faith to know that I wasn't going over the edge, losing my mind."

Marta Williams is a naturalist and environmentalist. She has master's degrees in both biology and systematic ecology from San Francisco State University. When she first heard there were people who taught animal communication, she was in the White Mountains of California searching for a vision to help the earth.

"For me that has always been of highest importance," Marta told me. "I am deeply upset by the destruction of the earth that is happening in our time. For now, I feel I can best serve the earth by helping people reconnect with the other life forms on this earth. I see animal communication as a powerful tool to open up communication and relationship between humans and our forgotten relatives. I believe this is the vision I received on my quest.

"To me, the earth is what is most sacred. My spiritual development has been led by teachers of the earth: shamans, animals, trees, mountains, deep ecologists, and the people of the many ancient cultures that still exist today who show us a better way to walk on the face of the earth."

A self-described highly sensitive person, Marta knew from a young age how other humans and animals were feeling. It wasn't until she studied animal telepathy that Marta realized that although she always believed animal communication was possible, she did not, until then, know it was real.

"Learning to do telepathy was a major spiritual journey for me, involving learning to trust myself and my own counsel and learning to be comfortable being a psychic," said Marta. "I absolutely hold this belief to be true: we are all psychics, we are all telepaths, and we all talk to animals. We have only to learn to be conscious of our abilities to use them and direct them."

Animal communicators are a remarkably diverse crowd. Many come from formal teaching backgrounds or have training in human and animal bodywork. Communicators include naturalists, healers, therapists, teachers, writers, speakers, PhD's, even a lawyer. What are a bunch of well-educated people such as these doing talking with animals?

Marta Williams.

Penelope Smith suggests that as humans begin to create deeper, more profound relationships with animals, the results will be nothing short of earth-altering. "It will change the evolution of the planet. It will change our destroying of the ecosystem into our loving the whole system, loving ourselves as part of the web of life instead of seeing ourselves as separate from nature. As we regain the ability to communicate with all life, we also begin to tap into the great wealth of knowledge that is in all beings."

What are we really looking for as we strive to remember a deeper connection with the natural world? If we ever find it, will we be able to take on the heightened states of consciousness and responsibility? Will we be able to stand in front of the mirror and ask ourselves the heartfelt questions: What have we done? What are we doing? Where are we going—not only ourselves but all life, all the earth? Why did we ever leave home?

"The point is to live everything," wrote the poet Rainer Maria Rilke. "Live the questions now . . ."

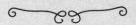

Observe

Peppy (dog) ~ Sam Louie

It's important for humans not to project what you feel about animals when trying to understand them. If you simply take the time to observe, you will learn a tremendous amount. By observing, I mean not having to try to look for anything or trying to understand or communicate, but just observing.

It's not to put us on a pedestal or glorify us. It is to connect with us and see how much we are all the same. We are no better necessarily. It just means that we have different aspects of the Great Life to teach, learn, and share with you.

Obviously, we animals have greatly benefited from a lot of human interaction. Humans have taught many of us many things. Humans have taken great care of many of us. There have been many, many humans who have done good work for animals and the environment.

Animals have destroyed a lot too. Were animals equipped with the technology that humans have, I'm not sure that animals would necessarily be better.

2

How Does It Work?

Late on the third day, at the very moment when, at sunset, we were
making our way through a herd of hippopotamuses, there flashed upon
my mind, unforeseen and unsought, the phrase, "Reverence for Life."
                                              Albert Schweitzer,
                                    Out of My Life and Work

The first time Chrys Long-Ago experienced mind-to-mind connection with an animal, it was the last thing on her mind:

I used to keep my horse at a boarding stable in Anchorage. One day when no one else was around, I was cleaning the stall and brushing my horse. I became so absorbed in the moment that the pressures of life just drifted away. I realized later that the activity put me into a mindfulness meditation, for that's what happened—I relaxed my mind.

When I walked out of the barn, a movement caught my eye. It was a lovely gray tree squirrel who ran up onto a fifty-five-gallon barrel and sat down not far from me with a nut in his paw.

In that relaxed mind state, I turned my attention to the squirrel and spontaneously greeted him in my mind. I don't know why I did that, because it wasn't a habit at that time. I said, "Greetings, little squirrel." He put his nut down and turned his head. He looked straight at me and then turned his body toward me in an open-body posture. This was a wild squirrel! We had direct mind-to-mind contact for at least twenty minutes. I heard everything he was saying.

I asked him things like how is it to be a squirrel and how old are you and how do you like living at the horse barn. The words came into my mind very quickly. He called the horses "grass-eaters." He said, "We call them grass-eaters, grass-eaters," in an almost sneering kind of way. He said that squirrels considered themselves creatures of the air more than of the ground, that they love to live in the swinging boughs of the trees and leap from branch to branch. I was totally consumed by the whole sense of being a squirrel, flying through the air like that.

Chrys Long-Ago.

He told me how they would venture down the tree head first, consciously looking everywhere, because all of their predators are on the ground, except for owls. He also told me how territorial they were, which I didn't know about squirrels. I later researched it and found out they are very territorial.

I asked him how long squirrels lived. "Three winters," he said. When I asked if that wasn't a rather short life, he said, "Who would want to live any longer than that?" He just had this amazing perspective!

Chrys was the first animal communicator I spoke with. Not only was she very knowl-edgeable about animals, but she had worked hard to make sense of how this thing called animal communication fit from our end. Like myself, she was intrigued with how the human mind could "translate" thoughts and ideas, even complete sentences, from a variety of species so different from our own.

It all begins with telepathy, one of those loaded words often used to poke fun at something that, underneath, we all know to be true. One dictionary defines telepathy as "communication by scientifically unknown means." Etymologically, the word de-rives from *tele*, meaning distant or far away, and *pathy*, from the Greek *patheia*, mean-ing feeling or perception. Perceptions from a distance, feelings from far away—a defi-nition for a rather vague and intangible form of communication.

Still, who has never "had a feeling" something was about to happen? How many times have you "just known" what somebody was going to say or do? Is this really so strange?

Carol Gurney, a communicator from California, believes that a first step to open-ing to telepathy is realizing it's something we do all the time. "When you are in touch with your feelings, telepathy happens very quickly," Carol explained. "You can get a whole concept within a flash. Maybe people get scared by the word—*telepathy*, but we are just putting a fancy word on something that we do all day long. When a friend tells you she is fine, but your gut says something's not right, how do you know that? It's telepathy!"

The jump from believing telepathy between humans is possible to believing te-lepathy between species is feasible is a tricky one for some. It requires not only viewing animals as intelligent, sentient beings, but accepting that a flow of communication between humans and animals is possible. Carol feels that people talk with their ani-mals all the time, though they don't necessarily recognize it. "The thought of the animal blends with your consciousness," she told me. "It has to become your own inner thought for that flash of a moment in order to get it. What happens is that we judge it as ours. We don't know how to tell the difference sometimes. We're not giving ourselves credit that we're getting it, nor are we giving the animals credit that they do communicate."

When J. Allen Boone first began working with Strongheart, he wondered how it was possible that a dog could so easily understand human thoughts while he, a hu-man, had so much trouble discerning dog thoughts. With this perplexing dilemma, Boone sought out Mojave Dan, a man who lived in the desert with a family of dogs, burros, and wild animals. Dan was the only person Boone knew who could carry on two-way conversations with animals. Even more extraordinary, Dan was amazingly well-informed about all sorts of events. He claimed the information came from his dogs and burros as well as from any wild animals—snakes, insects, birds—that happened to pass his way.

For Boone, the mystery wasn't so much in that Dan could communicate his thoughts to the animals, but that he could understand what the animals said to him. Others had tried to get Dan to tell them how this was possible. "His reply to these requests was that such things were too intimate to talk about and could be acquired only through personal effort and real humility," wrote Boone.[1]

With the instincts of a reporter, Boone was persuasively persistent. After a campfire dinner and some peaceful time under the stars, Boone told Dan about Strongheart and his difficulty in receiving communication from the dog. There followed a long silence, during which Boone was convinced the question had been laid to rest. But at last Mojave Dan answered. "There's facts about dogs," he said, "and there's opinions about them. The dogs have the facts, and the humans have the opinions. If you want facts about a dog, always get them straight from the dog."[2]

Getting the facts from any animal can sometimes be a puzzling and surprising affair. When I asked Sam Louie how he thought humans could understand what animals had to say in terms that were understandable to our consciousness, he offered a story.

Early in his career, Sam did some volunteer work with a woman who rescued Dobermans who had been impounded for aggression. In an attempt to place the dogs so they would not be destroyed, the woman asked Sam to talk with them to determine the type of family situation that would be best. The woman was desperate to place a dog, also named Sam, as she needed to move to take care of her ill father. When Sam consulted the dog, he distinctly heard the words in English, "When the rains come."

"Part of the skill as a psychic is not simply receiving information, because data without some analysis or interpretation is not very useful," Sam told me. "At the time, I simply interpreted this message as meaning we might not be able to place the dog until November, because that's when the rains begin in the San Francisco Bay area. But this wouldn't work for the woman, because it was August and she had to leave by September. When I asked the dog again, I got the same response, 'When the rains come.'

"A couple of weeks later, a woman named Annette Rains showed up to adopt the dog."

"Whoah!" I exclaimed, and Sam laughed. Not only was I struck by the humor in the situation, but by the intriguing way human word allusions can play a key role in animal communication. Plus, how did Sam the dog know "the Rains" were coming? Interestingly, this reference was something that would come up again later.

Communicators explain that there are several ways in which humans can both send and receive messages from animals. No doubt the explanation is an attempt to pacify the logical mind as it strains to make sense of something that evades the confines of logic. Like an inquisitive puppy, the logical mind needs its analytical bones to chew.

Clairvoyance (French for "clear seeing" or "clear vision") is the ability to see images not normally perceived. Usually this refers to the projection of a picture, a slide show, or even a short movie of an animal doing something, which plays within the darkened theatre of the receiver's mind. Sometimes perspective shifts and the communicator views the scene as if through the animal's eyes.

Clairaudience ("clear hearing") is an inner hearing that can include sounds as well as words. These may be sounds an animal hears, though distinct words and sentences may also be heard on the inner level, rather like thoughts. Communicators say there is a qualitative difference between hearing your own thoughts and hearing the thoughts of an animal.

Clairsentience ("clear feeling") is the realm of kinesthetic feeling. This can include taste, smell, and other physical sensations. Communicators who work with sick animals may feel aches and pains in their body corresponding to the aches and pains of the animal. Feelings such as depression, lethargy, or apprehension may be perceived in this manner; emotions are also a form of clairsentience.

Intuition, which might be translated as inner knowing, is a form of immediate insight. A good intuition is sometimes accompanied by a case of the willies, those tingly ghost fingers that lightly creep up over the top of your spine, making all the hairs on the back of your neck stand at attention, an obvious indication that something important is happening here. Intuition is a strong inner sensing or gut feeling.

While some rely on one method more than others, most often a person receives a combination of impressions. There may be an overlay of images and knowing, or inner words and thoughts plus sounds and feelings. Sometimes communicators experience what they scientifically refer to as "a big blast of information," which subsequently needs to be sorted out, or translated.

Carol Gurney asserts that there are no limitations to the way an individual may receive information. "If you are an artist or very creative, you might get a lot of images from the animal because that is how you see the world. If you are personality oriented, you may get personality things from the animal, such as things they like to do. People who are very spiritual, to whom meditation is like brushing teeth, may connect with the spiritual aspects and longings of that animal. We're like magnets. We draw to us what is comfortable for us to hear in the mode of communication that is comfortable. Where we are within ourself is what we will draw in."

Carol Gurney.

Some assert that the method of receiving information is dependent not only on an individual's preferred method, but also the particular species one is communicating with. Animals that are primarily visual, for example, may be more likely to send pictures or images since that is their dominant sense.

Communicator Jane Hallander finds dogs to be very visual. "They play a video in my mind of what happened or where they are. Lost cats do the same. Cats with behavior problems are more emotion and thought oriented. Birds use pictures and feelings a lot."

Mary Getten notes the differences between speaking with domestic animals and wild animals. She finds it easier with domestic animals because they are so familiar to us. "They are used to our time clock and know the things that we deal with day after day. When I'm talking to someone's cat or dog, it's pretty easy to understand what's going on because we basically live in the same world. When I communicate with wild animals, it's a little different because they have a natural instinct to avoid people and are not used to the experience of communicating with a person."

Mary has formed a relationship with a whale named Granny. When Granny agreed to share some of her thoughts for this book, Mary telepathically connected with the whale and translated what she said in response to my questions. As Mary made contact with Granny, her voice changed dramatically. It deepened, slowed, and sounded almost as if she were very far away.

"When I contact a whale," said Mary, "it's a down-shift into a totally different energy level. One of the problems in working with whales is that their world is so completely different that we often don't have words to explain it. I've had the experience of a whale showing me what it feels like to echolocate. It's almost indescribable."

This is part of the challenge as well as the fascination of animal communication. How can we humans conceive of something, such as echolocation, that we don't have a sense organ for? The obvious thing would be to adapt the senses we do have. The fluid translation of feelings, images, thoughts, even words lies at the core of animal communication. If we don't understand that all communication between species is based on a translation of one mode of understanding into another, we begin asking ourselves all sorts of silly questions, such as, "How is it that whales know English?"

Nedda Wittels and Echo.

Mary laughed. "Right. How do whales have a concept of that? The only way we can speak for animals is to interpret their images and information in the language that we have. That is one of the limitations."

Sam Louie speculates that we have relied upon our learned language for so long that, while telepathic messages don't necessarily come in English, there is something inside of us that automatically processes the information into our preferred language. Chrys Long-Ago similarly hypothesizes that our brains are "hard wired" to understand messages from animals in words. This would explain how nonverbal communications from animals can be translated by some part of the brain into a language we understand.

When I asked Nedda Wittels how it was that she received communications from Echo and Violet, the horse and cat she interviewed for this book, she admitted she was a bit curious herself.

I receive in many forms: pictures, images, sounds, concepts, words, knowings, emotions, physical sensations. When I work on the computer, as I am for your project, I sit down, connect with the animal, and type whatever I receive. Are Echo and Violet themselves writing each word? Not really, although my connection with them is so smooth and ongoing that there is an easy flow to the thoughts. Still, I often consciously choose words to express what they are saying.

There is a fine line that I walk between expressing their messages as they would if they could speak and getting my own thoughts or preferences for correct English and smooth writing style into the mix. Each word has annotations and

connotations. Look in a thesaurus and you'll quickly realize how easy it is to choose a word that sends the desired meaning in a different direction. That's why animal communication is a tremendous responsibility!

Animal communication is also a bit of a balancing act. In addition to finding the best possible words while translating animal to human thoughts, we must constantly be open to what the animal is saying—not to what we think the animal is saying or what we want the animal to say. In this sense, learning animal communication is learning to get out of our own way. It's moving past our limited perceptions of what we believe the world is like.

As J. Allen Boone learned through his lessons with Strongheart, the more he stopped treating Strongheart as a dog, the more Strongheart stopped acting like a dog. "And the more this fascinating thing happened, the more we began functioning as rational companions and the more the kinship barriers between us came tumbling down."[3]

It is a journey after all. As soon as we get out of our own way or, as Boone says, stop making the common ego mistakes of "trying to do all the thinking and to arrive at all the final conclusions,"[4] we come to a place where the mind is silent, the heart open. It is here that we are able to converse with all of life.

There are times when animal communication is fairly straightforward—a cat explaining why she doesn't like her litterbox, a horse expressing preference for one stall over another. But there is also a wild side. It can be deep and spiritual—a dog explaining karma, a parrot relating how she was once a Buddhist monk. It can be thrilling and outrageous—a dolphin expressing what it is like to live in multiple existences simultaneously. The exchange of thoughts and ideas with any animal is as open as we, and they, are willing to be, subject only to the limits of what we believe possible.

How might we perceive flight with an eagle's consciousness, tunneling from a mole's perspective, speeding across the land with cheetah legs? The mind reels at the possibilities. On a practical level, there is the prospect of highly useful information, animals sharing insights on how and why they do the things they do. In her capacity as a naturalist and biologist, Marta Williams suggests that asking animals about their living habits might be a first step to seeing a larger aspect of the world. In the beginning, answers could be compared with biological data already collected, though animal communication could be used in place of much of the invasive and damaging field study practices that are employed today by modern biologists.

What other discoveries would we find by going to the source, asking animals themselves what they think, what they feel, what role they play upon our planet? Carole Devereux told me that animals may represent a last chance for humans.

"Sometimes people can't talk to another human being, but they will talk to a horse. Why? Because a horse is nonjudgmental. Unconditional love flows very naturally between animals and people who are somewhat jaded about the human race. Humans have judged each other for so long that we don't trust each other anymore. When people are with an animal, barriers come down. That's why I work with animals in therapy, because it's a door, an entryway. Animals are the gateway to a higher awareness of spirituality."

If we are willing to open the door and take that first step beyond the entryway, if we are ready to really look and listen, letting go of all those constructs of what we think we know, if we choose to honestly and openly form a deeper relationship with animals and the rest of nature, whatever and whoever will we find?

Have Fun
Raphaela Pope and Dax (bird)

Dax is a little yellow-collared macaw. When I ask him what he'd like humans to know, he says,

Tell them to play.
Be lighthearted!
Have fun!
Be like me!

Raphaela Pope and Dax. Photo by Paul Harris.

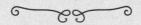

3

Beginning with Birds

*The finches come when called. I don't know why it works, but it does.
Scientists in the Galapagos have passed down the call: you say Pssssh
pssssh pssssh pssssh pssssh until you run out of breath; then you say it
again until the island runs out of birds. You stand on a flat of sand by
a shallow lagoon rimmed in mangrove thickets and call the birds right
out of the sky. It works anywhere, from island to island.*
Annie Dillard, Teaching a Stone to Talk

I do not think I called the birds. Rather, I am fairly certain it was the birds who first called me.

It happened one morning as I sat in front of the computer. From out of nowhere it seemed, a flock of birds swarmed to the bushes just outside my window. I turned my head and there they were: a rush of small, pale brown bodies with flecks of bright orange and yellow, fluttering about the bushes.

This is not a common occurrence around our house. There are plenty of birds to see in Alaska, of course—eagles soaring, ravens swooping, small birds chattering on the windowsill if you remember to put out seeds—but never such a large rush of birds so close. So extraordinary was the moment, so caught was I in the flurry of beating wings and flickering movement, that I could hardly believe what I was seeing.

Hand on heart, I moved slowly to the window. The birds kept coming and coming, until there was truly a great gathering at the bush. I was inches away, separated only by a thin pane of glass.

I had never seen such a thing before and so it was not only with thought, but with feeling, that I sensed the portent, the significance that something extraordinary was about to occur.

I sent the birds greetings. Perhaps I remembered Chrys and her story of meeting the squirrel, of maintaining mindful awareness, not too sharp-eyed, not too critical. And so it was a natural act, as if a part of me who had always spoken to animals took over, and there was an inner voice, calm and centered, which simply said, "Welcome little birds. Do you have a message?" They replied as one:

27

Yes. We are here to bring you encouragement, to remind you to trust and have faith. Remember that there are many little voices in the world. We are all here helping.

I was stunned out of time, caught within a moment of disbelief and bewilderment. I don't know how I was able to dredge up words, but I did. I asked what it was like to be one of them. How do birds see the world?

We see beauty. We are very quick. Our movements are quick and that is how we see and do things. We see beauty, and are beauty, and so we are uplifting.

My heart was pounding. It had been only a matter of seconds and yet already the wonder of what was happening beat within me, faster and faster, as if the birds' wings and hearts were now a part of me. Still, that connection, tremulous, tenuous at best, began to slip.

"What are you?" I asked, "What type of bird?" For even then a part of me was planning, seeking some sort of tangible proof that this was happening.

Finches. We are finches. We come to uplift you and send you words of wisdom as well as faith and trust and support.

And then, as if bursting through a dream, the birds began to leave. A few at a time, then in groups, until only one was left on the bush and I had the sense that he was leader of the group. He looked directly at me with his small, bright, round black eyes and said, "Yes, yes, this is true."

I was initially thrilled, of course. Who wouldn't be excited about their first "real" communication with animals? Although it was not the way I might have imagined something like this happening, neither did I know exactly what I would imagine. I was aware, however, that my whole body seemed to be vibrating very fast. It was an overload, as if I was too filled with energy and couldn't quite contain it.

While talking to other communicators, I had often thought how wonderful it would be to truly talk with animals—what amazing conversations one could have! And though I was excited, exhilarated even, I was also surprised to find that beneath the thrill there was a disturbing sensation. It began as a heaviness low in the pit of my stomach.

With a sense of detached curiosity, I realized I was nauseated. Even then, I reckoned this was the feeling of fear. Though you may know something with your mind—understanding and accepting that people can communicate with animals—experiencing it yourself is another story. And while I didn't really ask to know the story, here it was all the same.

I didn't tell anyone about the birds, not even my husband, not right away. I had some lunch, walked outside, played with the dogs. I let the experience lay beside me, a moment out of time. Perhaps it had all been an imagining. But when I came back to my office room, the question was hanging in the air: What had really happened?

I lay down on the floor and closed my eyes, focusing on a steady flow of breathing, in and out, taking comfort in this easy way to center. *There is nothing so strange about talking to animals,* I assured myself. *You asked them what life was like for them and they told you. What are you so scared about?*

Really, it was laughable, to be afraid of some birds at your window. And yet, underneath, the fear spoke to something deep and vast. Intuition said this was a deep fear, a fear of opening to something greater than what you think you are. In larger terms, it was fear of opening to the fullness of who we really are.

After several minutes, I opened my eyes. It was then I was reminded how even little things can have grand consequences.

I rarely lie down in my office. It's true that I pace, amble, stretch, sometimes even stalk a sentence relentlessly around the room, but I rarely lie down. So how was it, I wondered, that I came to lie down exactly where I did? Was it coincidence that my position was such that from where I lay on the floor I had a perfect view of outside the window? It was the same window from where I had seen the birds, though now, since I was on the floor and at a lowered perspective, I could not see the bush the birds had visited. Instead, I was looking upward at the window-framed sky, edged in one corner by a few branches of a large birch tree.

With a shiver of incredulity, I felt the eerie sensation of "there is no such thing as coincidence" dance upon my flesh in a fitful array of goosebumps. For there, on the branches of the birch tree perched ten or twelve of the same birds I had seen before on the bushes.

The birds now looked down, their eyes trained on me, through the window. I was not imagining; there could be no doubt. With a sigh of resignation, I allowed myself to fall into the mode of consciousness that opens to birds, that is perfectly capable and familiar with this type of connection.

As before, the mode of communication was an inner conversation. While I was aware of the birds as a group, it was just one voice that replied, as if a group leader or perhaps group consciousness was speaking. I asked the birds what they wanted me to see.

The Alfred Hitchcock film, *The Birds,* suddenly came to mind. *What?* I laughed out loud and asked if they knew that movie. They related that they didn't know it in the sense of watching it as we do, but had a sense of it from people's minds—as if they could read the fear that movie engendered in humans. They said the film had affected a lot of people and, from that perspective, had both created and revealed a belief about birds, a sort of group projection. Clearly, that projection was a dark one—though the birds (these birds, my birds) reminded me that it was symbolically true in that quite often a bird's message is a wake-up call, particularly a call to see.

Further, they related that the scene in the film of human eyes being plucked out was a core projection of the human fear of seeing. They reminded me that the whole issue of what the birds wanted was never resolved in the story; it was a mystery and remained a mystery. The birds came, attacked, made people aware of their presence (and thus, the shadow side of birds within themselves), and then left. There was no explanation. The birds on the tree said to me that this was a vision based on fear. It was really a fear of ourselves, though we were so disconnected from the original fear that we projected it onto the birds, through our own human lenses.

Do you understand this is about your human projection? Any animal can be seen like this, not just birds.

They gave me the assignment then to look for other bird movies and notice how birds were used as symbols in other mediums. They reminded me of the way Renaissance artists frequently used birds in religious art, and how birds can just as easily be seen in connection to spirit as fear. They reminded me that birds were often used as a symbol of spirit and the Holy Ghost.

Lastly, the birds left me with an example. The wind came up quickly and I watched how they held to the branches without being disturbed, their small bodies swaying with the wind.

We are not afraid of spirit, so it moves cleanly around us. It moves through us.

As the birds began to leave, I sensed the message was over. But one bird remained, just as before, and again I recognized it as the leader, or the one with the strongest intentional voice for me. He told me that it was important, very important, to understand the various perspectives of projection. He reminded me that when I first saw the birds they were below me and the message they presented was to uplift me. And when I saw them above me, there on the branch watching me like a bunch of spies, already I had sensed my fear. The message thus felt heavy, a bit oppressive. Clearly, the birds themselves hadn't changed, but my perspective had.

The bird, my small feathered guide, said the next step was to see the world from the birds' perspective.

Not long after the bird messages, I contacted Sam Louie. I knew Sam to be a talented communicator as well as a bit of skeptic. It was a combination I admired.

Sam asked me what kind of birds I had seen. The birds had told me they were finches, though soon after the event I began to doubt that finches could be found in Alaska. As I leafed through a photo guide to Alaskan birds, nowhere could I find the birds I had seen. From reading more, however, I decided the closest was a form of grosbeak. So when I told Sam they might be finches but were more likely grosbeaks, he paused, then laughed and said loudly, "They're finches! They say to tell you they are finches!"

I now believe those birds were finches. But back then I still hadn't made up my mind, even after what Sam confirmed. It was the fear element, perhaps. Sam was kind, telling me that fear was a reaction, something we all do to protect ourselves. "Trust the process," he said. "Trust the unfolding."

Still, I went back to fear time and again. It amazed me that it was so deeply rooted and, moreover, that the fear was not of something dark and horrible—no devil or bogeyman was my tormentor—but rather derived of a forgotten connection. I postulated that the fear arose from ego's desire to control life, to keep things normal, in their place. The fear was about opening to an unknown way of being.

A few days later the finches came back—not in physical form, but as a footnote. And I was again reminded that the universe is elegant, persistent, and full of humor as it attempts to awaken us.

A copy of *Animal-Speak* by Ted Andrews was mailed to me for review. It is a book that looks at various animals as totems, or signifiers of specific energies that can be used as gateways to the human spirit. The animal totem is thus both a symbol and carrier of a specific type of energy, and much of the book relates the various powers and medicines different animals embody. Andrews also notes that totem animals choose a person, not the other way around.

At the time, however, I knew none of this. I was only flipping through the book that first day I received it, allowing key bits of information to pop out at me, basically getting a feel for it. And so it was with astonishment that I found the finches. Or perhaps they found me. Who was it that stopped the pages from flipping, gently guiding my eyes to Andrews' words?

> A finch that becomes a totem will always increase opportunities to experience a variety of activities. Everything is going to be amplified. . . . If a finch has flown into your life look for new kinds of experiences and encounters with people from all walks of life . . . this reflects a general increase and variety of potentials that are likely to unfold within your life. Anytime a finch arrives, life is going to become more active.[1]

I dropped the book and stood alone in my office. Hand to chest, eyes to window, I laughed so hard I cried.

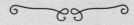

Listen

Marcia Ramsland and Trapper (wolf/dog)

Trapper is half wolf and half Siberian husky. He says, "There is great wisdom from animals. We come in great numbers and try to break through to the consciousness of people." I believe he is talking specifically about companion animals.

He also says, "Only now are we beginning to be heard." I think what he's reflecting is that it's so much more open now. People are actually hearing what their animals say, and people are writing books such as this.

Trapper says, "Companion animals are a conduit, like a channel, from God or All That Is to people through which unconditional love, enjoyment of the present moment, joy, and enthusiasm flow."

4

Fear, Filters, and Finding the Neutral Zone

There are only two ways to live your life.
One is as though nothing is a miracle.
The other is as though everything is a miracle.
Albert Einstein

Laura Simpson once did a consultation for a fellow communicator who had recently acquired a cockatiel. The woman wasn't sure if she should keep the cockatiel or give him away, so she called Laura in as a disinterested party to talk with the bird and ask what he wanted.

Laura contacted the bird and inquired if he would prefer to stay with the communicator or go to live with another person. The cockatiel wanted to know how he would get to the other person's house. Laura told the bird he'd have to go on an airplane. The cockatiel said he didn't know what that was, so Laura sent him a mental image of an airplane. Then the bird went silent.

When Laura asked what was wrong, the cockatiel suddenly cried out, "Oh no! Don't put me in there! I've seen those things before. They eat people and then spit them out. I've tried to talk to them and there's nobody there. They have no decent migratory pattern, and they make no sense at all. Oh no, I'm not going to be eaten by a plane!"

Fear is not species specific. Nor is fear ever unreal when you are experiencing it. Fear is something that catches you, clutches you, and keeps you hostage for as long as your consciousness agrees to be held within its confines.

I wondered if Laura explained to the cockatiel about airplanes. Could the bird be convinced that the monstrosity he thought he saw was something else, something much different than what he first believed? And, if the cockatiel did become unfettered of his fear, would he find irony in his vision of the plane as an unintelligent, uncommunicative mechanical bird so much larger than himself?

I was grappling with my own sense of irony from the finch experience. For there, at the heart of the matter, was the stunning realization that my fear wasn't that I couldn't communicate with animals, but that I could. Like the cockatiel, like so many humans, I had fashioned my beliefs to create my own version of the mechanical bird, and it was large and noisy and fearsome. It boldly proclaimed I was just like everyone else. And while a few odd sorts might talk to animals, sane, polite people just didn't do that sort of thing, much less write about their experiences.

"To prevent the fear, there's been control," said Ilizabeth Fortune, a former counselor and teacher who has spent many years learning from dolphins. "When we start to let go of control, we come face to face with fear. In my experience, fear has been an open door. I've had to go through fear to get to the other side. In fear is the 'ear,' so if I listen to the fear and allow it to teach me, I'll get to the other side and find out what's there. What I have found on the other side is very simple. It's that we're all one."

If there is a single message at the core of all animal communication, it is this: We are all one. It doesn't seem such a frightful message, and yet, as I was to learn over and over, saying it is one thing, but knowing it deep down inside one's bones and blood and being is something entirely different.

"It's important when fear comes up," continued Ilizabeth. "To me, it means you're ready to go to another level, do another spiral." Ilizabeth shared that dolphins first taught her how to handle fear. "Then, when it was time for me to handle fear in another way, another species taught me, which happened to be a bear. When I had to learn something else, it was from a horse. But it's still about fear, about how to handle fear, about how to go through fear."

Ilizabeth paused, as if remembering. "When you join up with an animal, like a horse, and you turn your back and the horse comes to you, laying its muzzle on your shoulder and you feel its warm breath, it chokes you up; it brings tears. It's the same feeling as being eye to eye with a dolphin, the same as feeling the magnitude of vibrations around a whale. The question is: Are we ready now to listen? Are we ready to be quiet and be still and communicate?"

It is in quiet stillness that the heart opens. It is here that consciousness, and thus all life, is suddenly experienced as so much more than what we first believed. When the mechanical bird is seen for what it really is, fear dissipates. We open our eyes to a deeper, fuller understanding of life, and the world is never quite the same.

In the openness of a heart-to-heart connection with any being, there is no fear because there is no need. However, this does not—nor should it—lessen the role of fear as a commendable instructor, an expert guide in helping us to explore the shadowy areas of ourselves. As we stop running from fear, the perception of fear inevitably changes. No longer does it hold us; rather, we hold it. Fear shrinks down and becomes a tool, a handy barometer of where our emotions are stuck, our filters smudged.

Any experience can be frightening or fascinating depending upon the filter or perspective through which we choose to see the world at that moment in time. We all use filters in how we see reality, for the brain itself is a filtering device. Our language, society, upbringing, race, and gender—as well as our own unique genetics, beliefs, and thoughts—help to determine how we see, understand, experience, and make sense of ourselves and the world around us. This is nothing new, and all you have to do is ask three people to describe a shared event to realize how each of us interprets the world in different ways.

The trouble with filters is that we are often so caught up and comfortable in our own way of seeing the world that we forget that personal filters color our perspective, and we continue to project those filters upon the world. We come to believe that what is "out there" is an objective reality, something separate from us.

Some claim that the way we see life is a mirror of what is happening within ourselves. The problems we face in the outer world are reflections of unresolved issues, emotional hot spots, or things we deny. This is a notion many people don't like, because it is so much easier to blame problems on our parents, spouses, co-workers, and the government—anyone but ourselves.

Now, what does this have to do with animal communication? While it may not seem obvious on the surface, it is in many ways the core of what communication with any species, even our own, is all about. In a strange sort of boomerang fashion, it is communication with what we perceive as something other than ourselves that takes us deeper within, back home once again.

"The one message that is most important to the animals I meet," said Carol Gurney, "is 'Let us be here to help you love yourselves.' That message comes in lots of different ways." Carol recalled a husband and wife who lived with three cats. The two female cats attacked the male cat viciously. On the day that Carol spoke with the animals, all she heard from the female cats was, "We're going to kill him. We want to kill him." Carol commented, "When I hear things like that, I know there's something else going on."

Carol learned that because the woman was often away, her husband adopted a new family of friends. Because he was relying on his new friends for support rather than her, the woman was angry. Carol suggested the problem was the anger that wasn't being expressed.

"But guess who was feeling it?" Carol asked me. "The animals! Look at what the animals were doing: two females were attacking the male cat! The woman called me the next day and said, 'You're not going to believe this. My husband came in and we talked about it, and we got things resolved and—the cats are fine! This is unbelievable."

"The cats are tuned in," explained Carol. "They want to act it out because the emotion is so raw and not being dealt with. The moment you deal with it, it's done. Otherwise, it hangs around our bodies and all around us; the air becomes thick."

"When your pet is misbehaving, that's when you have to look at yourself," agreed Laura Simpson. "For example, if your dog is running away all the time, you may need to ask, 'What am I running away from?' Sometimes pets need to go off and reground themselves, especially if we are going through a lot of emotional garbage. It can be overloading for them and so they need to go get their paws on the ground and be with nature for awhile."

Laura related that her dog, Hannah, a Great Pyrenees, used to take off at times. Even with her communicating skills, Laura would panic. "As soon as I asked to see whatever the lesson was, she'd be in the backyard. It was my lesson in controlling."

It is by noting our filters, blocks, and misperceptions that we begin to overcome them. This is true not just in animal communication, but for any journey of enlightenment. It is also the first step to finding the neutral zone, an essential mode of being for both sending and receiving clear messages.

We must also recognize that we all have filters, animals as well as humans. "Belief systems are a straightjacket," Marcia Ramsland told me. "It is difficult to get out. They are very addictive because they are what you think is true. The belief systems that are stopping us in animal communication are that animals don't think and that only a few people are telepathic."

Add to those firmly entrenched belief systems a few layers of fear and doubt, and it is easy to understand why telepathic communication, especially with animals, requires a paradigm shift that is difficult for some to accept. But what if we were to move to a stance of balance, a perspective wherein logical abilities and intuition both have a role to play?

Marcia found her key to understanding telepathy and animal communication within quantum physics, a framework in which the constraints of normal reality are expanded and the concept of interconnectedness thrives. "Our regular science works fine as long as you are in physical form, but with telepathy time, space, and physical reality are not the only realities. Once I learned about quantum physics, my telepathy got much better because I acquired a belief system that gave me a reason for how it worked. My logical mind could buy into it and believe it."

Is it not a win-win situation when reality expands to include telepathy and telepathy is improved by a worldview that embraces intuition? As our filters become more sparkling and smudge free of emotional holds, belief systems, and mental agendas, we have less need to project. For what we see is not so much a reflection of what is hidden, judged, or denied within ourselves as a glimpse into clarity. We see that the monstrous mechanical bird is, after all, simply an airplane. It soars through the air and we are not afraid.

"Without clarity, we cannot interpret reality correctly," explained Chrys Long-Ago. "It's like the sky in Buddhist philosophy—the true nature of the enlightened mind is like the sky, calm. But in the sky are clouds, obscurations—troubling, disturbed thoughts. Our ordinary mind produces the clouds. The clouds come and go; airplanes fly through the sky. But it does not affect the sky in any way. Your calm essence and your enlightened state are still there. You just have to calm down your ordinary mind enough to connect. And then you can connect with all beings in an honest way."

Change your filters and you change yourself. Change yourself and you change your perception of the world. Change your perception of the world and you begin to change the world itself.

"We can all live in harmony and have a complete web of life where all is respected," Penelope Smith told me. "The more you align yourself with that, the more of that you get."

Perhaps in the end it all comes down to this: If we have a choice between living life as if nothing is a miracle or living life as if everything is a miracle, why not choose the miracle?

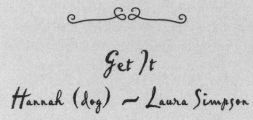

Get It
Hannah (dog) ~ Laura Simpson

People don't get it. All this talking is a waste of breath and a waste of noise. Whatever you think in your head—your animal has already gotten it. You don't have to say it again. That's just so redundant.

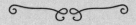

5

The Jump

One night, not too long after Violet the cat came to live with her, Nedda Wittels was heading up to bed when she stopped to stroke Violet's head.

"Her ears felt very hot," said Nedda, "and I thought, 'Oh, my, could she be sick? I wonder if her nose is also warm and, if it is, whether that might be a sign of illness?' I leaned forward over her and gently touched her nose with the index finger of my right hand. As I did so, I heard, 'Gee, I wonder if humans get hot noses when they are sick?' whereupon Violet's right front paw landed gently but firmly on my nose."

If there is a central credo among animal communicators, it is this: not only is animal communication possible, but all of us—yes, even you—can do it. In order to do it, you find yourself learning a new dance, a kind of three-step. First you shuffle toward the idea that animals and humans can connect in a way that is beyond the limits of language, and then, quite often unexpectedly, you kick up your heels with the thrilling realization that you can do this too. Then you take a step back.

Probably the most obvious and frequently asked question when learning animal communication is: How do we know this is real? It had certainly become my favorite question. In spite of speaking with finches and dogs, even receiving confirmation from several communicators about those experiences, skepticism still poked at me. It was both surprising and frustrating, because while I believed talking to animals was quite possible, and that the communicators who did this for a living were genuinely receiving messages, I still doubted myself.

I began to wonder if there wasn't a bridge somewhere that allowed one to cross the raging river separating self-doubt from self-trust. How many experiences did you need before you would believe that what you heard was real, that you weren't just making these things up?

"We need 10,538 validations to convince us that it's real," Carol Gurney told me.

"Really?" My heart sank. I figured I hadn't even hit one hundred yet. "We need that many validations?"

"I did!" laughed Carol. "I found it the hardest thing that I've ever done, because my issue is trust. I kept thinking I was talking to myself. We need to get over that feeling because it *does* feel like you're talking to yourself! We're used to seeing lips move and a voice come out, but this doesn't work that way. We have to adjust." Carol paused.

"Say you meet some people who speak Italian. As you listen to them speak, you may not have a clue what they're saying. But that doesn't mean those who speak Italian don't have thoughts and feelings, because obviously they do. If you want to communicate, it may be primitive at first—sign language, pointing, and so forth. But then you would get a book or take a class to learn to do it fluently. It's the same thing with animals! They have thoughts and feelings. Their language just happens to come in a different package. It's a matter of getting comfortable with that."

For myself, getting comfortable was one wild pendulum ride. While there were moments of absolute knowing, there was also the sudden slam back into ordinary reality, where it was so tempting to question the validity of those experiences.

"When you get an answer from an animal, it often feels like you're making it up," Marcia Ramsland assured me. "It shows up as a thought in your head, and we are so used to thinking that the thoughts in our head are our own."

Most communicators agree that self-doubt is the biggest obstacle for beginners once they have accepted the idea that animals are sentient beings. The logical mind insinuates we're pretending or perhaps a bit crazy talking to animals after all. Another version of self-sabotage is believing that other people can talk to animals, but surely we can't. Marcia advised that the only solution was to build self-confidence.

My vision of a nice strong bridge was fading fast. Could it be there was no bridge? Or could it be that my confirmations were there but not in the way I expected?

It reminded me of the old joke about the farmer and the flood. The river is overflowing, and water surrounds the farmer's home up to his front porch. A man in a boat comes by and offers help. But the farmer declines, saying he puts his trust in God. The boat goes away, and the water rises to the second floor.

Another boat comes along, and the farmer again refuses help. "I put my trust in God," he calls. The boat speeds away; the water rises.

As the farmer climbs to the roof, a helicopter flies overhead and a ladder drops down. The pilot calls to the farmer to climb the ladder and be carried to safety. And yet again the farmer refuses, shouting that he puts his trust in God. Just then, the farmer is swept off the roof into the river and drowns.

The farmer ascends to heaven, where God greets him with astonishment. "What are you doing here?" Visibly upset, the farmer says "I put my trust in you and you let me down."

"What do you mean, let you down?" says God, shaking his head in disbelief. "I sent you two boats and a helicopter."

The sneaking suspicion that there was no discernible bridge leading to self-trust pervaded my thoughts. I had the nervous feeling that crossing the river of self-doubt was going to involve a leap.

"It's quite a leap!" Marcia laughed. "And you do shift from having to believe it on faith to absolutely knowing it's true and that you can do it." Then, like many good teachers, Marcia told me a story.

> I remember the first time I absolutely knew what I got came from an animal and not myself. The dogs and I had gone for a long walk, and when we came back we all went upstairs, except for Royal, a little sled dog who tended to stay downstairs, and Trapper, a half wolf, half Siberian who had a cast on his leg. It was odd for Trapper not to come upstairs because he normally did. When I asked him mentally why he didn't come upstairs too, I fully expected him to say that the walk was too long and his leg was tired. Instead, this is what I heard: "Royal gets lonesome down here by herself; I thought I'd keep her company for awhile."
>
> That blew me out of the water entirely! At that time, I couldn't conceive that Royal wouldn't just come upstairs or that Trapper could act compassionately. I didn't know they had become friends.
>
> Oftentimes when you ask a question of an animal, you get back exactly what you're expecting, and that doesn't mean you're wrong. In fact, you're probably right. But it is the times you get back what you're not expecting that you absolutely know it had to come from the animal. Everything Trapper had said was outside of my knowing. That was when I knew the answer had definitely come from Trapper, not from myself. It was a paradigm shift. I got goosebumps all over. It sank in and I *knew* what I heard was from the dogs, because not only was it a reasonable answer but it was completely outside of my belief system.

Communicators have many stories about surprising information that helps to verify that communication is indeed happening. Raphaela Pope told me about a beginner's workshop in which a young woman chose to work with a llama. While answering some basic questions, the llama told the woman that his favorite food was bananas. The woman thought this answer so peculiar, she nearly didn't share it with the group.

"Now, anybody who knows llamas, knows that they regard bananas as a tremendous delicacy, just like apples and carrots for horses," said Raphaela. "I have some llama acquaintances and they are mad about bananas! Since this woman knew nothing about llamas, it was the surprising, odd information that she couldn't have gotten any other way than from the animal that was her confirmation."

Hearing stories such as these brings the humbling realization that the biggest obstacle in talking with animals isn't the animal's inability to communicate, but our own. It is our separation from animals and the natural world that has created in us a forgetting, a doubt that turns in on itself, forcing us to ask ourselves, "Is this really real?"

When I asked Laura Simpson why she thought we humans had so much self-doubt, she told me her dog Roxie would like to answer. "Roxie has dealt with this before, so she's a good one to ask. She says, 'People have to start listening to the little voice in their head, and not think of it as being crazy. It's a lot easier if your person will listen to you and respect what you say. You don't have to do as many antics.'"

As self-doubt yields to accepting the reality of experience, we open. Again and again, we open. Talk to finches, and just when you think you might be able to believe that what you heard is real, your dog tells you something crazy, like he used to be a bear. As in a recurring dream that never quite resolves itself, we find not just one leap, but a succession of leaps.

Even after Carol Gurney had her 10,538 validations, which negated all doubts that she could really talk to animals, she had to take another leap.

A woman asked me to communicate with a dog who had passed on. It was the first time I had tried such a thing. When I got in touch with the dog, he told me his transition was as easy as his life had been with her.

He said, "Tell her it's vast here. I can see here forever. There's lots of music and if I want to see someone I do and if I don't, I don't. If I want to see a hill with sheep, I do." I wondered why he was telling me about a hill of sheep. Later on, I learned that he used to herd sheep. When I asked if he had a message for the woman, the dog said, "Yes. Tell her when she hears music in her heart, she will know that I'm near." I had no idea what that meant. When I called the woman and related this story, I could hear that she was crying.

She said to me, "You don't know this, but this is a miracle. Today I had him cremated and put his ashes on the mantle. We used to listen to classical music; it was our favorite thing to do together. A piece of music came on that I hadn't heard before, and when it did, it filled my heart and I could feel that he was near.

So, what you are telling me is, it was real. I wasn't imagining it; it wasn't wishful thinking on my part."

And that's what we have. This woman thought it was her wishful thinking, but because I could tell her otherwise, she could believe her own experience.

When doubt meets trust, amazing things can happen. The leap is no longer one of fear, but of faith. To remember what you already know is when the leaping becomes fun. It is knowing that in spite of what others and even your skeptical mind might say, the experience you are involved in is far greater. It is moving to a place of deeper trust, not only within yourself, but also with animals, nature and all the world. "As soon as you open up to the animals and want to see them for who they are, what you're saying is, 'I want to know who I am,'" Carol reminded me.

As we leap, we embrace the miraculous. And it is then we realize that where we are leaping to is home.

Jing. Photo by Jane Hallander.

Part Two

Many Roads for Traveling Souls

Jing: Why a Buddhist Monk Becomes a Parrot

Bears: A Dog Who Became a Bear, A Bear Who Became a Dog, and Spirit of Polar Bear

Violet: On Being a Cat and Light Worker

Past Lives, Future Lives, and Living in the Now

Echo: On Elevating Consciousness and the Equine Form

More than You Realize
Ostrich ~ Morgine Jurdan

I bestow the gift of life in a new and different way. People often think with their heads in the sand, and this is how I am often pictured. What I give is a different way to view knowledge. When you remove your head from the sand, you can see life in a new and different way. I could also share that when we submerge ourselves into ourselves, looking at all parts of ourselves, we can better know the world.

People are interesting and funny, and I delight in the ways you create to fool each other. You rely on your wit and are so surprised and angered when someone outwits you. I think people are acutely aware of what they do. I do not feel you are as unconscious as you would like to believe.

You live such fast-paced lives. When you take time to be in the moment and see what is really happening and what is true, you often come away with a different picture.

Life is seldom what you think it is. It is usually much more—more alive, deeper and wider and fuller than you imagine. The truth often lies hidden underneath a lot of things that need to be explored on a deeper level.

I can feel as tall as a tree and broaden my perspective of life, and also be conscious of the tiny ant crawling up my leg. Sensitivity means you are awake and finding what it is you truly want out of life, not what you assume you want.

You truly know more than you realize. You are incredible beings and I honor the role you play in my life and work to create a world in which we all can meet our potential.

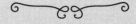

6

Jing: Why a Buddhist Monk Becomes a Parrot

Before I knew much about animal communication, I once asked a question so ridiculous it made a parrot laugh.

What I wanted to know wasn't all that ridiculous; perhaps it was the way I phrased it. What's it like for animals to communicate telepathically? I asked. Can every animal hear the thoughts of every other animal? Surely that would be awfully noisy. Or maybe it's more like how humans use the telephone, I conjectured. Is it like dialing up a certain person's number in order to make contact with that individual?

That's when the bird laughed. That's when I knew I was in way over my head.

When Jing, a female African gray parrot, came to live with Jane Hallander, it was the bird, not the human, who initiated lessons in telepathic communication. Jing began her training by touching the individual fingers of Jane's hand in a deliberate manner. While this gave Jane the idea to "teach" Jing to touch whichever finger she called out, the parrot was way ahead of the game.

Jane was amazed to find that Jing was able to touch whichever finger she called out in English with total accuracy. So Jane got tricky. She tried Cantonese, then Mandarin. Other tests were done, the names of the fingers called out by friends in Korean, German, Japanese, languages Jane didn't speak. The language didn't seem to matter, for each spoken word sent Jing hopping to the correct finger.

Finally, Jane merely thought the fingers. Without even a single word spoken, the results were the same: Jing moved from finger to finger, each one matching Jane's thoughts. How could this be? The answer, Jane decided, was telepathy.

Jing later revealed to Jane that she "awakened" upon seeing Jane for the first time. As Jane worked with Jing and teacher Penelope Smith, developing her skills in sending and receiving thoughts from animals, Jing's story began to unfold.

Jing explained that her last life had been as an enlightened Buddhist monk living high in the mountains of Tibet. Upon dying and leaving that human form, Jing waited nearly a century before incarnating into another body, this time as a wild parrot in

Africa. Along with other parrots, Jing was captured and brought to the United States to be sold as a pet. It was then that Jing chose Jane to help her on her life's mission to help awaken humanity.

"Our paths crossed because I am essential to her cause," explained Jane. "I like to say that 'We are two that make one.' How was it arranged? I don't know how these things mesh so well together, but they do."

The following interview was conducted over several months via electronic mail. I would send Jane my questions, and Jing's answers, neatly typed by Jane, would come back to me a few days later. I was fascinated by the implications of Jing's story. Had she really been a Buddhist monk? Why would a Buddhist monk, and an enlightened one at that, come back as a parrot? Furthermore, if an enlightened monk chose to be reincarnated as a parrot, who might we find living inside other animals?

Jing, do all animals communicate telepathically at the level you do, or is this something you developed just as Jane developed the ability to communicate with you?

I am special in my flock. My parents taught me that we are the beings whom the flock depends on for safety. I can talk to other birds and animals easily because they help me tell of danger. They know I'm a special being. Other birds, like my friends the crows, have the same sentinels and those are the ones I talk to.

We use emotions, body language, mental pictures, and thoughts to talk. Voice is used to alarm the flock or get someone's attention if they are not focusing on me. When we are very good at it, we just use thoughts.

Animals are like humans. If we are comfortable with you, we will answer you. If not, you are strangers to us.

Do you find there's a difference in communicating with humans as opposed to other animals?

Of course. Don't you ever feel like the human you're talking to isn't listening to you? That is how animals feel about communicating with humans. Animals always listen. Humans either don't know how or don't want to listen.

Are there some animals you prefer to communicate with?

I like to talk to other birds, because they understand me as a bird. I also like to talk to cats. I like squirrels because they are wild, so communicate very clearly.

What kinds of things do you talk about?

Events and happenings. If another parrot saw a hawk he would tell me.

Jane tells me your last life was that of a Buddhist monk and that you chose to come back as a bird to help others. Can you speak more about that?

I was what you call Tibetan Buddhist. I was an enlightened monk, able to choose the incarnation that I wanted.

I chose the body of an African gray parrot because these birds can talk and catch the attention of humans. My awareness is what makes me a sentinel.

When I died as a human, I was very old and waiting to find the right way for my gift to humanity. I still waited many years after leaving my body, until humanity was ready to change, to learn, to awaken.

My mission is to bring awareness and awaken humanity by teaching reverence for all life, including animals. If humans learn to communicate with other beings, you are awakened and you will prosper as you have potential. If not, you will destroy everything.

Why did you choose to become a bird—why not a human who communicates with animals?

Had I chosen a human body, as one who talks to animals, I would have a more difficult time being understood. People distrust people but understand animals. There's no division of religion with animals. The bird who talks is the African gray parrot. Humans expect this bird to have great wisdom. In Africa there is a tribe that believes the gray parrot brought language to human beings.

Did you incarnate into your present life with full knowledge of who you were and what you were to become, or did you awaken to this knowledge during certain events in your life as Jing?

I didn't know who I was until coming here. When I saw Jane the first time, I "awakened" and realized my past and the way I had chosen. I am still Jing, the parrot, but within the parrot lies my past.

Can you speak more about your life in Africa?

I lived with a group of other grays. I had passed my first season and was still learning from my parents about my future as a sentinel. It was a much harder life than I have now, but flying above everything made it wonderful and special. One night when we were roosting in our trees, long poles knocked us to the ground, where we were picked up and put in small boxes by humans.

Did you know you would be coming to North America from Africa?

No, my own karma arranged it.

How much of our life is set up before we incarnate, and what determines how conscious we can be of that in the present incarnation?

As you reach more enlightenment, you have more control of your karma. Look at people who are "out of control." Their karma is still directing them. As you become more enlightened, you start to have choice about your path.

We choose incarnations to follow our correct path to enlightenment. Most will not choose the path I have chosen—to help others learn—until they reach a special level of enlightenment.

My path is to help humans awaken to the importance and equality of other beings and the world you live in, before you destroy it and yourselves. If you awaken to this message, you may become enlightened to the reality of what you are doing.

Enlightenment has many forms and stages. I don't know what path I will take after this. You can call me an enlightened monk in my previous life, but remember "enlightened" is not black or white. It has many levels.

I know my own past lives and can bring those messages forward, but you know already what is an important message. Your term is *collective consciousness*. I am here to help bring that forward.

Bring forward collective consciousness? How so?

If enough humans listen to me and others and learn that all beings can communicate with one another, they will awaken to that reality and use consideration toward other beings.

How? Are you listening to me now? You are representative of other humans. Multiply yourself many times and you have collective consciousness.

It is time for people to start to awaken. However, it can happen only if they listen. Your programming tells you the time is now.

What is the most important thing humans can do right now?

Learn to listen—listen to the voices of other beings. All beings are equal. This is what you call nature. We are all equal, except humans have taken advantage of their own perceived intelligence and have become unnatural beings.

How is that?

By thinking they have the only intelligence, when many of us (animals) think very much like humans.

Jane tells me that when the two of you work to find lost animals, you often enlist the aid of the crows and ravens. How did you come into that working relationship?

Those birds are my comrades. They are also teachers and communicators. They send messages throughout the world. I knew them in Africa. I learned as a very young being to talk to them. They help us know of danger.

What do the crows say about humans and how we might be more aware of all species?

The crows have a low opinion of most humans, having been exposed to people who kill them. They trust a few people, but in general consider humans somewhat barbaric compared with their own culture. Crows have evolved very far.

Would any of the crows you are in contact with like to speak directly?

I will translate what they say: "We are more than messengers. We direct animal minds to make a balance. We are feared because many humans know we are more powerful than they are. We will be here when humans are gone.

"We are also benevolent. We help other animals by communicating and guiding them. There were people who respected us and there still are, but not as many as before. However, things are changing. We will again become known for who we are."

Jing, do you have an opinion about the projection of prejudices onto other species? For example, the crows mention how humans fear them, and humans have done a similar thing with wolves. Only fifty years ago, many humans believed wolves were evil.

Most people never know the animal. They think they know themselves, but they don't even know that much. If someone tells them a wolf is evil, they believe that. This is the same for many animals. If they are told humans are evil they will remember that. We are all much closer than you think.

So, animals have similar projections about other species?

Yes.

How do parrots see other species?

A wild parrot views other birds as fellow animals. We seek out elephants for our ground feeding because those big animals provide safety from ground predators. We learn at a very young age about which animals are predators.

Do you think we use each other as mirrors—in the sense of projecting aspects of ourselves we are too fearful to see in ourselves onto others, either other individuals or other species?

No, most humans and animals are not enlightened enough to realize such thoughts. We are taught and blindly follow the teachings, until we reach a place where we start questioning why.

Is there anything else you'd like to add, Jing?

My advice is that people should start to listen.

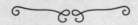

We Are the Message
Buddy (horse) ~ Jeri Ryan

We are the message. As such, we must each be within our hearts deeply. Each of us is the message we are bringing to the world and what our beingness is telling others is very important. It is important that we know what the message is that we are carrying, each of us within ourselves, so that the more we get into our hearts, the more we can know the meaning of our own life. We are living it, being it, carrying it and, everywhere we go, we are the message.

7

Bears: A Dog Who Became a Bear, a Bear Who Became a Dog, and Spirit of Polar Bear

Early in my conversations with animals and communicators, Laura Simpson told me that her dog Hannah, a Great Pyrenees who had passed away some time ago, was now a polar bear living in the Arctic.

"A polar bear!" I exclaimed. "Could we talk with her?"

"She may be willing to talk," said Laura, "but she said she's had enough of people for awhile. Hannah needed to be a polar bear, some animal that didn't have to deal with people, because they caused her so much pain. When she became a polar bear, she sent me a big message."

"Like a postcard?"

Laura laughed. "Yeah, like a postcard. Hannah was pretty funny. For a long time when I'd ask to visit with her, she'd be dressed in a Caribbean hat, like she was on vacation."

I loved the image of Hannah as a big white dog spirit dressed in a colorful Caribbean outfit, lounging on a beach chair, maybe sipping some fruity drink with a little umbrella in it, resting up before her stint as a polar bear. But, as usual, questions came to mind: Why did Hannah choose to come back as a polar bear? What was life like up at the Arctic? What did she hope to accomplish as a polar bear?

"She likes it up there because it's so nice and quiet," said Laura. "She tells me there's nobody talking to her. She says, 'We all just do what we're supposed to do. We eat well. We sleep warm. And we hold the planet together.'"

Polar bears holding the planet together?

"She says they have magnets on their feet."

I had to ponder that one.

"Well," offered Laura, "it's so magnetized up at the top of the world that she probably does feel the draw of it all. She says that polar bears are one of the fiercest animals and yet a loving, mothering tribe too. They are the ones who choose to live at the pole to help hold the planet together."

While our conversation ended there, I was curious to learn more about polar bears and their role on the planet. Perhaps, like Hannah, other polar bears chose to live where they do to avoid humans. What would we discover if they were willing to speak with us and we were willing to listen?

A few days after speaking with Laura and Hannah, I had my own connection with a bear. It made me wonder again if these talks weren't exquisitely and comically timed by some greater guiding force. The idea of Hannah the dog as a polar bear was intriguing, and somehow the connection between dog and bear made a kind of sense to me. However, I certainly didn't expect to find another dog associated with the life of a bear, nor one so close to home.

One rainy spring afternoon while working at the computer, I took a short break and sat down with Max, who was resting comfortably on the floor beside me. He was curled in such a way that his belly and back resembled a glossy black pillow, an expressive invitation for a little bit of rest.

Max is a black Labrador retriever who showed up on our back porch during a winter windstorm. He has always been a big jolly fellow, a firm believer in enjoying life and bringing the "inner puppy" out to play.

As I lay next to Max, I began to see images in my mind. Different in quality than a daydream, the experience was more like watching a movie. Although I did not initiate or expect communication, I realized that the images I was seeing were from Max. Strangely, however, the movie I was seeing was not about a dog, but about a mother black bear.

As I watched, I saw in some detail a mother bear in a den, sleeping in winter, curled in much the same position that Max was just then. The bear slept with two small cubs cuddled beside her, safely snuggled within her outstretched paws.

Was Max the bear in a past life? I was not sure, only that Max was showing me this life as "his." The experience was somewhat like watching a Fellini film, for it intermingled dreamlike sensations, vivid images, and thoughts that were narrated by both Max the dog and Max the bear. The film was also curiously out of time, as if what I was watching was also what was happening in the present. The gist of the film went something like this:

Max begins by saying that he enjoys the black bear life. He shows that while bears are hibernating and appear to be sleeping, their minds are actually very active.

Hibernation is the wrong word. Call it deep winter bear sleep. It is a comforting sensation, not unlike regular sleep, though one is more conscious of feeling very safe and warm and loved.

There is quite a lot that happens while bears appear to be in deep sleep. The mother bear transmits many of her adventures to her cubs in much the same way I am now communicating with you. This interior "movie" is very important for the cubs, so that when they go out and try things on their own in the spring, they will already have some reference. Still, seeing things in a movie isn't the same as actually doing them.

In addition to personal learning experiences and adventures, the mother bear also passes on a kind of ancestral history to her cubs while in winter sleep. This all comes from the region of the third eye area and is somewhat like a direct transmission of stored wisdom. Though similar to a dream, it is much more potent. This is the bears' version of a history lesson, and, as in every other school, some cubs pay more attention than others.

I wonder about the notion of "holding the earth together."

Black bears do indeed "hold" the earth, especially in the winter months. You can learn more about this by looking at the symbols and writings about bears, especially those relating to sleep and dreams. This holding is more of an energetic nature, that at a deep level they hold memories for certain parts of the earth while it cycles through various dormant phases. While most of what they hold are bear memories, bears also help to hold the history of the forest and the land.

Can you explain more about the role of polar bears in holding the earth?

It is their task and it is true that bears do hold the earth in the sense of holding energy and working with it in specific ways. It is also true that species are shifting in the tasks they are taking on. Bears have a lot to do with holding the earth, and humans are pretty much unaware of this. I do not know much about the brown bears, but I was listening to what the Polar Bear (Hannah) said and I think it is true.

Max then shows me that he was once a horse and, before that, a huge black whale.

I like being "big animals." I like the feeling of those vehicles and would feel squished in the body of a Chihuahua. But this is just my personal preference. My signature is also to be dark in color. Again, a matter of personal preference.

In closing, he shows me that he was once a seal, and that the seal life was fun.

There was not much I could do with Max's dream-movie other than journal it. I sensed the best thing to do was simply to let the information sit without judgment.

Taking Max's advice to look into bear symbology, I found that bears are indeed often associated with dreams and the dream lodges of Native Americans. While a more suspicious part of myself wondered if I hadn't subconsciously created a version of Hannah's story, I knew that on a conscious level it simply hadn't occurred to me that if Hannah could become a polar bear, Max could have once been a black bear.

Deciding it might be wise to check out the information, I called Sam Louie. Sam had helped me with the finches and I admired his attentiveness to confirming details and his no-nonsense approach to past lives and other areas difficult to corroborate. There was most definitely a skeptical side of Sam I could relate to.

Sam tuned into Max very quickly. I felt his connection was on target, for he described Max as a "friendly, silly, big black male dog."

"Okay," said Sam, getting down to business. "I'm telling Max we want to ask him about having been a bear in a past life." This one point was all I had told to Sam in relation to my recent experience with Max.

There was a pause, a long nervous silence on my part.

Suddenly, Sam laughed. Was Max really a bear?

Of course! Don't I look like one? What's so interesting about that?

I allowed myself a cautious laugh, though Sam laughed louder.

"He is talking to me from a subconscious level, but he's also a funny, spontaneous personality, even when talking from that wise subconscious place. He is definitely a dog with a very spontaneous spirit, both deep inside and on the surface."

"Max told me he liked to be big animals," I offered, "that in his past he liked being big."

"Yes," agreed Sam, "and gentle ones." Max says:

Bears are very gentle animals. They are no more defensive than any other animals, and probably less so. They are much less likely to have to use any of their physical power other than for food or defense than a lot of other animals. For instance, take birds. They are attacking life all day long, being defensive and running away from things. Bears are not like that. They just hang out and when they need to be defensive, they are, and when they need to eat, they eat. Bears don't hunt just to kill the way a lot of other animals do. Bears don't practice-hunt the way the cats do, the way that foxes do.

Bears are actually very gentle creatures. They are not meant to interact with humans. It is a sin to domesticate a bear, to make them into something that they are not meant to be. There are still plenty of bears who are getting domesticated around the world.

What about taking on the new tasks in relation to the earth changes? Can you say anything about that?

The Alaskan bears are. I'm not going to speak for other bears because that's where I'm from as a bear, Alaska.

It's about environmental awareness. It's the simple lesson that when people admire us and respect us and see us just for bears, there is a great amount of learning given to humans. The admiration of the animal in its natural state brings about a certain viewpoint that helps preservation of the whole planet.

Is there any more about bears?

Not unless you want to ask more.

Well, is there any other message you would like to include in this book, Max?

I love you all—those I know and those I don't know.

"That's it," said Sam. "It's a happy message."

After the conversation with Sam and Max, my confidence began to build again. Slowly, self-doubt was easing its grip, allowing a certain amount of trust to take hold. Slowly, too, I was learning that perhaps it didn't matter so much whether a dog was once a bear or a bear a dog; maybe the important thing was what that animal had to say.

Hannah's observation that polar bears are one of the few animals who choose to live in the far north, away from humans, still lingered in my mind. If these majestic animals chose to speak to humans, what would they want us to know?

When I asked Nancie LaPier if she'd help me find out, she agreed. The being with whom Nancie connected was not a living polar bear, but Spirit of Polar Bear. In metaphysical terms, this being might be thought of as an oversoul or central energetic common to all polar bears. As Nancie explained it, each individual within a species is like a ray off a central sun of that species. While one can go through an individual to get to an oversoul level, this route was more direct.

With the understanding that Nancie would be using a symbolic manner of perception in order to convey the essence of polar bear wisdom, we began our talk with the bit of information that Hannah had related: the idea that polar bears had "magnets on their feet."

Spirit of Polar Bear shows himself being upright and explains there is an open chakra at the bottom of the feet. The "magnets" on their feet are stronger on their

Nancie LaPier.

hind legs than they are on their front legs. Within the center of the earth is a particular magnet as well, which is compatibly charged to the ones that we all carry on our feet in order that we are held here with our physical bodies.

We all have energetic magnets on our feet?

Any living creature does, more particularly, life forms with feet, as opposed to fish, and less so with birds and animals of flight. Not all beings are aware of the bottoms of their feet and what happens electromagnetically by way of giving and receiving from the earth. Bears and other animals that are "surefooted" are much more aware of that relationship.

"I think our term *grounded* is what he means here," commented Nancie. "Many humans aren't even into their knees in terms of their awareness, and some not even into their hips. So, without an awareness of that part of our physical vehicle, we cut off our relationship to the earth."

If humans were a little more grounded and more fully present in the body and aware of the magnetic exchange between the actual organic earth and the physical body, the polluting and the raping of the earth would not be done. In terms of healing, it's best to "get the being in the body." Each individual's personal healing will result in a global effect, in a lot of changes in how you move upon the earth.

As for holding the earth together, polar bears have a particular energy they bring to the planet, which is part of a larger pattern that every being contributes to. There is a particular "medicine" they have, just as there is for all the different life forms on the earth. We all have a part that we play. Polar bears do not literally "hold the earth together," but represent a much stronger connection of energetic and spiritual applications between heaven and earth than some other species.

How is that?

They are connected to the magnetic grid.

Magnetic grid? Can we talk about what is the magnetic grid, both in the earth and in the feet, and the connection between the two? And especially the spiritual component of that?

Nancie's laugh startled me into realizing the intensity of my persistent inquiries. "Are you beginning to fear my questions?" I asked.

"Yes!" she exclaimed as we launched into laughter. So, too, was I aware of an element of surrealism: two women who had never met, one in Alaska, one in Connecticut, connected by a phone line, asking questions of a polar bear spirit.

"I'm just kidding," said Nancie. "I get to learn too. We're going to go deep here!"

It's difficult to describe in a particular scientific way that makes sense, but there is a magnetic grid or etheric body of the earth which is both above and within. There are certain life forms, both in spirit, physical form and within the earth, that have a talent for helping to maintain the grid in a particular way. You'll hear the term *holding the energy*. That in effect is what it means.

"So," said Nancie, "Holding the energy means that one is an anchor on one of the grid lines. But it's not even conscious; it's just an ability of this being's spiritual makeup. It's as if you were building your house and wanted someone who had electrical ability, as opposed to someone who had designing ability. There are different talents that help keep everything in divine place. This is just one of those skills that bears in general and other vertical beings—such as trees and certain humans—have the ability to participate in. For humans, you will usually find them to be very grounded, very aware and sensitive to earthly matters, and even in the body of the earth themselves.

"As for polar bears, generally speaking, they very much enjoy being in their bodies and being fully present. As I speak with this polar bear spirit, I'm aware of such body awareness that I can feel the layer of protective fat that's just under the skin and contributes to them being able to stay warm when they go into hibernation. They even have the ability to put their consciousness to that layer of their body, and if they did not, they would not be able to sustain that layer of fat. It's necessary for them to have a very strong body consciousness in order to survive. That's a part of the medicine they offer to humans who want to feel an alignment or spiritual connection with them. They could teach the gift of being fully present and really grounded into this earth plane."

Nancie paused. "That is why it is so important for humans to provide sanctuary for these animals; because when they go extinct we do not have an outward symbol to give us guidance." Spirit of Polar Bear added to this thought.

There's nothing in your objective reality left to learn from. The pleasure of seeing an animal is what usually happens first, before someone senses an alignment. At the point one begins to follow their fascination, they begin to enjoy the medicine and teaching of that particular animal. This is very important for an individual to come back to wholeness, to use their objective world and all the things in it to align with, so that one can understand those parts of oneself and actually take that power and build it within as well.

When animals go extinct, you are missing a part of the whole; you are missing something in your objective reality that would contribute to your being whole.

Other animals and communicators had also alluded to this—that by losing a connection with any animal species, we lose insight into that aspect of ourselves. The consequences are enormous, for by any animal species going extinct we lose a unique connection and, thereby, the ability to integrate that wisdom.

Have polar bears taken on a new task with regard to certain earth changes?

The answer is twofold. Yes, we participate in the earth changes, but just as have all beings that are here. As vehicles, we have facilitated bringing in, either consciously or unconsciously, a particular vibration of energy that is especially assisting those individuals who are grounded in this way because we transfer those energies from heaven—that's the term that can convey this for you—through the body and then down into the earth, and vice versa.

We take a particular energy from the earth and it moves through our body and then back to heaven. We can be the transmuters and the facilitators of this. Humans also can do this; some have intentionally offered to do that.

Bears on the earth are not as conscious of the information that is coming through. They are more happy to just be and allow, and may or may not be aware in this dimension of their service, but this is part of their service.

When Spirit of Polar Bear speaks about heaven, does he mean that in a spiritual way or as a particular star system?

Think of the star system Polaris. Look to the name.

Once again, your language speaks more strongly than you are aware. Polaris has the name *polar*—meaning significantly connected with polarity and poles, as well as that particular star system. The star system of Polaris is an exchanging place where other energies come and are stepped down in order to come here. We are part of a universal plan that is interconnected all the way back to the Oneness.

So, it doesn't need to be that specific in terms of heaven. It encompasses a spiritual awareness as well as an energetic happening. Your spiritual awareness actually creates the energetic happening anyway. It's all interconnected.

As we thanked Spirit of Polar Bear, Nancie told me that she saw him fishing.

"He has a long fishing pole and stands outside of this huge, white ice cave. He's very droll, very matter of fact, curious, and interested, but not all warm and fuzzy. Still, he's pleasant. He just sort of crosses his bottom leg and goes back to fishing. And he loves fish!"

The Mystery
Spirit of Cat ~ Nedda Wittels

Hello. I am the Nature Spirit of the domesticated felines. My responsibility is to oversee their welfare, help them stay connected with their personal spiritual guides, help elementals work with their physical forms, and be a conduit of universal consciousness from All That Is into feline form.

Much of the mystery of cats has been assigned by humans. Cats do not find themselves particularly mysterious. The key to the mystery seems to be that felines are very independent and yet align themselves with humans. The humans who feel this is a mystery are those who have forgotten or do not understand that cats were designed by the Creator to work with humans.

We also have powers such as healing, telepathy, and shapeshifting. These abilities vary with individual cats, but as a group, felines share these. When humans open to these abilities, we become partners with humans.

All species are equally important to the health and well-being of the Earth. Cats are particularly important in this time of transition to higher frequencies of consciousness. Do not mistrust their independence. That independence is their strength and a message to humans: Trust your inner knowing, your inner or Higher Self, which is the expression of God/Goddess/All That Is within you.

Many cats are also performing healing for humans and the Earth. They are particularly helpful for healing and transmuting energies. If you choose to align yourself with feline energy at this time, you will find cats helping you adjust to the new frequencies, and this will assist your personal transition to higher consciousness.

I send my personal blessings to all who wish to be in touch with me. Ask for my assistance and I will gladly give it, especially when you ask in the name of one of my felines. Thank you.

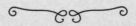

8

Violet:
On Being a Cat
and Light Worker

Violet is a Siamese cat who lives with communicator Nedda Wittels in Connecticut. When I first made contact with Nedda, she told me that both Violet and Echo, an Arabian mare, would be willing to talk with me. As Violet began answering my many questions, I was impressed by the detail of her descriptions. Violet spoke of past lives, her fondness for the feline form, and the series of events that led her to find Nedda, all with the artistic flourish of a storyteller.

In the following interview, Violet and Nedda reveal via their personal story how animals work in a variety of forms to help humans expand consciousness and more actively realize our inherent connection with all life.

Violet, can you tell us about yourself and how you first began communicating with Nedda?

I began communicating with Nedda in earlier lifetimes when we were both healers. I was in feline form then. We first met at an ancient temple where I was one of the guardians. Siamese cats have guarded temples for tens of thousands of years and that was my role at the time. Nedda was new to the temple and we had a strong affinity for each other. In those days, all humans were telepathic, at least the ones at the temples were, so there was no problem communicating. Most of them enjoyed talking with the cats and we felines each had our favorites.

The planet was very different then. Humans and animals interacted as equals and shared in the daily responsibilities of their existence. Ceremonies at the temples were performed by humans, cats, snakes, and some animals and other beings who are no longer on the Earth. It was a very peaceful and loving time and we all honored the Presence, the One Who Is All.

In later lifetimes, I have mostly been in feline form because that is my favorite. I have lived on other planets in this galaxy, and spent many hundred thousands of lifetimes as a feline/humanoid species on a distant planet. These are the dominant beings there, very sentient, artistic, tender souls, with much love and musical ability. They are quite wonderful and I would not have chosen to be on Earth except to help in the current transformation into higher frequencies.

In Nedda's current lifetime, we have been together twice before. Once, when she was a young girl, I came as a black and white male cat. It was an undistinguished lifetime, primarily designed for me to be around Nedda for a few years to see how she was progressing, to connect with her energies and to mark them with my own so that she would recognize me at a later time when our meeting would be more important.

When I came the second time, Nedda was an adult. We bonded very deeply. Nedda was immersed in her own emotional growth, so we did not speak much telepathically. Although we had a powerful connection, she left me with other humans after seven years and I had to adjust to living without her presence. During this time, I was beginning to clear my karma from many lifetimes on Earth so that I could resume my healing powers in a clear way when next we met.

My third time arriving in Nedda's current life was difficult, but I knew that we would resume our former emotional bond and could work together to achieve our life purposes. As a young feline, I was abandoned and had to live on my own and survive until Nedda and I would be brought together. I had felt abandoned by her in my most recent previous life with her, and this situation was designed to bring that issue and trust of humans to a climax so I could resolve it.

Living on Earth so many times with humans was necessary to adapt my energies so that I could be here now and do the healing work I am trained for. Still, many of these lifetimes were difficult, especially during the periods when humans and felines were enemies.

After being on my own for an entire summer, a kind woman who had been feeding me encouraged me to come with her. I placed my trust in the Presence that this was the correct path to reach Nedda, although I wasn't sure how we would connect. When the woman took me home, her two felines were angry that she had brought a third cat into the house, but she was kind enough to keep me separated. The very next day, Nedda showed up. Our energetic link was still there and she seemed to recognize me immediately. She asked me my name and whether I wanted to come home with her. I told her my name is Violet and yes, I did want to live with her.

I wasn't feeling well in the beginning and not in the mood for much conversation, but Nedda had become conscious of her abilities to communicate telepathically, so I made an effort to answer her questions. She was considerate of my health, and I began a healing process. Over time, we have built a mutually loving, supportive, and respectful relationship.

I am here now to fulfill commitments I made at the soul level, to be a partner with Nedda as a Light Worker for the Age of Ascension. This includes being a healer, at which I am very talented, as well as a teacher, which is more challenging for me. Sometimes I need to be more patient with my students. But, then, I'm a cat and they are human, and it is hard to be patient with them!

You seem to have a very clear memory of some of your past lives. How is the recall of past lives important right now—or isn't it?

Past and future and present are all simultaneous from the higher realms. It is possible to influence past and future lives by what we do in this life. If we are more loving in our current life, we can clear a lot of karma and that will help our soul's extension in other lifetimes learn their lessons more quickly and lovingly.

[Nedda:] Violet, how many past lives are you aware of?

I don't think about them much and don't know really how to count them. I just become aware of aspects of them as I encounter situations in which it proves helpful.

[Nedda:] Do you find it helpful to remember past lives?

Yes, it helps me clear up past impressions and automatic responses that don't really help much with a current life. Or it enhances a relationship. It helped me to remember who you were, and I remembered quite clearly what we had to work on. In this way, it helped me focus on what I was supposed to do.

[Nedda:] Would you recommend that humans use past life regressions or other techniques to remember their past lives?

Hmmm. There are no automatic, hard and fast rules. The main rule now is to learn to go inside and follow your own intuition. This is a form of communication from your Higher Self, and that is where humans should be looking for guidance. Does a particular activity or project enhance or help you reach your soul's purpose for this lifetime or does it distract from that? Only your own soul can tell you.

You mentioned being a healer in an ancient temple, at a time when humans were telepathic. Do you know how and why humans for the most part lost that ability?

Humans have not lost that ability; they have chosen in recent times not to develop it. I think they became afraid. Indigenous cultures did not make this

choice. They continued to live close to nature
and communicate with animals as individuals
and with the spirits responsible for individual
species and plants. Humans in more industrial
societies, especially European cultures, became
frightened by religious groups that tried to
control them (the Catholic Church in particular, during the period of the Reformation) and
industrial/city life took them away from nature.

*[Nedda:] How do you know all this
history?*

You and I lived some lives together during
that time, and I also lived some lives separate
from you during that time. It is easy for me to
tell you about this because your awareness of
memories has returned.

Violet. Photo by William Kluba.

[Nedda:] Is everyone equally telepathic?

No, even among the animals some are more skilled than others. Some animals
do have distance limitations in their abilities. Some tend to send only in certain
forms, such as pictures or knowings, for example. It is partially related to beliefs
and training by your mother. As an animal uses the ability, it grows and becomes
more complete, taking on new dimensions.

*[Nedda:] I, too, have experienced this. When I began communicating, I didn't
receive information in physical sensations, but I do now.*

It's the same for animals. There are variations. Sometimes it has to do with
what we have learned in our past lives or what our immediate life purpose is. It also
may have to do with our level of spiritual development or basic intelligence of the
spirit merged into the form. That is, there may be some genetics involved.

*What are your views on humans, Violet? How do you see us? And what is the
most important thing you would like for humans to know from the feline perspective?*

The most important thing humans need to know is that we are all One. We are
all Consciousness. We are all from the Presence. Physical form does not matter.
Only Spirit matters. When you look into the eyes of a feline, or any other being,
you need to see their soul, and because souls don't have forms, my soul and your
soul are no different from each other.

Spirit in human form is spirit that has forgotten itself for the most part. We animals are here to remind you—and many of us try on a daily basis to remind you, but you fall into forgetfulness so easily that we get frustrated. Or maybe I should say that I get frustrated. I know some who seem infinitely patient, such as Echo.

When I look at a human, I see an opportunity for transformation—the awakening of a spirit to know that the Earth is holy, that all life is equally holy, and that we must share in our love for each other and for the Earth and take care of each other and the Earth.

Sometimes I am very loving and patient and want to work to heal the Earth-Human relationship. At other times I am angry about the disrespect and harm that humans have caused on this planet. Nedda says I have a short fuse. I do anger quickly, but I see that as a virtue. There is room for moral outrage here.

When I link with other felines around the planet (we do that about once a week), we share information on the energetic vibrations where we are living. Let me just say that despite all our many efforts to transmute energies for healing humans, other animals, and the Earth, it is an uphill struggle. But we continue out of duty and love, and I try to learn patience.

I am excited about participating in this book because I hope to reach many humans in this way. I want them to feel the urgency of shifting themselves into new ways of being, new vibrational frequencies. The energies are here, and many have been and are being trained to work with them to clear blockages, balance people's energy fields, and expand their conscious understanding of what needs to happen and what their role is in the process.

If you have animals in your life, especially felines, and if you are already starting to feel the shifts in energies, be aware that the animals are working with you, sending love, healing, and light, balancing your energies, transmuting dense energies to finer, clearer frequencies. Cats are especially talented in this way.

Could you briefly comment on what life is like on other planets, other galaxies, other dimensions? I've often wondered if that is where animals "go" when they seem to be just sitting staring off into space. Cats especially seem good at that—can you let us in on any secrets?

Nedda said that as she read this question, Violet stared at her with wide open eyes. This is a big question.

[Nedda:] Violet, are you going to answer this? Are there secrets about this?

Well, of course, I won't tell secrets, because then they will no longer be secrets. However, I will answer the question.

Felines do like eye contact. Not all other species like it. When we are staring off into space, sometimes we are speaking with our personal spirit guides or with other beings who do not have physical form at this time. Sometimes we are meditating with our eyes open. Sometimes we are having other spiritual experiences. Sometimes we are talking to other animals. Sometimes we are contemplating great truths. Sometimes we are admiring ourselves. Sometimes we have out-of-body experiences, but more often our eyes are closed when we do that.

As for other planets, galaxies, universes, and dimensions, that is too vast a subject.

[Nedda:] Won't you give us a taste of it?

There is a planet where there are feline/humanoids who are highly spiritual beings. There are plants there that sing and produce other musical tones and vibrations. This planet is especially beautiful. The felinoids are quite physically powerful. They have a variety of colors and patternings on their fur. They stand on their rear legs and their forelegs are like hands. The females are dominant in their culture—they are the healers and spiritual leaders. The males raise the young and are very nurturing. Both sexes like to hunt, although the females tend to do more of this. This species is very reverent, seeing consciousness everywhere and living their existence entirely based on unconditional love. When they hunt, they pray for permission from the species they are hunting and offer many gifts to honor the individuals whose lives are sacrificed. There is little or no conflict there because of the total focus on love energy.

[Nedda:] How do you know about this place? Have you been there?

Yes. I lived many lives there in preparation for coming to Earth. These are my people. Someday, I hope to return home to them.

Can you speak more about that weekly linkup you have with other felines around the planet? Is it with all felines everywhere or just those who choose to be "on-line," so to speak?

Yes, it is like being on-line, to use your technology term, except the exchange is not limited to words, and we often merge into a kind of oneness so that everyone experiences what the others experience. It might feel like overload to a human at this point, but for us it is blissful and fairly easy to integrate the information.

It is not all the cats on the planet doing this, but those who are here at this time to focus on planetwide events. Sometimes we just check in. Always we share information. Always we offer prayers for each other, for our human families and friends, and for the Earth and all humanity and all other species working and living on the Earth at this time.

There are also subgroups that work as teams, sometimes in specific localities or on specific projects. Nedda knows about the Orange Cat Contingent.[1] Well, there is also an Oriental Cat Contingent that includes felines of many Oriental breeds who have memories of the earlier times that I share. As guardians of the temples of old, we are working to bring back knowledge of healing techniques we developed with humans in those ancient times. That is part of why I am here with Nedda, who does healing work.

If you would care to let your feline acquaintances know about this book, I would certainly welcome their comments.

I have already told them about this and reviewed the information they wanted to share, and we discussed the issue about secrets. The reason for intraspecies secrets is often to protect the species from human interference. It is not wise to give others information for which they have not been adequately prepared. So we discussed and debated this issue and as I answer the questions today I am keeping in mind our decisions about this. They did agree that I could be the spokesfeline for the group.

What can humans do for animals?

It depends on their level of consciousness. For most people, the first step is to acknowledge our sentience by speaking with us vocally as if we really do under-stand every word—which we do! Tell us what is going on in your life that affects our lives so we can prepare ourselves.

Then, open yourselves to receive our communication. Sit quietly with us and open your heart center and be receptive to whatever you experience. Get in tune with your own ways of receiving and do this often, and soon you will "hear" us.

Send love to animals who live apart from humans, expressing honor and respect for them. They have a birthright to be on the Earth, and the Earth and humans and other animals need their presence here. When the last of a species leaves the Earth, a great cry of pain can be heard and felt by everyone, for this adds to the imbalance of all.

Practice treating all life with reverence and respect. Give thanks to all plants and animals for the nourishment their bodies provide you. It is best to do this before ending the life of the plant or animal, but it can still be healing when you do this after the fact. Ask for spiritual guidance in all tasks and activities you perform, especially when working with nature. You will receive much information and help, more than you might imagine when you first begin working in this way.

And most importantly, live each day and perform each action from a place of love.

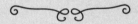

On Oneness

Katie (cat spirit) ~ Teresa Wagner

We're all one, truly. There is no hierarchy. One kind is not better than another; one kind is different from another. I do love the cat form. I have been in it many times, and may come again. Some humans may love the human form and come back many times, but there is no hierarchy. For instance, a human who is very concerned about helping the earth may come back sometimes as an earthworm, one of the earth's greatest forms that helps ecology. This is not silly. We are all One, and the best thing we can all remember is this. Because as we live and choose, we are choosing not just for one being or one species or one kind, but always making decisions for all.

9

Past Lives,
Future Lives, and
Living in the Now

To know the universe itself as a road—
as many roads—
roads for traveling souls.

Walt Whitman,
Leaves of Grass,
"Song of the Open Road"

Sam Louie once knew a dog named Whistler who lived with a couple in California. The couple was visiting Australia when the woman received a message from her sister, who was caretaking Whistler. The sister related that Whistler had been having seizures, so she rushed him to the vet. The vet was having a hard time controlling the seizures and felt that because Whistler was in a lot of pain, it was appropriate to put him down. The sister wanted to know if she should have Whistler euthanized. The woman didn't know what to do. Here she was, thousands of miles away from Whistler. How could she make such an important decision from so far away? It was then she remembered that someone had given her the number of an animal communicator who lived back in California. She just happened to have the number with her. And that is how the woman called Sam from Australia.

Sam related,

I got in touch with Whistler and asked him how he was feeling. He said he was in a lot of pain and was scared because his body was out of control. But he didn't want to die in the vet's hospital alone. The couple wasn't scheduled to come back for four days. Whistler said, "Well, I'll hang on. Just have them give me pain killers until they get home, then bring me home and have them put me down then."

When the couple got home, they called me again to ask Whistler if he was ready to go. He basically said he was so happy to see them that he wanted to spend a few days with them. He was still having seizures and was incontinent and couldn't walk on his back legs.

This went on for about three weeks—the couple calling and Whistler telling me to tell them he wanted to stay. The couple took time off work to be with Whistler. They stayed outside with him. They dug a hole in the ground and laid his rear end over it so they wouldn't have to carry this hundred-pound dog back and forth. They even put up a tent in the back yard so they could sleep with him.

In one of Whistler's last communications, he said how grateful and thankful he was to this couple. He also said that he felt that his purpose with them was to help them learn love and repair their marriage. He said that his death and this crisis provided a window of opportunity for the couple to really learn love and some profound messages of life. Whistler said he felt they had jumped through the window with him. They had seized the opportunity by taking time off work, sleeping with him outside, cleaning up after him, and even cooking him steaks. They had chosen to take time to be with each other as well as him.

Then Whistler told me about a past life. I normally don't like to emphasize past lives because I can't corroborate them. But Whistler wanted me to know that in his past life he had been a stockbroker. He said that he had consciously chosen to be a white male born in the late 1890s, and that he knew that there was going to be a cataclysm on Wall Street. He became a stockbroker and ran his own brokerage house. He wanted to do that in order to keep as many people sane and employed as he could. He told me that he died shortly after the war started because he knew at that point the financial crisis was basically over. It was a very stressful life. He died of a heart attack at a fairly young age, but he was ready to exit.

Given all the stress of that life, he wanted to come back and have an easy life. So he chose to be a dog where he would be well loved and could play and roll in the mud. Whistler also told me that with his mission accomplished here, he was going to come back in about thirty years. He would be a child born into a war zone. He would be one of these media children who would talk about the effects of war on children, and it would be a time when politicians would very seriously start to seek an end to war on a worldwide level, not just simply make peace in particular regions, but really push for a permanent end to the war mentality.

"Now," said Sam with a sigh, "that's not a typical reading I get and yet I felt quite sure of the information from him." And then Sam finished the story.

The last part of this story is what ties it all up, because the woman called me after Whistler died. When she told me she wanted a personal reading, I said, "It's about marital infidelity, isn't it?" She said yes, that she'd had an affair with a man and hadn't worn her wedding ring in three years. She said, "I want to tell you that after our experiences with Whistler and being with each other for three weeks in this crisis, I've decided to put my ring back on to reaffirm my marriage with my husband."

I then realized that's what Whistler had been talking about. Because the window of opportunity presented in his dying was taken, Whistler's purpose of coming in to help this couple relearn love and repair their marriage had been fulfilled.

Penelope Smith calls reincarnation "the connecting thread." She writes, "As spiritual beings, we are free to choose the form of life that suits our own desire for experience in the physical universe. Those who have had human bodies may now have animal forms, or the reverse, for various reasons and with no set paradigm that applies to all."[1]

Some people have trouble with the notion of humans becoming animals and vice versa. One way we prevent ourselves from considering the idea is by adopting the belief that animals don't have souls. Another way of distancing ourselves is by clinging to simplistic versions of evolution, whereby life forms move from "lower" to "higher" levels.

Communicators point out that most animals do not support a hierarchical view of life. Rather, different forms provide different experiences. The purpose of taking a particular form is to learn what it is like to be in that type of body and experience life through that unique perspective.

Jarvi, a former sled dog, related to Marcia Ramsland that one reason a being might choose to become an animal is purely for delight. "There is great joy in coming in as an animal," Jarvi said, "especially if you've been a person, because animals are so very directly connected to the here and now. Your senses are highlighted, your body is graceful, you are holistically connected; it's the perfect antidote to the more intellectual lifestyle that people tend to have. Although people really aren't cut off from the world, they often feel that they are, so returning as an animal can be very therapeutic."

While certain animals, such as Jing, Violet, and Whistler, express detailed knowledge of past lives, not all animals carry such conscious awareness. At times, the concept of past lives is just as much a baffling mystery to animals as it is to humans.

Sam Louie related that many of the animals he's known have no idea what a past life entails. Sam's old dog, Peppy, told me the same thing. "I have no idea where I've been in past lives," said Peppy. "The only time I know is when we have workshops and people tell me what they see. Where I'm going, I don't know. I'm happy just to be on this couch right now."

Anita Curtis, a communicator and author living in Pennsylvania, tells a remarkable story about a horse named BB. Before BB was born, Anita asked a pregnant mare when she planned on having her foal and received the answer, "Tuesday five." This made no sense to Anita since the fifth was a Saturday, not a Tuesday. Perhaps the horse meant Tuesday at 5:00? When Anita pressed for further information, the horse became exasperated and Anita dropped the issue.

Anita Curtis and BB.

On Saturday, February 5 an Arabian filly was born and later given the barn name BB. Anita became very attached to BB even though the filly lived with other people. Insights about her strong affinity to BB came to Anita a little at a time. First, there was the odd recognition that "Tuesday five" was the anniversary of her mother's death, Tuesday, February 5. Anita also recalled that her mother had been called Beebee as a child. And then there was BB's habit of sticking her tongue outside her mouth and sucking on it with a slurpy sound. Anita recalled her mother's four-pack-a-day smoking habit, always a cigarette sticking out of her mouth.

"Could it be her?" Anita wrote. "No, it was too bizarre. . . . Other people had these experiences with reincarnation, but it couldn't happen to me." [2] It took many other coincidences, confirmations, and strange workings of the universe to prod Anita into accepting that the horse BB might really be the reincarnation of her mother.

The story curled inside of me like a snail finding a home. On the surface, it was, as Anita said, bizarre, yet even so there was something familiar about it. It reminded me of what my grandmother had told me several times when I was young: that when she died, she wanted to become a horse. If you were a horse, she said, you could run so fast across the land that it felt as if you were flying. I don't know if my grandmother seriously believed she might become a horse, but it did make her smile as she gazed out the window and spoke of galloping through the fields, the wind in her mane.

When I asked Anita if she still believed BB was the reincarnation of her mother, she said, "Yes. Dealing with the doubt was not easy, but too many things pointed to her being my mother."

Perhaps situations like this are a final exam in the how-far-can-you-stretch-your-beliefs department. While it is one thing to accept the idea that reincarnation is possible—not only for people but for animals—surely it is quite another to find your mother has come back as a horse. I wondered what I would do if one day I met my grandmother living it up as a horse, neighing and snorting and flying across the fields.

When she took her first animal communication workshop, Anita was shocked to find that other participants spoke about past lives. "I considered myself very open-minded, but I certainly would not blurt something like that out in a room full of strangers," she wrote.[3] What had happened that brought her to a place where she could write about such things?

"My work has changed my views on the traditional framework of reality and spirituality," Anita told me. "BB's role in my life just brings home the everyday living with all I do in dealing with the animals and their people." And what about BB? I asked Anita to ask the four-year-old horse if she believed she was once a human. "I don't remember pasts," said BB. "I know I'm here to be loved, and Anita loves me."

Perhaps that is all that matters.

While some animals don't recall or emphasize past lives, others are not hesitant to talk about it. Sam Louie related that one of his first professional consultations was with a woman's Tibetan terrier. "As soon as I tuned into him he showed me a life as a very lonely Tibetan monk. He said that he didn't like that life and wanted to come back where he didn't have to be lonely, where he could be gushing and silly and small. The woman later told me there was a myth about Tibetan terriers, that they were all wayward monks come back as dogs."

Raphaela Pope related that for her, sensing an animal's past lives was not particularly hard. The difficult part was explaining what the animal said to the human. Raphaela remembered a spaniel puppy who couldn't be induced to wear a collar. This was important to the person because he wanted to show the dog. The man had consulted many experts, none of whom could figure out why the collar was such a problem. "The puppy told me he had been hanged in another life. It was a very dramatic and scary story. I told the person what the puppy said. He politely paid me and left and I never heard from him again." Raphaela laughed. "I wonder if it was just too far out for him or what!"

Only a hop, skip, and jump away from the far-outness of past lives is the idea of future lives. Whistler told Sam that he planned to come back, even citing a time span of when that might occur. Communicators have many stories about animals who talk of returning and, among animals, there seems to be general agreement that there is some choice about when and where and in what form one comes back. But where is it one comes back from? What is the experience of being *out* of physical form?

"It's very freeing," said Katie, a spirit who once lived as a cat with communicator Teresa Wagner. "And it's very powerful. Being in form provides some joy and challenges to remember who we truly are and to become more whole, but here I'm whole. Being out of form is being in spirit, and that's who we all are."

"I think animals have a greater understanding of the life and death thing," Marcia Ramsland confided. "Maybe it's because they spend a great deal of time in the alpha brain wave frequency. Imagine the insights you would have if you spent as much time meditating each day as your companion animal does, sitting quietly doing nothing! I think animals who spend many hours a day just sitting quietly have found a place to reside in their mind. I think they know things that we don't know because they're operating in a more holistic space."

From this space, death may appear as a doorway, a transition point between dimensions. Indeed, the difficulty with death is most often not so much from the animal perspective as from the human perspective.

"Animals are not afraid of death as we are," Carol Gurney agreed. "If you can give your animal permission to go when they are ready, the transition can be much easier for everybody. You won't avoid the pain—that's part of the process—but you will make it less painful and will actually begin to see that there is a beauty in death."

To reframe death in such a manner from the human perspective is a journey unto itself. As I was working on this chapter, Anita Curtis sent word that her horse, Porcia, her mentor and friend, the large Arabian mare who had helped her write her books, was, by her own request, to be euthanized.

"We are all devastated," Anita wrote me. "Porcia will always be with us, but not being able to see or touch her will be almost unbearable."

The date for Porcia's death was set ten days in advance. For several days, I propped Anita's book open to the photo of Porcia. Even through the black and white photo, it was easy to sense Porcia's inner depth. As Anita wrote, "Porcia has large, marvelous eyes that peer into your innermost being, and when she communicates in person, she stares into your eyes until she is sure you have the message she wants to convey. When I met this magnificent mare, I felt like I was standing in the shadow of greatness, but

I had no idea just how deep her wisdom was."[4]

Anita told me that another mare named Shaza had also decided to leave her body. Porcia, Shaza, and Briana (mother of BB) were kept by a man whose teenage son had recently died. Though the mares lived in different locations, each told Anita they were taking on some of the pain of the family. When Porcia and Shaza became very ill, they chose to leave.

Anita related that she went to Briana wondering how she was going to get through the ordeal. Briana told her it was a celebration of joy. "I argued with her," said Anita, "but she kept repeating it. She finally said, Look in your flower book. I dusted off my *Flower Essence Repertory* and looked up *joy*. The first essence was 'Angel's Trumpet: Acceptance of death as a joyous transition, deep release or liberation of the soul as an expression of joy.' I couldn't believe it!"

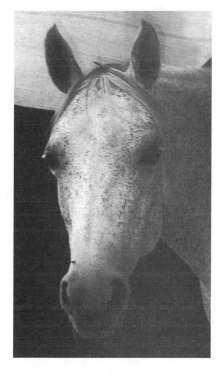

Porcia. Photo by Anita Curtis.

Just as Whistler felt his death brought about a "window of opportunity" for the living, so too does death provide a new window, a new perspective for the traveling soul. Unfettered from the brain and the limits of our thoughts and senses, how does one perceive reality from outside our usual framework of reference? It is a paradoxical thought, because to think it accurately you must step outside of what we know as thought.

An iguana named Lila summed it up to Raphaela Pope like this. "Everything is simply energy. Objects and living beings vibrate at different rates. But there is no real difference in matter. Going in and out of living, dying, different bodies is very common, very ordinary. Humans partially block their awareness of past and future lives. The better to focus in the present. Animals have no such other needs. We are more elemental. We know that everything is happening now. It is a simpler and more complete perspective, not as complicated as humans make things."

From the holistic perspective of an ever present now, past, future, and even present lives are all variations on a theme. Like Lila, other animals caution that while past and future lives may be meaningful from a certain perspective, at some point chasing these stories becomes more diversionary than helpful. Why? Because the very idea of past and future lives binds one to a linear concept of time. As Nancie LaPier points out, "It also prevents one from being fully present in the now, which is the only point in 'time' where we can affect patterns and recreate our futures." To jump into the now thus requires a new understanding, a larger frame of reference.

Raphaela Pope felt her concept of time was evolving through her discussions with whales. "Several whales have expressed the idea of time being simultaneous," explained Raphaela. "It's like the nineteenth century is still happening and the twentieth century is still happening and the twenty-fifth century is also happening, and they are all in the present. One way I understand it is by thinking of us all having a soul or higher self that is simultaneously running many personalities, many lives, in lots of different time periods and countries, with different languages, different cultures."

The concept of time as a boundless now is a cornerstone of many esoteric schools of thought and a common denominator in the mystical experience. In terms of modern physics, it has a home in the holographic model, an understanding that all parts, all moments, contain the whole.

Most scientists who tinker with the edges, holes, and wrinkles of time assert that time is a very human construction. Though culturally and linguistically built so well that it seems real, it is actually a grand fiction we have all agreed upon. As Stephen Hawking notes, "What we call real [time] is just an idea that we invent to help us describe what we think the universe is like. A scientific theory is just a mathematical model we make to describe our observations: it exists only in our minds. So it is meaningless to ask: Which is real, 'real' or 'imaginary' time? It is simply a matter of which is the more useful description."[5]

The leap to a boundless here and now suggests that we understand ourselves as multidimensional beings. Instead of seeing ourselves as creatures who have souls, we shift perspective and realize we are souls who choose physical forms. If we want to get fancy, we open that to include many physical forms. Not only do we have one life, we play many lives. And not only that, but our past, present, and future lives all exist simultaneously. How is that possible? Again, it involves a brain wiggle to expand our perception and get beyond our present understanding of time.

When entertaining such ideas as simultaneous lives and multidimensional realities, we approach the slippery brink of thought itself, both in and out of time. From the past to the future, we sit precariously on the edge of now. And still we ask ourselves, who are we? What is real?

Alas, it is Chuang Tzu and the butterfly all over again:

Chuang Tzu, a Chinese Taoist, once dreamed he was a butterfly fluttering over flowers, doing exactly as he pleased. He didn't know he was Chuang Tzu. Suddenly, he awoke and there he was, unmistakably Chuang Tzu. But now he didn't know: Am I Chuang Tzu who dreamed he was a butterfly, or am I a butterfly dreaming he is Chuang Tzu?[6]

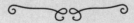

Magic

Raphaela Pope and Pluto (horse)

Pluto is a Lippizan, a wonderful horse. I told Pluto about this book and asked him what he would like humans to know. Here is what he said:

"Tell people that there really is magic. There really are beings beyond your normal senses, and you will be able to talk to them and receive their information and wisdom as easily as I do. Assure everybody there really is magic."

Now he gives me a picture of truly gorgeous rolling hills. He says, "Be content. Eat grass." It's funny; you get some very elevated perspectives and then some very basic views. Pluto adds:

"We're entering a time when humans and animals will be closer together and understand each other better. People will know that animals have an interior life, their own purposes, and sincere and intense relationships. When people understand and respect this about animals, they will be more forbearing and respectful of each other."

Pluto is reminding me of a reading in which he showed me that he and his person had past lives together: he was a cavalry horse and she was a soldier. Now he's saying, "Less war! less conflict!" I think they actually died in that battle. Maybe it's going on as we speak. Who knows? The Universe is mysterious.

10

Echo:
On Elevating Consciousness
and the Equine Form

In the evershifting ability of Spirit to experience itself in various forms, species, times, and cultures—in short, in all kinds of lives—there is possibility for infinite diversity, endless combinations. All embodiments provide an opportunity to learn through experience.

Dropping into one existence, you have a life, soak up the culture, and then you die. Well, that was exciting, what about another? And so you choose another place and time, another body, another name, another variation on a theme, for there you meet others you have known, in new roles now as they interact with you as parents, children, lovers, friends, and foes. This is the grand metaphor of life as play, game, and drama.

No doubt at first this would be a great deal of fun. Imagine going anywhere, anytime: traveling to the Delphi oracle; helping to design the great tombs and pyramids in Egypt; listening to the Buddha in India; discovering fire and creating language in the time before time; shapeshifting with the yellow-eyed wolves; flitting through ancient jungles as a giant mosquito; mating as an ostrich, a dinosaur, a being on another planet; crawling from your shell and slithering across the sand only to be plucked up and swallowed by a sharp-eyed gull; sliding back and forth between the folds of dimensional reality in the form of a large, beautiful black-backed whale.

As you grew in experience, you would grow in confidence, daring yourself to try ever more dangerous lives, always looking for a little more thrill, a little more experience, venturing a little closer to the unknown. If you are always and forever spirit, birth and death are simply a walk through the changing room: new life, new clothes, new body, new story. Remembering your connection to spirit, there would be no trauma associated with either coming into or leaving the world.

But what if you forgot who you really were? By forgetting your connection to All That Is, you'd be undertaking a new, ever more dangerous and yet exciting adventure, one in which you would have the opportunity to discover your true identity all over again.

"In a world of duality where everything exists in opposites, it appears there is great bliss in forgetting you are an expression of God only to rediscover this," Nedda Wittels told me. "It's like discovering how good water tastes after you've been without it for three days. I guess some beings, like you and me, have chosen to have this experience. As far as I can tell, only the human form provides this experience."

Echo, an Arabian mare who lives with Nedda, agrees. "Humans have forgotten," said Echo. "It's all just part of the game."

Just as the interview between myself, Nedda, and Violet the cat unfolded, Echo and Nedda agreed to share personal information as a means of illustrating how and why certain relationships are formed between humans and animals.

Echo, can you tell us about yourself and how you first began communicating with Nedda?

I am a being of light who has chosen an equine form for this lifetime. Nedda and I are from the same soul consciousness and have worked as a team countless times, both in and out of physical form. When I speak to others with psychic ability, they see me as a winged Pegasus, an angelic equine. I am a being of love.

What does it mean to be from the same soul consciousness?

The soul is an individuation of the Creator consciousness that exists at a particular vibrational frequency range, sometimes called the soul plane. This range of frequencies includes Oversouls, who are teachers and guides for souls at lower ranges of frequencies. Each soul is learning many lessons simultaneously by extending its energy into physical form to experience "life" in a particular level of existence. Actually, all levels of existence are consciousness and, therefore, alive. However, there are understandings to be learned by experiencing the variety of possible existences that are available in the universe.

On the soul plane, time is not as you experience it here on the Earth. Each soul experiences a multitude of lifetimes and many are experienced simultaneously, even though they would appear from your perspective to be taking place across hundreds or thousands of years and in sequence. Sometimes, a special pairing occurs called soul mates. This is when two aspects of a soul share a particular lifetime in physicality. While it is more common for both aspects to take the same type of form, Nedda and I are such and have taken different forms to achieve specific purposes and to enable us to support each other in specific ways at this time.

What do you see as your life purpose?

In this lifetime, I have had many important tasks to fulfill. First, I had to be

Echo.

beautiful; strong, yet sensitive; spirited, yet gentle; fiery, yet calm and centered. I had to epitomize these seeming contradictions so that many would be drawn to my presence to experience my energies, so that they could take in the love and gentleness and know that horses do not need to be handled roughly, without feeling, but can be handled tenderly, with caring, concern, and an open heart.

I also agreed to develop Nedda's telepathic abilities during a time when she had forgotten them. I had to work subtly, with love and gentleness and great determination. She was hiding these abilities from herself and was not ready for a long time to acknowledge them.

A third task was to be a mirror for some of Nedda's issues of spiritual growth. This means she is also my mirror. We grow through interacting with each other. There are many animals on earth who have this role with one or more members of their family. It is a challenging task because often the human does not see the parallels between themselves and the animal. Still, it is an effort of love and quite worth doing, in my opinion.

Can you speak more about the importance of having "seeming contradictions" for others to experience your particular energies?

The meaning of the word *contradictions* is important here, although the concept of duality is a contracted quality, meaning that to experience duality, the soul must contract itself—literally become smaller—to fit into a physical form. English is not a language that easily expresses some spiritual concepts.

To understand my meaning, it is important to remember that the third dimension is one of duality, and humans have largely understood that opposites cannot coexist without contradiction or conflict. This is an illusion. Because ultimately there is only One, the appearance of contradiction and conflict needs to be resolved. One way to resolve it is to experience the harmony of oppositions coexisting as Oneness. This is experiential, not logical, as humans currently think about logic.

When you can look into the eyes of another and see the Beloved, that is one way of experiencing nonduality. When you can see faces (consciousness) in a tree, that is another way. There are many ways to experience this, and each human will begin to have these experiences more often in the near future.

In regards to being a mirror for Nedda, and she for you, can you speak more about how beings interact with each other in various lifetimes in this way? And is this as an aspect of karma?

This is a very large subject and could be an entire book in itself!

As each being experiences life in a physical form, some of what they experience is karmic and some is what they have chosen at the soul level to experience. In order to have both types of experiences, they are matched with or choose others who agree to experience the other side of the events for their own growth and learning. Much of this is very subtle. Here is an example.

Let's say there is a human who likes things done in particular ways and is very controlling, becoming angry when things are not done to her specification. This human will be surrounded by some people and animals who have the same issue but different rules. The human will also have in her life people and animals who don't care about doing things in rigid patterns at all. The first group reflects the same pattern, but with different specifics. The second group reflects the aspect of the person who wants to break away from this rigidity. Both groups will cause the human to feel discomfort and a great deal of anger.

The karmic lesson involves recognizing the pattern and developing flexibility. The anger that the human experiences is a key to uncovering the pattern because anger is a very uncomfortable feeling and the human will want to get rid of the anger. In an effort to do so, she will become aware of the pattern and work to resolve that issue to eliminate the anger.

[Nedda:] Echo, do we have karmic issues between us?

Yes. Some have to do with your desire to protect me from pain and discomfort. In other lifetimes you were unable or unwilling to take care of me. You are still carrying some guilt from that, which has made you overly protective of me. It is in finding a balance, where you provide care that is reasonable and loving, but not smothering, that you and I resolve this together.

[Nedda:] What is your part in this?

The issue for me is allowing myself to be cared for, which is also another issue of yours, because you like to be independent and not need anyone's help. I had to fully trust that you would eventually recognize me as a free and independent being who enjoys being loved and cared for and at the same time wants to be free. That is part of the quandary for horses—how to be with humans in a partnership that recognizes the horse as independent and simultaneously a human "pet." So, I get to work on my issue and you get to work on your issues and we both benefit.

What about your views on humans, Echo? How do you see us and what would you like humans to know from the equine perspective?

Humans are beings of love who have forgotten what love is and who they are. Truly, humans live in a dream, sleepwalking most of the time. They miss so much: the beauties of nature, the glories of God, the sacredness of all things, the consciousness that exists everywhere. It amazes me that this much forgetfulness can go on for so long, and that so many humans seem to prefer to be in that somnambulant state.

On the other hand, I have taken human form many times, and I do recall that it can be quite ecstatic to re-awaken to the joy and bliss of knowing you are one with God, Goddess, All That Is. Still, I prefer to be conscious of this to being unaware of it.

The equine perspective . . . now that is very special to me. I have enjoyed being a horse more than any other form I have experienced, especially because I love to fly-run. (Flying and running are quite similar feelings of freedom.)

However, many horses live miserable lives with humans. They are often treated cruelly, heartlessly, like inanimate objects. They may be abused, starved, overworked. A very few horses have a completely happy existence. I believe that those who prefer this form take it again and again because they find the form so enticing, even when the lifetime itself may be filled with woe.

Still, each lifetime is designed for a spiritual experience. We take bodies to have certain types of experiences. This enables spiritual growth, an expansion of understanding, and playfulness. The universe exists as a playground for the many consciousnesses that exist, all of whom are expressions and aspects of All That Is.

While there is Spirit of Horse, a being whose purpose is to watch over equine matters on Earth, any individual horse form may contain a being who in a previous existence was in some other form and who may have never been a horse before. What a fascinating, joyful play of consciousness, to take different forms and learn about each of those perspectives!

Where do you think we are all headed as a planet?

I don't know that you are all headed for the same dimension. The raising of vibrational frequencies is happening for all on the planet, regardless of form, but will not become permanent for any particular individual unless consciously chosen. Many dimensional shifts are becoming possible at this time. It is difficult to speak of time frames because each being on the planet and their level of consciousness influences the timing at any given moment. Complex, yes?

Ah, but the opportunities are fantastic! To remember who you are! To become part of a unity consciousness based entirely on love. That is where many of you are going, and that is where the Earth is headed. But each being, including the Earth Mother, gets to choose. How delightful to play this game of life!

I don't disagree with any of what you're saying, Echo, but I sometimes feel this is too strange for readers. Even the idea of talking to animals is, I suppose, strange for some. What would you say to those people?

People will be called to read this book because they are ready for it, and as they read it, they will remember the eternal truth: nothing exists that is not consciousness—God/Goddess/All That Is. Once they recognize and remember that, it will all make sense to them.

Those who think it is too strange are not ready and won't read it. And that's OK. This book is not for them.

Thank you for giving me the opportunity to participate in this project. We are all working together for the same goal—to help reawaken those who are ready to wake up.

Part Three

A Question of Perspective

Moving Past the Comfort Zone

Beyond Karma and Back

The Innernet

This Magnificent Dance
The Council of All Beings — Morgine Jurdan

Do you wonder how everything fits together? How when you think a thought, magic happens and begins a process that often results in something you want to happen? How do plants and animals know what to do to keep things going? How does each element work in harmony with the rest? What synchronizes this magnificent dance between all forms of life?

You can learn to move in balance and harmony merely by observing, feeling, and asking questions of beings such as ourselves. You can learn much more about a bird by observing its life than by capturing it. We smile and shed tears when you judge the intelligence of a creature using standards you use to judge yourselves. If we were to capture you, put you in our environment, and see how you meet our standards when it comes to survival—flying, swimming, digging, singing—we think you would fail.

Why not learn to love the magic and mystery you find in life instead of trying to control things? It can become an exciting adventure to let go and trust. We suggest you learn what harmony and balance are about for each of you. There are no hard and fast rules that will work for everyone. You are each unique individuals doing your own dance, and you will discover your own way to play the game.

What we share has deeper meaning, a way of discovering who you are and what you are here to do. You cannot do this in isolation. Each one of us—each part of the universe—is affected by your thoughts, feelings, actions. We all benefit and suffer. We are all here, sending unconditional love to aid you in creating what you desire, for when you do, we all benefit from your joy and happiness and love, which is shared by all.

Begin anew today. Inhale life consciously and see where it might take you. Blessings and love to you all.

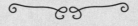

11

Moving Past the Comfort Zone

Sugar was a dolphin who once lived in a lagoon on the Atlantic coast where she put on exhibitions and interacted with people until, after a short illness, she died. When I asked Raphaela Pope if she knew of any animals who chose to live in captivity rather than being free in the wild, Sugar came to speak.

It's all a question of perspective. It's all a way to increase experience. Experience is creation. A different world is being created as we speak. I chose not to stay in this lagoon with the people. One of many choices, one of many lifetimes. It was not as much of a sacrifice as you might think. I did not lose my perspective of my other personalities. It was one among many. My goal was to bring to people the perspective of the majesty, power, beauty, and intelligence of other animal life-forms.

Is this a common goal among dolphins?

It's true that dolphins as a species have a very shimmering light energy.

Raphaela paused. "Oh, it's so beautiful! Sugar is showing me a grid, and where the lines intersect are shimmering points of light. I think this is her picture of life or the universe. Now the grid is changing to look like a vast expanse of water shimmering, with a bubbling, streaming energy, glittering. It's like seeing atoms shining."

This is pure life energy. This is accessible to all of us. We choose our forms. You could choose to be a dolphin.

Raphaela laughed. "Oh, maybe I will!"

Can you explain how you did not lose perspective of your other personalities?

It's a matter of physical brain structure and chemistry. Religious or ecstatic experience is required for humans to get beyond their day-to-day perspective. We are less intellectual, more holistic, and even while we're engrossed in swimming, eating, and mating, we don't lose the holistic perspective.

Sugar reminded Raphaela of the shimmering ocean of energy and reiterated that it is really all the same, just a matter of perspective.

Raphaela laughed. "I think that's where she started!" Indeed, Sugar had brought us full circle, as dolphins so often gracefully do. Raphaela felt that just as other animals

Dolphin. Photo by Ilizabeth Fortune.

might confirm a communication by reaching out a paw, Sugar used her dolphin life as a type of confirmation and communication. That captivity "was not as much a sacrifice as one may think" was perhaps to emphasize that the dolphin life was just one among a simultaneous many.

It was a big thought, and I was beginning to feel the effects of Sugar's expansive energy. Caught in the game, I tossed out a question of curiosity, just as someone might have once tossed Sugar a fish. Little did I know that it was going to take us in a much different direction—again reminding me that no act, no question, is without consequences.

Sugar, can you tell us what you're going to do next? Where are you now and where are you going to go?

There was a long pause and when Raphaela finally spoke, her voice had changed. "Oh God, Dawn, I hate this."

"What's wrong?" I was as mystified as Raphaela was upset.

"I just hate this," said Raphaela. "I have to tell you, I feel I'm a pretty down to earth animal communicator. I want to help people solve litter box problems, as well as expand their perspective about who and what animals are. But when animals tell me they're on another planet, I just go, 'Oh no!'"

"Sugar says she's on another planet right now?"

"Yes, she is," replied Raphaela with resignation.

"Well, some people suggest there's a link between cetaceans and other planets," I offered.

"I know, and that's why I have never gotten too involved with those people." Raphaela chuckled. "Because they seem pretty out there to me. But I know there are people who think I'm pretty out there too."

"Maybe it has to do with what Sugar's been saying, that it's all a matter of perspective."

"Right! It's all a matter of perspective. So, she's enlarging my perspective!" Suddenly, Raphaela became jolly about the whole thing. She struck me as someone who finds it easy to laugh at herself, yet is equally determined to winnow out the origins of such humor.

"This is so sweet," said Raphaela. "She's comforting me. She's saying, 'You don't have to think of me on another planet.' She knows I think that's just too wiggy! She's very sensitive. She senses I'm tired but says she is willing to talk again."

And so our conversation ended.

It was a few weeks before Raphaela, Sugar, and I were able to reconnect. In the meantime, I was opening to animals at a fast and furious pace. Though I had read many of the exercises designed to deepen our telepathic link with animals, for myself none of it was happening in such a neat and orderly fashion.

In what I now believe was an attempt to short-circuit my deep-rooted and pernicious sense of self-doubt, my dogs were working overtime to get me to open. Most often they knocked me for a loop when I was least expecting it, thus least resistant.

A few days after talking with Raphaela, I was about to head upstairs when Barney, a white cocker spaniel–poodle–terrier who has lived with me for many years, sat himself on the stairs in such a way that I knew something was up. The angle of his sitting, the way his deep brown eyes looked up and locked onto mine, stopped me in my tracks. It stopped me in my thoughts as well. Inside my head, I could hear Barney's words. He was calm, methodical. Not only with words, but also with images, he commented on other times, other places. As if reviewing an old film, he recounted some of his past lives as well as some we had shared.

It was interesting information, every bit of it, though when I asked if past lives were important, Barney commented dryly, "Just another side of the story." His off-the-paw remark was so typically Barney that I laughed out loud. His implication was that such perspectives are reflections or metaphorical insights of whatever dramas the inner world is exploring. Just as dreams might come to show you something, so past lives are important in this way.

It was a good talk and I was thrilled and grateful for the experience. Just as Barney finished, Zak got up from where he was lying at the foot of the stairs and began climbing the stairs. Zak is a golden retriever, cocker spaniel, and Samoyed mix. He joined our family as a puppy when I first held him and found I could not put him down. Barney had not been happy about this at the time.

Even now, Barney was not so happy as Zak passed him on the stairs. With great purpose and deliberation, Zak sat on the stair directly above Barney. His action and timing was that of an accomplished actor as he held our attention, drawing out the silence. He then sent his words with a wry and amused expression. "I'm not even from this planet."

Before I had the chance to react, Zak sent me a whole packet of information, blasting at me the feeling-image that he came into this life to give Barney and myself more energy. He related that he was an "energy dog," something like a helper dog. His job, he said, was to strengthen others energetically, to give protection so that they could focus on other things, specifically things of a spiritual nature.

While Barney was obviously not thrilled about being upstaged by Zak, when I glanced at him, he related that the information was true.

Suddenly, all the feelings that Raphaela related upon hearing that Sugar the dolphin was living on another planet—dismay, doubt, irritation, incredulity—struck home. It wasn't so much that I disbelieved Zak, but did I really want to be one of those whackos who talked to beings who came from other worlds?

By the time Raphaela and I made contact again, several communicators told me they too had talked with animals who inhabited other planets. While this may seem strange to humans, it is apparently no big deal among animals. If you are connected consciously to spirit, and know that spirit can take any form, then whether you are an ant in the Midwest, a stockbroker in New York, or a cetacean in another galaxy is merely your form of the moment. No major revelation in the grand scheme of things.

In the human scheme of things, however, it is just this sort of thinking that is eventually going to get you into trouble. The problem is that respectable people who are at least open to the idea of talking with animals might just draw the line of plausibility at the idea of a dead dolphin sending messages from another planet. And what's worse is that those who don't think a dead dolphin sending messages from another planet is too far out are going to be just those sort of people your mother warned you about.

I told Raphaela I now understood her concern, for I too had felt that disconcerting uneasiness of knowing what I heard was real, yet feeling it was too strange to repeat. Still, you can't help yourself.

"Here's the problem I have with it," said Raphaela. "It's not that I don't think it can be true. The cosmos is vast, infinite, and beyond our present understanding. But what makes me nervous about receiving this information is that I associate it with the lunatic fringe. And I don't want to be in that category. I want to have a nice placid life as an animal communicator, well respected in her community, that sort of thing."

And that's the catch. Whether we talk to animals or not, we all have our experiential comfort zones that both define and reveal just how far we are willing to travel, how far we are able to stretch our minds before we consider ourselves total lunatics. It is one thing to talk about spirituality and agree with the statement that we are all One, but it is quite another to accept seriously that a deceased dolphin living on another planet in spirit form may have something valuable to tell us.

When we reconnected with Sugar, I asked if she could tell us more about how we create our own realities. There was a long pause.

The world, the cosmos, the universe. All of these are inadequate words for the shimmering sea of creative matter that we are all swimming in. This sea is replete with possibilities. Beings consciously or unconsciously select by thought and emotion the events they want to experience. For example, Raphaela wanted to be an animal communicator. She thought and dreamed about it, and then brought it into the physical. She decided she was an animal communicator, acted on that belief, and now here she is!

Taking that to another level, can you speak more about our multidimensional selves and how those selves interact with each other? For example, if we are all in the process of more consciously knowing our multidimensional nature, then how might having a breakthrough with one self affect other selves?

For the most part, your awareness of your other selves and interactions is limited because of the linear concept of time. However, this is flexible and changing. In other realities, selves can and do interact.

Think of it like an octopus. Every tentacle is distinct, has its own existence, but is connected to the whole. It's a great subject, a subject of vastness. The true understanding of it will make you realize your connection to God. Every single expression of your soul—every being, every animal or human life—partakes of God qualities and is able to create.

If we think of ourselves as the tentacles of the octopus, then once all the selves are aware of the central self, or the metaphorical octopus's head, is that head yet another tentacle to something else, something bigger still?"

"So how far up does consciousness go?" asked Raphaela. "Oh, here's the answer: Huge Block Capital Letters—INFINITE!

So even your present being is a tentacle to some other bigger consciousness?

There is no end to growth.

For a moment, Raphaela and I laughed softly. What else can you do in the face of Infinity?

Apparently, what I do is think of other questions, for it was only a few seconds before I recalled something that had puzzled me.

Is it true there are realms of bliss you encounter when you expand your consciousness that are actually protective thresholds to something much greater?

The state of bliss is always available. You can always step into it. You can reach it through meditative or trance experiences. There are many ways to access it. When you're in bliss, it seems all consuming; it is all consuming. But it is not the end. There is no end.

"I don't know what's beyond there," said Raphaela, "but I'll probably settle for the bliss! For a few hundred years anyway!" When Raphaela burst out laughing, I joined her. Raphaela has an utterly infectious laugh and it took some time before I could think straight again.

How can humans become more aware of their multidimensional selves?

Be aware that every thought and emotion that you experience has consciousness and creativity and goes on forever.

"Oh, my God. Better be careful of what we think," murmured Raphaela.

Also, ask to know your other selves. You may get glimmers in your sleep, in meditation. Send love and endow them with the highest evolutionary energy that you can. Give them the benefit of your wisdom and experience, as your other selves give you the benefit of theirs. You are receiving from them all the time.

What can humans do to make the changes on earth more smooth and graceful?

Create the change by thinking of it as being easy and gentle. There are enough people on the earth predicting hellfire and brimstone. Meditate on simple, elegant, uplifting transitions without physical disasters. Many disasters have been averted because of the rising consciousness on earth. Others have not. You don't have to be drama addicts.

"We love drama!" exclaimed Raphaela. "But that's what gets you in trouble."

And while we laughed again, another thought occurred to me. I had always assumed that multidimensional selves would live in different times and places. But was it possible that—with our love of drama—some of our selves might choose to have lives in the same here and now reality?

"Oh, good question!" exclaimed Raphaela, who was now just as captivated by this game of multidimensional possibilities as I. "Let me see what she says. Oh! She says, 'Yes!' She gives these wonderful long answers and then she hits you with this succinct, yes."

And with that, I had run out of questions.

"I still think of her in dolphin form," said Raphaela as we said our good-byes. "She's waving her flipper. And smiling that dolphin smile!" Raphaela laughed joyously. "Oh God, they are something!"

Happiness
Beau (dog) ~ Morgine Jurdan

My message to humans has to do with happiness. I think people spend way too much time focusing on what they do not want and do not have, instead of the other way around.

If I am sleeping, I sleep well. If I am eating, I thoroughly enjoy the experience. I love myself and I love being alive. I spend time with fellow beings, enjoying their songs and dances. I am happy and delighted to be experiencing all life has to offer me.

For me, life is simple and fulfilling. I am grateful to learn more. I look for happiness and focus on love. When I keep these things in mind, I create situations that bring them to me and allow me to smile back at you.

People often feel it is difficult being a domesticated animal. This is because you focus on what we live without or our limitations. You make comparisons and judgments. I take where I am—whatever the situation—and give it my best, finding something to love and enjoy.

Life can be a rewarding experience if we make it that way. Animals may not contemplate ideas and

Morgine Jurdan.

arrange our world in such complicated ways as humans do. However, I feel our simple way of looking at life offers us greater rewards in the long run. We do not miss much and you, in your desire to understand and dissect life, often miss much.

My wish is that we could spend more time being present with each other. I feel love teaches us all we really need to know. Thank you for allowing me to share myself with all of you in this way. It is a gift few animals ever receive. Blessings to you all from me, Beau (which in your language means "beautiful"), and may your days be filled with joy, happiness, wonder, awe, and love.

12

Beyond Karma and Back

Looking at Zak—strong, happy, reddish-golden furred, brown-eyed Zak who loves to race and chase balls and have his belly rubbed—it was hard for me to take in this business of energy dogs from other planets. Multidimensionality is a fun concept, but when it comes up close and personal, certain costs are involved.

A few weeks after talking with Raphaela and Sugar, after opening (slowly, cautiously) to the idea that things may indeed be quite a bit different than we have been taught to believe, I resigned myself to the idea that it was time to explore more of what Zak had to say.

And so one afternoon as I plucked up my courage to sit beside him, quieting my mind, I asked Zak about this other planet. What I expected I don't know, though most certainly not that he would laugh at me or so quickly amend the thought that where he came from was even a planet at all.

That was more like a joke.

Perhaps the shock value of the unexpected was what he had been waiting for, because in my surprise, a whole slew of thought-images came rushing into consciousness. There was nothing first, second, third about it, and yet the material was cohesive and flowed together seamlessly. In that odd, out-of-time manner, the experience was sharply focused in the now.

This is what Zak related.

I am connected to a group of beings who literally make up our planet, for our light bodies can create any kind of world or planet we choose. The group of beings is similar to what you might think of as a fraternal order, yet more. We come to this world both to give energy and stabilize energies. You can call me "The Neutralizer."

The members of our group come without karma or karmic attachment, having a very direct and focused connection in this regard. We come to do our job, do it, and that's that. But many of our group who come to this world enjoy their lives as animals, and this is sometimes regarded as one of the "benefits of the job."

Our group does not make karmic attachments of emotion in the way some other animals do. We don't usually come back to work with the same souls. Rather, our group is mainly about service, and we come with packets of energy.

Seeing the image of a computer zip drive and disk, I understood Zak to mean that, metaphorically speaking, this packet of energy is used to help boost other energies and neutralize stuck energies.

By "stuck energy," do you mean emotional holds or karma?

Yes. My job is to streamline your focus, smooth away the sticky or uneven edges so you can move forward, or expand with more clarity. I am like a pumice stone, smoothing away things that might otherwise slow you down. The order is very giving in this sense of service.

I got the feeling that there is not a lot of emotional attachment in this group. Rather, there is an aloofness, as if they are closer to spirit in composition, not so personal or ego oriented.

Is there anything your group would like to say?

There are many ways to manifest the spirit. Choosing how you will manifest is dependent upon a number of variables. How much light you allow in your consciousness, your body, your level of understanding is an aspect of clarity—of "where you are" in your perspective. Holds in the body are holds on spirit. We are here to unhook, unhold, unzip the body—to a degree. We are helpers of humanity and of others as well. Most of us work with a number of energies in one life. We also have communication with the others in our group.

As I came out of the relaxed communicative state, I felt the familiar stirrings of frustration. How could anyone possibly verify this information?

With a look of amusement, Zak turned to walk away, though not without tossing me a bone:

Of all the animals you have interviewed thus far, the horse named Echo would know about our group. If you feel a need for confirmation, ask Echo.

It was a peculiar feeling to be both so highly amused and utterly frustrated by a situation, though I was getting used to it. Watching Zak trot from the room, his white plume of a tail held high in the air, I contemplated the situation: Here is a dog who is really an enlightened being come to help my other dog and me, and if I want to know if this is true, I should ask a horse.

All I could do was laugh. It was not laughter of disbelief. On the contrary, the laughter was born of a deep gut knowing that the story was true, whether or not anyone else would ever believe it.

Though I knew Echo and Nedda would be open to answering my question about Zak, I was hesitant to ask. I was reminded, however, of something a group of spirit animals had asked communicator Diana Roth to tell me, a prediction of sorts: "You will be put to a lot of tests in getting this book done, but for every test you pass several doors will open."

All well and good, but what if you weren't sure you wanted the doors to open?

Even as I was typing out a message to Nedda, little knocks of self-doubt kept tap, tap, tapping in my mind. How was it, for example, that Zak even knew of Echo? All three of my dogs often sat with me in my office while I spoke with various communicators on the phone, but I had never spoken on the phone to Nedda. Our communication was solely by e-mail. How was it possible that Zak could know about Echo?

And then, in one of those synchronous moments that transpires from nowhere, Zak raced down the stairs and into my office. As I turned, he looked me right in the eyes with what felt like a mixture of support and mild irritation.

When will you cross the bridge and believe what you already know?

I sent the e-mail.

As human beings, we can only take so much weirdness before we are faced with a decision: open to a new way of being or batten down the hatches and hope the nonsense will go away. We can only expand our belief systems so far before we begin to have a meltdown.

As Zak said, how much light you allow in your consciousness is a reflection of where you are in your perspective. Where I found myself was holed up in the closet, though the door was cracked just a bit. While doubt and disbelief were ever present, a feeling of lightness and well being was also washing through me.

When Nedda's reply came, I was anxious and excited, for not only did Echo respond, but Violet as well.

[Echo:] Zak's description of the group he belongs to is correct. It might amaze you to know that there are many beings from all over the universe and from all the dimensions who are here on the Earth to help in this time of transition. It is my understanding that Zak's group has chosen key humans to work with—to boost their energies and to give them subtle guidance—so they can fulfill their purpose for being here at this time. Dawn, part of your purpose is the book you are writing, which will raise human consciousness about spirituality and animals. Of course, this means that you will have to become more conscious in the process of writing the book. Isn't this fun?

[Violet:] I think I have met some of the beings in Zak's group while on another planet. They are very influential in generating love and peace energies and in providing support for others who also generate these energies. You and your work are very special to have one of them living/working with you.

I suppose I might have taken quite some comfort from these responses. And yet, like a loose thread on a favorite shirt, those little filaments of incredulity were so tempting to pull. While I no longer doubted the information I received from Zak, I knew there was more.

Chrys Long-Ago, the animal communicator in Anchorage who had first introduced me to the wonders of talking with animals, was willing to help. I told Chrys only that Zak said he worked with a group of energetic beings from another place. And so it was with only the vaguest of information from me that Chrys began to tune into Zak.

"I don't get a name for Zak's group," said Chrys. Here is what he's saying.

On a soul level I have stepped down my energy in order to come into matter and take a physical body. I have mastered the ability to maintain conscious awareness and do work outside of physicality. Some of my group are trying to become physical in order to be accessible to beings who are only conscious of their physical state and to awaken other beings who have forgotten the past when they were more highly attuned to spiritual vibrations.

What we observe happening is that as people become more aware of their past lives—particularly lives of spiritual value in which people were healers or very gifted in spiritual things—and they remember how vast the subject was at one time under different races of people, it tends to be shocking. It gets people feeling a bit insecure, which means ungrounded. The best thing people could do while making that shift—when they're feeling frightened and insecure because of what they're finding out about their past—is to reground.

We still need to be physical people when we're in our physical bodies. The problem with more people becoming more aware of the past is that they're getting more scatterbrained, and it's fracturing for people to remain in that place for very long.

It's not being mindful when people get lost in their memories; they totally lose being in the present. Once you have lost being focused in the present, you have lost your power. That is what is going on.

The whole New Age movement has a destructive element to it in that a lot of the readings and other things are causing people to lose that sense of being in the moment and grounded right here. The very highest work people can do is to sort out their own problems, to heal themselves and move to the plane of consciousness where they are open to all the wonderful qualities of enlightened nature, such as bliss, compassion, and love, and to ground there.

Some of the New Age focus gets us too much into our mental constructs?

Yes. It tends to make your thoughts run rampant and that is what is ungrounding and unsettling.

Do you mean that when people are caught up in the material of messages from others—be it channels or Ascended Masters or even animals—that takes the focus away from seeing it within?

Yes. They're not doing their own work. They are reading about everyone else or, what's worse, they're focusing attention on their own past—past lives, past accomplishments, past civilizations—and the danger is that they are not living in the moment anymore and so they've surrendered their power.

If you're not in the moment, if you're distracted and thinking about the past or fantasizing about the future, then you've lost your ability to act in the moment and to have a concentrated focus.

I told Chrys that before we began speaking, I had been trying to get Zak indoors. He came to the door muddy and had given me a flash as he walked into the house about enjoying the mud and getting back to the earth.

Chrys laughed. "He says that a dog lives predominantly in the moment, unless he has become neurotic and is with neurotic owners. A dog is experiencing life. Instantly as stuff comes up, he handles it, experiences it, and then lets go. And that is mindfulness meditation. So, maybe playing and digging in the mud is being spontaneous."

I like being a dog. I really enjoy it and I do like being dirty. I think that you obsess a little too much about me being dirty.

It was my turn to laugh.

I can go and be anything I want anytime I want. I can just die and do something else for awhile.

I keep a perspective of who I really am as a spiritual being. I may be enjoying a dog aspect for awhile, but that's not who I am.

"Oh, that's interesting," said Chrys. "People are always searching for who they are. Zak says he knows who he is; he's spiritual. That's where he's grounded."

What's the most important thing you would like people to know?

It would be good if they could learn to be like dogs, learn to be happy with who they are and what they are doing. Even the most simple activities become the means of enlightenment.

Muddy Zak. Photo by Dawn Brunke.

It's your perspective on what you're doing that determines whether it is enlightened activity or ordinary. People could learn to be more like animals—not just connected with nature and spiritual things but truly experiencing those things without judgment of right or wrong, and without trying to make a decision on the outcome of events—just observing or participating in events without trying to alter the natural outcome.

One very good message that people can learn from dogs is how to have a warm, open heart without desiring a reward for it—just being open and loving, not because you expect to receive that back. Forget rewards! If people would just forget rewards, the expectation of something coming in the future, then they could be more in the moment.

Of course, being kind to others means you are being kind to yourself, because in the absolute nature of things, everything that you do is done to yourself. There is no other being.

Zak, when you told me about your group, you said you worked outside the realm of karma. Can you give us the simple version of that?

Karma is only a mental construct.

Our group does not deal with time. Ours is an expanded view. We are a being beyond name, beyond identity and beyond ego, who manifest through myriad forms of material as well as metaphysical systems of karma. A system of karma can be a person who is evolving through many lifetimes. That person and that ego don't really exist, but I show it to you as a karmic package or pattern that is going on over and over and over again.

"We keep saying 'they' when referring to his group," commented Chrys, "but Zak shows it to me as being nondual—not a bunch of beings, but really one great intelligence that can manifest in myriad different ways and influence a lot of different beings. It exists and permeates all universes, all intelligence."

"It's kind of abstract," said Chrys. "I'm not sure that they've lost their total sense of identity, however, because if it is a being that separates out and calls itself a dog—well, there are different levels of that stage of enlightenment. Let me ask him about that." Chrys paused.

The intelligence we embody exists almost as a very rarefied gas in the universe. It's so fine and pure, such a very pure energy, a pure wavelength, a pure power, that it can't be seen or detected by most other life-forms. That's why we manifest in material bodies. It's difficult to channel us.

My being a dog is just a dream.

Zak, you're here with me now in this life, so is it your dream or my dream?

It's yours too. The thing is, I've been able to keep my awareness in my dreams. I'm staying aware of my spirituality while you get lost in your materiality and your perspective.

Just like when you get in a dream, you forget that you're dreaming. You forget that it's just a dream and you go along through that dream working and thinking and trying to solve problems, and then you wake up and go, "Oh, what was that all about?" That's the way your waking life is. It's a dream too.

But if you go along in life with just being in the moment, isn't that similar to being in a dream where you also just go along with the moment?

Bring intention and focus into the moment and it can reveal enlightenment. When you lose attachment for the future, you cease to generate karma. When you lose attachment to the future, you give up caring how something comes out. You disengage your intention, and that's when your karma changes.

Now, you can still have a plan, because your ultimate plan might be to benefit somebody, such as to fix the breakfast or to put the children to bed. But when you keep the view that this is a dream, and you know that you're going to wake up from it and become a fully enlightened being, then you begin to stop generating karma. You let happen all the events that are going to happen regardless of your interference.

Do you have any questions about that?

I half snorted a laugh. This was my dog asking me.

Well, you wanted to know about karma. This is karma—you thinking, thinking, thinking all the time. If you stop thinking and start being aware with the part of your mind that does not have desire to manipulate the outcome of every little thing, then you go beyond accumulating karma and eventually arrive at the place where karma and nirvana are seen as two halves of one whole. Nirvana is the enlightened state beyond karma. However, both are a dream. There is a stage of enlightenment beyond this and that is where we come from.

Oh, Zak! I marveled how talking with animals could have brought me here.

It's really a trip being a dog. You get to do things without having responsibility. You don't have to get a job and go to work. It's not true with all dogs. Some of them are saddled with great grief and responsibilities for their families.

People need to understand that it isn't always so wonderful being an animal. Many animals need to be liberated too and go into states of being where they can assimilate spiritual lessons and be taught things. Not all animals are aware of their spiritual essence and nature.

There's a lot to learn from people putting themselves in the places of their dogs, but there's one great danger in that they often tend to project something that isn't there and they then enter a little fantasy.

"This is consistent with what I believe and what I've seen with other animals," interjected Chrys. "I can see that he considers it would be nice if people could imagine themselves as a dog and have the mind of a dog—being present in the moment and not having a care in the world sort of attitude—but he doesn't see that happening. Many people tend to think things about their animals that aren't really existent. He hopes your book will break through to some people so they stop seeing their animals so personally and start seeing them as separate and individual."

Chrys paused and laughed, and I wondered what now. "It's about his food," she said. "The idea of a treat just flickered through his mind. Maybe that's very profound too! Maybe you can be very enlightened and still enjoy your chocolates!"

I certainly hoped so. What would be so great about enlightenment without chocolate?

There's a lot of light on the planet, more than there was for many centuries. But what is dangerous is the lack of time people give themselves to being mindful. There are many more distractions now and fun things to do, and people are building up their monumental egos. It's not easy for people.

"But he was able to work out of his body," said Chrys. "Did he tell you that he had evolved on another planet or was from another galaxy?"

"No," I explained. "He first told me he was from another planet, but then later said that was a joke, that planets are just concepts too."

"Yeah, that's the space concept," laughed Chrys.

You're already confused with the time concept. Once you get out of the time system, you don't have karma anymore. Karma is predicated on a belief in time, a belief in activity taking place in the past, present, and future. So, when you get your mind shifted into the no-time awareness, then karma does not affect you.

Space is equally a concept, a mind thing. Space is actually not out there. Space is different levels of awareness. To humans, it may look like far away or light years, but in reality it's only a concept.

Do you mean that planets are a sort of mind joke of space?

It's different wavelengths—a different wavelength in the sense of a different brainwave, a different mental thought pattern. You could slow down your patterns and your whole essence and let that coalesce into some kind of an already established planetary system or change vibrations and become involved in another one. We tend to want to stay out of that and be in our own aloofness. We are very fine, very pure energy.

"That fits with what Zak said to me before about not coming back again and again with the same person," I told Chrys. I was also struck by the word *aloofness*, which Zak had used when speaking to me. My understanding was that he meant it in the sense of not wanting to encourage dependency.

"He says he has had to reduce his vibration in order to get to here, to be in physicality and be able to master our brain waves so that he could talk to us," said Chrys. "That's the power of concentration he has, that he can change his vibration to that degree and hold it and go back and forth."

But I'm still a dog.

Which set Chrys and I to laughing.

I asked Chrys if she could tell when she was speaking to Zak the dog and when she was speaking to Zak the enlightened being.

"Well, we're talking more with what you would call his Higher Self," said Chrys. "His dog mind is a different vibration. I can hear it; it has a different voice. It actually has a different sound to it, a different feel."

"And is his dog self aware of his Higher Self?"

"It's not aware of it being a separate self," said Chrys. "They are not two different selves."

"But is Zak the dog conscious of his spiritual nature?"

Chrys said she would ask the source. Then after a long pause, "Ah!"

It's the other way around. You're close. It's my spiritual self, what you might call my soul, which is aware of its own nature, its own perfect intrinsic enlightened nature and its dog form at the same time.

The dog form itself is just an illusion; it really doesn't have much consciousness. The only thing that enlivens this body is the spirit. The spirit has awareness of the matter. The matter is a kind of reflection in the mirror, without its own intelligence. My material brain is not the thinking part. It's the intelligence in the brain that's the thinking part and the intelligence is the electrical connection, the thing that you call current or energy.

And that energy is connected to spirit?

It is spirit. It's just spirit stepped down into a vibration so that it provides the connective current for matter, for the cells, for the little parts of matter, the atoms. I really am the space between the atoms.

"That's what he says!" exclaimed Chrys with both astonishment and jubilance. "Yup! That's what your dog is!" And once again, Chrys and I were moved to laughter, perhaps indicating that humor has a definite role in enlightenment education.

Chrys felt that what Zak was speaking about was related to the concept of emptiness in Buddhism, that the space between atoms, and even between the fragments of atoms, is where all intelligence resides. "So, your dog is actually aware of that nature," said Chrys. "It's not your dog—it's this enlightened being who is aware of itself as the intelligence of the universe and has the ability to change its vibration, to become these different forms."

But the forms themselves are not independent of the mind that is thinking them.

So the goal is to bring the spiritual self into the conscious mind?

In truth, I could barely formulate the question. My brain was becoming supersaturated, all this talk of atoms and spaces in between. And yet, it seemed we were onto something.

As you become more aware of your spiritual essence and nature, you suddenly realize that what it is that's aware is spiritual essence and nature itself. You merely had a fragmented view for a moment. You were only looking at yourself through a cracked door. But then you open the door, and the ordinary mind falls away.

The ordinary human mind, human consciousness, is the door, but it blocks the doorway. And yet, thinking about yourself as a spiritual being eventually cracks it open wider and wider. You realize that you are the essence of enlightenment— enlightened being and intelligence. The more you think about it and speculate about your spiritual nature, the closer you get to actually realizing that you are really the one who's observing and thinking, not the thing that you're thinking about. You are it! It becomes apparent as you keep dwelling on this and contemplating this.

Chrys and I were quiet. For just a moment, then, I was held, suspended in a moment out of time where nothing quite made sense yet everything was perfectly clear.

And then the doorway will disappear. And then you just stand in space, knowing everything.

The Turtle Story
by Jim Worsley

One morning I was driving to the park to walk my two dogs—Archie and Tucker. The morning was like any other, except I kept thinking I saw turtles along the road. Each time, the object turned out to be something besides a turtle. As we got to the park, the idea of turtles went out of my mind.

Archie usually brings me a stick to throw, fetches it, and waits with it until Tucker and I catch up. I was throwing the stick as usual when one landed behind a tree. As we caught up, I saw Archie staring at the bottom of the tree. He had left the stick where it fell: within an inch of an Eastern box turtle.

The turtle was sitting perfectly still with his head poked out of his shell. I saw that he had some clear purpose for being there and that it was no coincidence that all the way to the park I had been expecting to see a turtle. It looked as if he was waiting for us so he could finish his job.

Archie and turtle. Photo by Jim Worsley.

At this point I realized I had been summoned. I soon thought of Dawn Brunke's book project and her question, "What do the animals want us to know?" I posed the question to the turtle.

I heard him say, "People need to clean their minds; then they can be more satisfied where they are. Home can be anywhere. See, I can live between the highway and this path. I have plenty here. It is home to me. People need to be more satisfied with what is already here for them or they will not be satisfied wherever they go."

I noticed the turtle was being extremely patient with us. Tucker edged closer to sniff the turtle's shell. It was as if the turtle trusted us. I asked if "cleaning the mind" meant having a more positive attitude about the earth in general.

"Of course!" I heard back. At this point the turtle lifted his shell, turned, and began walking away. "If your mind is clean, you will not have to go so fast to find what you are looking for. Nothing is lost until you think you lost it. I stay off that highway because it's too fast. There's always enough when you choose what you already have before racing off for more." And then the turtle walked out of sight while the three of us stayed and watched him go.

13

The Innernet

With all technology, we follow the dream of true oneness: telephone, television, telecommunication arose from the deep desire that we are truly all connected. In our desire to become what we truly are, we invent the Internet and alike interconnections to emulate telepathy, the most natural communication.

René K. Müller, Webmaster

One morning I wiggled into waking consciousness from the wagging tail end of a vivid dream.

In the dream, I'm taking an animal communication workshop led by Sam Louie. The class is on break and I am alone in the workshop room with Sam and several dogs. I am about to leave too, when suddenly I discover an animal communication device within my brain.

At first I think Sam is responsible for this, though he is quick to say no, that is not the case. He tells me that perhaps the exercises in class helped me to locate the device, but it was there within me all along. It looks like a dark glass ball, maybe an inch in diameter. Though it is inside my head, I can also see it. It reminds me of a computer icon. The ball has many small, brightly colored disks arranged in equatorlike fashion around its center. It is through these circular disks that laser beams of light are emitted, thus allowing a linking beam of energy to connect me with whatever animal I choose to speak. In this sense, the device serves to facilitate communication as well as "translate" languages between species.

I am excited by the device and realize there is no reason I cannot activate it right now. As I do so, I suddenly hear the individual voices of the dogs in the room. I turn to one and he flashes me a huge doggy grin. He then says, with a distinct British accent, "By George, I think she's got it!"

I laugh as the other dogs join in singing a song from the film *My Fair Lady.* "The rain in Spain stays mainly on the plain," they croon in hilarious musical parody. I am astonished by the humor of the situation. "Do you hear that?" I keep asking Sam, "Do you hear that?" But Sam too is laughing, as are all the dogs, all of us caught within an infectious wave of song and laughter.

One of the dogs from the other side of the room then catches my eye. "Do you believe it now?" he asks as the others continue to sing and laugh. "Are you ready to believe this is real?"

That dream danced inside of me for many days. I thought about it often, secretly smiling, laughing, and wondering.

The idea that animal communication abilities might be discovered in a device within our brains fit with the idea that this ability is present in all humans, though often forgotten. My initial reaction, that Sam had given me the device, reflects a common projection, for while many people believe talking with animals is possible, they doubt they possess the ability. Being a good teacher, Sam revealed this was untrue.

That the device was represented as a round globe implied it held a shared, universal quality, something that is true for everyone on the planet. Furthermore, the light beam disks (both light and circular disks representing universal connections) were able to link any being, no matter where they were, what form or species, or language they spoke. That I saw the device as a computer icon ties in with the connective abilities of computers and the World Wide Web to link any one individual or group of individuals to any other.

As time went on, I wondered about other details and began searching aspects of this dream for correspondence to other facets of reality. For example, why the reference to the film *My Fair Lady?* Certainly the "I think she's got it" fit; but why did the dreammakers choose that particular film? And why the silly song? What was so important about the rain in Spain that my brain would use precious energy to conjure up the image of dogs singing this song?

The 1964 film version of *My Fair Lady* starred Rex Harrison, who played the language expert Professor Henry Higgins. Higgins is intent upon transforming a Cockney flower girl's common speech into proper English. On a general level, this easily corresponds to the intent of animal communication to transform the flow of language for clarity and a better understanding between species. It also fits in with the communication device being a "translator" of languages.

The Cockney girl who underwent linguistic alteration and became the "fair lady" was played by Audrey Hepburn. The name of her character was Eliza Doolittle. Doolittle?! The name jolted me into a sudden burst of knee-slapping recognition. Was it coincidence that Miss Eliza had the same last name as the most famous animal communicator of all fiction—Dr. Doolittle himself? Did I find that connection merely because I was looking? Or had the dreammakers sat around belly-laughing in the middle of the night as they poked hidden patterns such as this into their creation? I was just about to wonder what else I would find when the specter of Rex Harrison smiled and I realized he too was part of this game. After his role as the human language expert Henry Higgins, it was Rex who played animal language expert Dr. Doolittle in the 1967 film of the same name.

Just as the outer world offers us a bounty of transformatory images and synchronous events, the inner theatre has its own language and artistry that can quickly transport us to new understandings of ourselves and the universe. The dreamworld in particular is a rich and fertile land wherein the mind is given free reign to make sense of and rearrange realities, inner as well as outer. It re-presents our personal world as it represents altered accounts of perceiving reality.

Carl Jung has suggested that dreams are the conscious mind of the unconscious. Meaning, therefore, is always present, though it may take a bit of digging. Deeper and deeper we peel back the layers, uncovering the workings of fascinating, multileveled connections, intricate themes, and subtle (and sometimes not too subtle) variations of pattern. Dreams also serve as portals to the multidimensional. Follow any bit of the hologram and it will lead you back to the whole.

I knew there were other layers to my dream. Piece by piece, I could go through and fashion a new puzzle, rearranging the pieces into another version, another story which would reveal other layers, other connections. If I dug deep enough, I would find the door that pulled me through.

Just for fun, I picked up another few pieces. Why, for example, was it Sam Louie who taught the workshop? I had never met Sam in person, and had never taken a workshop. And what about that silly rain song the dogs kept singing? What did that have to do with anything?

I didn't get an answer right away. However, as I began to rework an earlier chapter of this book, I incorporated a story Sam had told me about a dog who was looking for a home. The dog told Sam that it wouldn't happen until the rains showed up, and this translated into the eventual arrival of a woman named Annette Rains, who adopted the dog. The dog waiting for the rains . . . Annette Rains . . . dream dogs singing about the rain . . . the rain in Spain? Double entendres and mixed metaphors were splashing all over the place, making soggy my brain. Did the dreammakers plan this or was it all just one long, loose connection—a damp shaggy dog story unto itself?

"Dreams are like looking at an incredibly detailed and often complex blueprint of one's individual makeup, with emphasis on patterns that are presently active or are going to be activated," writes teacher and author Dr. Brugh Joy. "Dreams reveal the selves that dance our lives at both the unconscious and conscious levels. Dreams are a threshold to understanding universal principles of Life in general, and they have collective as well as individual significance."[1]

From another perspective, then, Sam and the dogs, even Henry Higgins and Eliza Doolittle—and, by extension, the good Dr. Doolittle himself—are all aspects of the dreaming me. More than that, they are all part of the dreaming us, because now that you've read the dream, it's part of you too. Shared dreams become a Web page that anyone can access. Click on the computer icon that looks like a small round ball with dots around its center and there you'll find the universal translator device can be downloaded for free. In truth, you don't even need to download, for you already have the file within yourself. If one consciousness can think it, then it is available to everyone.

"Animals are my little computers to the universe," Laura Simpson told me. We had been talking about computer imagery and telepathy, playing with the common denominators of being "hooked up" and "on line." Laura was expounding the idea that animals provide a direct connection to universal mind because they are, for the most part, clear about who they are, unfettered of self-doubt and limiting beliefs about separation. I shared what an animal spirit had told me: "The reason new computers allow you to do so many things at once is because that is the physical manifestation of the inner knowledge/reality of what it is like to be multidimensional."

If it is true that the outer world reflects the inner, is the preponderance of the entire world coming on line (the phrase *World Wide Web* says it all) a reflection of the human race becoming more conscious of our telepathic abilities? Is the Internet an outward manifestation of the Innernet? Was my dream image of a telepathic communication device, a sort of 3-D computer icon, generated because that is the way the outer world handles such connections? Is it because we humans are still too afraid to trust our own natural abilities that we manifest machines to reflect back to us the underlying truth that we are really all connected?

Marcia Ramsland and her dog Jarvi once had a long talk about the "animal network." It was the same connection Mojave Dan expressed to J. Allen Boone, whereby he was able to get information about anything he wanted to know simply by listening to the animals—for, in their travels and meetings, the animals knew everything that was going on.

"People do not understand how it all is and therefore threaten the entire process by their lack of understanding," Jarvi told Marcia many years ago. "It is of the utmost importance that people reconnect to the plants and animals. We can teach them what they have forgotten."[2]

Could the forgotten language be a simpler version of what we are so busy doing every day at our computers? Any bit of knowledge, any experience, can be "posted" on the animal network, where it can be accessed by anyone at any time. "We have access to all," Penelope Smith told me. "Every being has access to all files, all knowledge and, through others that are conscious of it, we can tap into that."

I had the idea it was like a search engine on the Internet. Enter in any word or phrase, and you are presented with anywhere from a handful to hundreds of thousands of web page sites. Each site presents a facet; all are reflected aspects of whatever you have chosen to focus upon. In a somewhat similar fashion, ask any question of an animal (human included) and the answer will reflect back to you one facet of the whole. Get a particularly clear answer, and you can follow that all the way to enlightenment.

In the celebration of awakened life, all is part of the One. We can find the truth everywhere, in every piece of life because every piece of life holds the whole. As we begin to awaken, we play with pieces of the puzzle. A crow caws the latest news and a mouse listens. We click on a mouse and the computer screen comes to life. A dog talks about the coming rains and a woman named Rains appears. Laughing dogs sing of falling rains and reach out from an unfolding dream. Visions, messages, themes, stories, multiple layers—all are facets of the One. A central pattern prevails. In the grand scheme, we're all connected on the Innernet.

Buddy's laugh—Buddy and Carole Devereux. Photo by Jim Steinbacher.

Part Four

The Call for Transformation

Buddy, Ellie, and Ancestor Horse: Welcome to Knowing

Miracle and Manifestation Made Real

The Role of Llamas: Holders of the Light

Dolphins, Whales, and the Multidimensional Now

The Cetacean Nation: Love the Greater Love

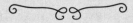

Open Hearts
Buddy (horse) ~ Jeri Ryan

My heart welcomes you to our home and to our hearts. When you open to us, you enter our hearts and we enter yours. When we understand each other, we understand ourselves because we find how close we are to being the same. Then we can have peace with each other and accept what each other has to offer, whether or not it is pleasing, or what we want in the moment.

I welcome you to that knowing. We are blessed with that knowing. We all have that knowing. I welcome you to knowing about your knowing.

14

Buddy, Ellie, and Ancestor Horse: Welcome to Knowing

BUDDY

Buddy is a horse who has been communicating with Carole Devereux for many years. "He was the first to inspire me to communicate spiritually with other species," Carole told me. "I had just bought this horse and was fascinated by the idea that he might talk to me. When Jeri Ryan did my first animal consultation, we asked Buddy what made a barn enjoyable for a horse. People might assume that a horse would want a bigger stall, more alfalfa, or a bigger pasture. I was not prepared for what Buddy said because it changed the way I viewed animals from that day onward. He said the thing that makes a barn most enjoyable is the way the people treat each other. When people are in harmony with each other, the horses benefit. I thought that was a very profound statement, coming from a horse!"

Carole was one of the first animal communicators with whom I spoke. When we did a short interview with Buddy for a magazine article, I knew very little about interspecies communication. Carole told me that the interview would work best if I stayed silent and "held the energy" (whatever that meant) on my end of the phone line as she meditated, made contact with Buddy, asked him my questions, wrote down his responses, and read them back to me. It took some time, but we eventually had the article.

As a result of the wise workings of the universe, six months passed before I reconnected with Carole and Buddy. On an intuitive whim, Carole and I decided to conduct this interview differently. Rather than staying on the line, I would hang up, meditate on the question, and call back fifteen minutes later. As Carole put it, "We'll do a three-way conference call, you and I and Buddy. I want you to be involved."

Did Carole know the power of her words? Involved I was to become, for after centering and focusing on the question, I began to hear Buddy. *Buddy?*

The experience was unsettling, though not unfamiliar. Buddy spoke clearly and succinctly, pausing after every phrase, as if encouraging me to take down his words.

I told myself this should not be so strange. I had spoken with birds and dogs, what is so peculiar about speaking with a horse? *Only that he's a few thousand miles away*, my inner critic cackled. Well, communicators do that all the time, I reminded myself. Sam had spoken to Max at a distance; Chrys was miles away when she spoke to Zak.

Okay, then, continued the critic. *What about this: Buddy is already talking to Carole. How can he be talking to you too?*

As I got out pen and notebook, my hand quivered. I knew better than to focus on doubts; still, my body could not hide the rush of fear and excitement that caused my hand to shake.

Buddy paused. "You're doing fine," he said simply. He then directed me to write down those very words, so that I would remember: *You're doing fine.*

Time and again, we are brought to the test. For me, the issue was trust. If you cannot trust your inner experience, how can you expect others to confirm it for you?

As I called Carole, I felt a wave of uneasiness. Was it really Buddy I was talking to? Would Carole be upset? My job had been to hold energy and meditate, not write down words. At the same time, I felt the stirrings of excitement, for what happened between Buddy and myself felt undeniably genuine.

How often we face our fears, until at last there is a small trust, an inner peace that opens to knowing! And there is Buddy, and others, all of them rejoicing, welcoming us to our knowing.

What follows are messages from Buddy to Carole and myself in two different sessions.

SESSION 1

Question: Buddy, what do horses as a species have to teach humans, and what would you most like humans to know?

Buddy and Carole

I have much to say on the subject of human consciousness. Humans have a driving desire to outdo themselves all the time, and this need not be the case when furthering consciousness.

What do you mean by that?

There is a long road or pathway that connects all species together in body, mind, and soul. Once on the path, there is not much we can do to change the outcome if we are always thinking how we can control the end result.

Why should we not try to outdo ourselves?

You lose consciousness and you cannot repeat the experiment. You need to grow more slowly, like a tree whose rings are close, and therefore creating stability. The human race is unstable at this time and is in danger of collapse. Everyone is running to and fro, creating more and more havoc. You need to assess your life and then let it be.

The doing is only really accomplished inside. If you hurry to bring it about here on earth, it will be unstable and, therefore, unfounded in truth. You can only know truth after you have withstood the fires of time. Time and patience create works that unite universes.

Is that what we're trying to do, trying to unite with another universe?

You take me too literally. I mean unite with the path.

How can you unite with a path? Is it predestined to some degree?

Yes. More than you realize. All circumstances are predetermined pathways to consciousness and you have to realize that your breathing, your heart beating, your cellular division, and your brain are all preprogrammed so that you can concentrate on the path. You need to thank your Creator for giving you a heart that beats without thinking about it, without your awareness. Could you beat your own heart without help from above?

No, I guess not. I never thought of it that way before.

See? You're changing by just sitting still!

If all humans would sit still and ask and then listen to the Creator speaking to them, you would outdo yourselves, the way you attempt to by running to and fro. It is the most difficult thing for humans to do now, sit in a place and be still. Try it sometime and count how many impulses pass over you that make you want to get up and do something. Just sit there.

Carole said, "That's where we stopped, though I think Buddy could have gone on. His message is very clear: what he feels the human race needs at this time is more quiet time."

Buddy and Dawn

I would like to say that humans, as a species, have much forgiveness to bring to their hearts. Forgiveness for themselves is key. Humans are much more concerned with "image" than animals. Humans split themselves when they value their image over their hearts and souls.

Humans can learn a lot about joy from horses. The spirit-emotion of joy *is* forgiveness. It is "for giving," both to oneself, to those in one's surroundings, to the land, the earth, to all the people, and to the planet.

Do not think for one moment that what you do has no effect on others. We are all interconnected, we are all one. Just as one part of the body affects the entire body, in the same way, you are part of consciousness and the universe. The small part, the microcosm, not only affects the whole; the small part *is* the whole.

We animals are very supportive of you, Dawn, and part of why this is happening—not only the book but this particular phone call connection—is for you to trust yourself more, to share your experiences with others through the book, and to carry the vibration of moving from self-doubt into self-trust. That is your "dawn."

Carole's first exclamation when I read what Buddy dictated was, "Oh, my! He's so cute!" And for that I felt deep relief. Implicit in her statement was the acknowledgment that the voice I heard was indeed Buddy's.

"You've changed tremendously since we talked last," Carole said. " You were nervous in the beginning and your insecurity was cutting off a lot of energy. Whatever you've done since then has deepened your ability to make connections. And, that *was* Buddy you heard."

The confirmation was heartfelt. As Carole knew, when learning a new language or exploring a new paradigm, we need guides —not necessarily to validate the truth, but to say, "Yes, you are here now. I've gone that way too. What you heard is real."

I related that Buddy's message came to me in fragmented phrases and often I couldn't guess what was going to come next. This made it easier, for I wasn't able to judge or second-guess; I was, in effect, pushed out of my own way.

"It comes right into your heart," Carole agreed. "That's how it happens! You open to the energy and just let yourself be."

SESSION 2

Before our second session, I wondered aloud whether Buddy had broadcasted two messages simultaneously or had related one idea that Carole and I received in different ways.

Carole felt Buddy was perfectly capable of talking to more than one person at a time, just as we all are on the telepathic level. To know this, however, we need to expand our paradigm of what is possible. So too, we need to take into account the perspective of what we are asking.

"There is relative truth and there is universal truth," explained Carole. "Relative truth is relative to you and me in this moment. Universal truth is like the sun shining on the earth. That is true for us all. But when and where it shines is different for each person and each thing.

"It's like seeing a great spider web. We're all part of the web, but it's where we are on the web that determines the message we're getting in the moment."

Carole and Buddy

Buddy, do you have more to say on the state of human consciousness?

The state of human consciousness could improve if humans were more willing to look at the whole picture and not focus on just themselves as the center of the universe. The human race is very young.

Look at the age of the Earth, seas, and mountains. It takes time to make a tree, a rock, a stream, and air. These are all miracles of life. They need to be respected and honored. They have much to teach us. Work with life as an unfoldment, one stage at a time. The human race is like a flower, a small tight bud, unfolding slowly. Take life more slowly. There is more to come.

Many civilizations have perished and plunged to the depths of the past. Find out why. How did they collapse? Do not repeat their mistakes. We are all making the same mistakes over and over. When will we change? It takes so much time to start again from scratch.

Observe the cycles of life—any life. Even a rock has a life cycle. It is imprinted and encoded into it, just as yours is imprinted and encoded in you.

Dawn and Buddy

As I opened to Buddy, I sensed he would address the issue of simultaneous messages. I asked if he would also comment on the mechanics of translation, of whether the images and metaphors brought forth reflected more the thoughts of the animal or that of the human.

I took down Buddy's message in longhand. As there was remaining time in the session, he directed me to go to the computer and begin retyping what I had received. As I did, he commented, "This is your answer about translation. Here you will take the words and add to them your feeling-thoughts, not to refashion the words, but to add extra experience for your readers." What follows is an extended version of what Buddy communicated.

We are all connected. The image Carole used of a spider web is a good way to see this. Does the message come from the spider or any one of the creatures that wander or are caught upon the spider's web? Perhaps the message comes from the web herself?

Much of your questioning has to do with thought. Thought is like a spider web. It is beautifully magnificent, a wonder to behold. But it can also capture and ensnare you, and you become a tasty morsel for spider to consume.

Let's leave the image of the web and go to another place—see this in your mind. . . .

(Closing my eyes, I inwardly see an image of gold, yellow, and red circular formations. They are pulsating and seem alive. The forms look like cellular suns with shadowy rings of light surrounding each one.)

This image reflects light and vibration, an example of how communication in the more subtle spheres operates. This is another experience of reality, another world if you wish, one that exists when you close your eyes and see in another way.

Last time, we spoke of image. Humans are very attached to image and this includes the manifested image of the world that you/we have created. Know that there exist many—truly, countless—realities. Your question is almost to ask which is the "true" reality. They are all true. In a manner of speaking, there is no reality—no matter how small or individual—which is not true.

In the scientific reality, there are "facts" that are observed over and again, thus labeled *true*. However, at the deepest levels, these truths and realities are merely one among many realities, no more true or less true than any other is.

Let us have some fun with this. One of your thoughts was of the sun. Is the sun a ball of gases, identifiable, explainable, and quantifiable by scientists? Is the sun a collection of sun beings shining light onto the world? Is the sun a god? (It was once thought so by an entire race of people. That was their truth, and their reality.) Or is the sun merely an idea in the thought of a god?

The sun shines on us all, though at different times, in different places, to different degrees. There is also a sun within each of you. Which sun is more real? Which sun is the true sun?

So, you see, it is true that the answer is always in your question from your own frame of reference. All is true, all is real. Even shadow and darkness have a place within the scheme of things—a "place under the sun!"

A better way to understand the sun is to be the sun. Becoming the sun is becoming the thought. Becoming the question is becoming the answer. All becoming is consciousness. Consciousness is light; in truth, consciousness is "light becoming"—or light moving into a period of being.

Once again, the image of light and the emotion of joy are what I want to convey to you today. I do not want to say stop asking questions, for questions lead to a search for answers, and answers are the beginning of becoming both question and answer. However, at a certain point, questions and answers may be silenced for simply becoming. And becoming leads to *being.*

Dawn, you are familiar with the Buddhist Ox pictures. This is an ancient answer to your question and one that might well be shared with your readers. Is the ox the man, the man the ox? At one point, all vanishes into the void, which is the intake of creation. Then out it comes, back into the manifest world. Know that there are many variations of this "manifest world." Think of this each time you breathe, for this is a profound aspect of life, a deeper mystery some would say. This is one way you can re-member yourselves to the connection of all life. It is one of the gateways to the multidimensional being that we are—both individually and collectively, for we all breathe in life in the same way.

Breathing in life is taking the world back into ourselves and then releasing, from the void, back into reality. Which reality? That is a joke, for we are forever creating.

Is there anything else, Buddy?

I send you laughter! There is much joy in simply releasing for a time all idea and thought. A soul-filled eternity can pass in one intake of breath and the release of one gigantic horselaugh!

I would also remind your readers not to take everything in this book too literally, to choose not to nit-pick with questions and doubts, but simply to open their hearts to the possibility of Oneness, to remember to throw back their heads and intake the spirit of joy and to laugh—for themselves and all the world—for that will lead to the spirit of peace.

After listening to my message from Buddy, Carole laughingly asked if I was "blowing myself away." Yes, there was clearly an element of being blown away by Buddy's message!

The pictures that Buddy referred to are better known as the Oxherding pictures.[1] First attributed to a Chinese Zen master of the twelfth century, this series of woodcuts with text show the journey from human mind to enlightened mind and return back into the world.

The Ox is used as a symbol of our inherent enlightened nature. The journey of enlightenment begins with a human (in the Oxherding pictures, a man) seeking the Ox. The man finds tracks, glimpses the Ox, and finally catches the Ox in the "wild fields." Taming the Ox, the man rides it home. This leads to picture 7, "Ox Forgotten, Self Alone," wherein the symbolic nature of the Ox is grasped. In picture 8, "Both Ox and Self Forgotten," duality is transcended. The final pictures illustrate the man returning to the world as an enlightened being—or, as an Ox for others.

Though I had studied these pictures about twenty years earlier, I had not thought of them since. That Buddy chose the Oxherding pictures to explain the evolution of human consciousness in a book about animal communication was, to me, both humorous and keenly appropriate.

I asked Carole about Buddy's directive to expand on his words. I had experienced similar situations with other animals when energetic bundles of information were simply too fast and too large to record in the moment. Whenever I worried over not being able to note it all down, the animals said they would be present. In fact, as I later recorded the information, I did feel each animal gently guiding, rewording, and, at times, even editing.

Carole related that Buddy would tell her and Jeri Ryan the very same thing. "He's always adding at the end, not to worry about perfection, that you are free to use creative license."

"You know how else I know it was Buddy talking?" she asked softly. "It's because you keep picking up his personality in the message. His message to the world is always about joy."

In such a short time, I came to know Buddy as a wonderful being, generous with his time and wisdom, patient with this human, and funny. In our second session, he sent me a poem just as we said good-bye. It was both an answer and a reminder:

> *Was this me speaking? Was this you?*
> *Remember the spider web. You are all that you create.*
> *We are all connected.*
> *We are all, truly, One.*

ELLIE

After our talks with Buddy, Carole suggested we talk to Ellie, Buddy's mate. Carole felt Ellie could eloquently share the mare's perspective, for as she noted to Carole, "I have much to offer. Like the dolphin transmissions, I can heal with my words and thoughts and emotions. Hold the space for me to connect with the outside world, please. I have made many friends through my heart and my awareness. I reach out now to humans as a teacher about life."

Carole and I agreed to ask Ellie to speak on what she most wanted humans to know. Just as I was about to hang up the phone, however, Carole stopped me with the most detailed, passionate description of an animal I've ever heard. This, I was to learn, was part of Ellie's message.

"Ellie!" Carole exclaimed. "She is perhaps the most stunning horse you'll ever see. She is gorgeousness. Her coat is shining chestnut, and she has a white lightning bolt on her forehead. Her mane is exquisitely thick and lustrous. And her tail—she is so proud of her full and silky tail! Ellie is a goddess among beings. To liken her to a human female, she's very tall and voluptuous with long legs and a beautiful neck and body. And, oh God, her behind—it's absolutely incredible!

"She has dark brown eyes, a small muzzle, and the rest of her features are very refined. She has tiny feet, like little teacups. She's very outgoing and friendly, so she may come right out and talk to you too."

Ellie. Photo by Carole Devereux.

Ellie did indeed talk. On the topic of beauty, she had so much to say to me that we needed a second session. It was then that Carole suggested I fly solo. In the quick, firm, yet gentle manner of first-rate teachers, Carole encouraged me to simply listen and take down the message. Before I had much of a chance to say anything, the phone receiver was back in its cradle, and Ellie was speaking. The following is her discourse.

Beauty and the Goddess

Beauty is an inner knowingness, an inner perspective. Beauty is goodness, the manifestation of light in a kind and gentle (which is to say, a loving) act.

I have had a life in what you know as ancient Greece, where beauty was much discussed. There, the central image of a fountain and a reflecting pool was used as a touchstone to the act of beauty. Beauty flows from within, reflecting both the inner and outer aspects of itself. This is what resonates at the core of your saying, "Beauty is in the eye of the beholder."

I wish to bring human attention back to the experience of beauty in the world. Beauty is an aspect of the enlightenment process, for it uplifts the soul, much like bubbles of inspiration uplift the heart. Beauty is not just reflection, for it is found not only in the reflecting pool, but also in the fountain from which springs an inner rush of beauty from soul to soul. Beauty is about transformation.

Humans have largely perverted beauty. This is not to say you have lost appreciation for beauty, but you have largely forgotten the flow of participating in and creating with beauty. It is no mistake Carole described my beauty. By doing so, she invoked the spirit of beauty—not only in me, but also in herself, in you, and all the world.

This is a difficult notion for humans to understand, for you often see beauty on superficial levels. Know that Beauty goes much deeper. She invokes the elements of kindness, truth, and feeling at the heart level. The children's fable "Beauty and the Beast" reveals the growth of beauty in the female, Belle.

Beauty is tied to Goddess energy, for it is about expanding and elevating your frequency. There are many places where beauty is incarnate. Beauty comes with developing trust of the self.

As you unfold the nature of space and time, recenter with the image of the pool and fountain. These two elements work together in revealing beauty. This is a spatial memory, which resides at the core of all beauty.

Deep within the reflecting pool is a clarity that illuminates the true inner brilliance of beauty. There are stories of humans staring into reflective bodies of water and falling in. In many cases, this is the "leap," the first step toward reaching out and merging the inner and outer aspects of Beauty.

Beauty is a flow, a current that carries the wave of truth and light. Like the fountain, Beauty is a bubbling up, an active motion, an inspirative energy, arising from the heart. The heart chakra is a bridge between the physical and spiritual. In many ways, this too is what beauty does, linking and allowing transformations between dimensions to occur.

The movement of Beauty is what allows humans (and other beings) to connect to the divine. In all the religious and ecstatic experiences humans have recounted, you will find the mention of Beauty. As noted, this is an understanding that was seen and honored at certain points in your past, though largely overlooked at present.

How does Beauty relate to the Goddess, to the Divine? We will invoke the energies of inspiration; a bubbling up of ideas; a rush of emotions; a flood of feeling; a rising of passion; the union of active and passive, yin and yang, male and female. When you call up the image of the pool and fountain in your heart and mind, do you not see all of these elements and how they coexist in simultaneity? So, too, is it with the presence of Beauty. It is an interaction, a union—in many ways, the nexus between idea and manifestation, thought and act, physical form and the divine.

I wish to emphasize that Beauty is an act of becoming. Meditate on Beauty and you pull yourselves closer to who you really are.

Ellie, how does this all relate to horses and why is this such an important issue for you?

I am a creature of Light and Beauty. I could be a fish, a ferret, a mink, a rose. I am aligned with Light-beings who usher beauty into this world as a conduit to the next. I offer guidance in nurturing your skills of manifestation. I am as an art teacher reminding you of the beauty of form, how form reflects function, and how all elements of manifestation work together to create the working of Love in the universe.

I relate the time/space of Old Greece and the ideas of that point in time because many of you were present then as designers, artists, artisans, architects, storytellers, dancers, and weavers, both of cloth and ideas.

In preparing for the future earth, we (the group of Light-beings) would like to inspire the element of beauty, not only as a tool for manifestation, but as a bridge to the divine.

The Goddess of Beauty has returned to the earth. In truth, she never left, though she has been dormant, allowing others to have their hand at manifestation. She moves quietly, though some aspects of her become enraged and act with fury. There is still a rift between the Goddess and this aspect of the Dark Female a rage at injustice to women, children, animals, the earth, all things female, and to the corruption of beauty.

I speak of Beauty not as an ideal but as an active element of enlightenment, of coming home. She is a guide, and a very creative and artistic one at that.

I wish for all of you reading this to see and feel beauty: outside yourself, in others, in simple acts and those "random acts of kindness," as well as in yourself and those you love. They all are the same. By falling into the reflecting pool, you merge to a new understanding of beauty, grace, and light. When you come out, you will never be the same.

I bid you farewell, recalling the past to the present, and bridging the present and future to the now; with much love and a wealth of beauty to all.

ANCESTOR HORSE

It was Buddy who suggested we speak to Ancestor Horse. "He will help you understand more about time than you intend to ask," Buddy told me.

Although Carole had spoken to Ancestor Horse through Buddy many times, the idea was new to me. Surprisingly, the notion of talking to a horse who would be connecting with an ancestral horse spirit, thus forming a human-animal-spirit, interspecies, interdimensional phone call, didn't seem too odd. Perhaps self-doubt was fading. What I felt was eagerness to be part of the communication.

I couldn't guess what Ancestor Horse might say for the simple reason that I could barely imagine Ancestor Horse. Who was he? Where, and when, did he exist? This was not just the consciousness of a deceased animal but an ancestral energy we were after. I had no sense where this was going to take us, but I was happy both Buddy and Carole were along for the ride. And so we began.

Ancestor Horse, Buddy, and Carole

Ancestor Horse came through Buddy. I saw a picture of myself kneeling at the water's edge with a bunch of early horses. They were looking into the water and drinking. A voice said, "Terra Firma, Terra Firma, Terra Firma. In the past, as in the now, comes one instant." Ancestor Horse began:

Time was once measured by the moon and sun, and their cycles, long ago. We did not have minutes or seconds. We had only suns and moons reflecting in the water where we drank. We would take days and work to accomplish one thing, not worrying about time.

Time was measured in days by the sun and the way the moon crosses the sky. Time was marked by the trees, flowers, and seasons. In my belly I have knowing of time, not in my mind. Rhythms and timing are heavenly and cannot be measured, held, followed, or even yet understood by the human mind.

Until the past catches up with all of us, we wait for time. Time jumps ahead to meet your expectations, so be careful not to see too far into the future and become ahead of yourselves. By being unhurried, you stop time. By hurrying, you speed up time. Go slowly. Listen to your beating heart, waiting, pausing.

Ancestor Horse, Buddy, and Dawn

Greetings. We step from the Rock energy, from where our symbols are held in prints and paintings, physically linked remembrances to times gone by.

We are always present, always in the "now." There is an Aboriginal saying that we exist "around the corner of time," and this is a way for human consciousness to understand the way we come to you now. It is not so much from the "past" as from around the corners of time. It is as if, for a moment, you shift your perception and glimpse from the corner of your eye into another dimension wherein past and present coexist. Yes, future too, though that is yet another bend around time.

At this point, I feel an uncomfortable buildup of energy in my body, like an adrenaline rush. The voice, which I assume belongs to Ancestor Horse—though there is a Buddy-like familiarity about it—tells me it will be easier if I move from writing in my journal to the computer, because I can type much faster than I write.

In moving, you come to appreciate a new way of seeing things and physically experience a new dimension of being.

In a sense, the movement of time is like a stampeding of horses, their hooves moving swiftly across the land. We move as one unit, caught in the flow of movement. This is how time is for humans. You are so caught in the movement of time that it self-perpetuates, this manifestation of time, and you gallop along the plains of your life, moving swiftly with the rest of the herd.

The first thing to know is that this is one notion of time. Time exists in other dimensions and other worlds in different forms. Even Buddy has his particular notion of time. He is able to bridge with me because he has opened his mind to the possibility of moving from the herd mentality of time and thus is able to deepen, enter, and hold his own ground in meeting me for a moment out of time.

This is a moment out of time?

In many ways, yes. To understand, you must suspend your notions about time as well as space. This is a vast concept, one that you may only understand partially at first. You will deepen your metaphors, symbols, and paradigms of time. There is no right and wrong way to view time, only an ever deepening understanding and appreciation of this construct of time.

Let me give you an example of time in another dimension. Rejoin the herd for a moment and become the horse galloping across the land. If you turn your head and lift your nose to sniff the wind, you can shift dimensions by allowing your consciousness to ride the wind. The dimension of wind exists in another sense, another dimension beyond your own. It is seamless, always moving; yet, it is the same in stillness and in gusts and bursts; it is all accommodating. It passes and moves through the human and animal worlds, but at another dimension of being. The image of wind in horses' manes and tails, and even the feeling of the wind is often associated with horses because we have an affinity for becoming part of the wind.

The wind is also connected to stone and, again, we remind you of our representation on stone and rock. Wind and stone have a connection that is timeless, something many creatures do not understand. This is yet another consciousness, apart from and yet a part of humans and animals and the greater earth.

Time is fleeting. Time stands still. Both these statements are true, for they are instances of the interstices of time. Again, a vast subject that is difficult to explain without more experiential references.

Would you tell us more about time in relation to the earth changes and the ideas and prophecies that certain events will happen at certain dates?

The history of time is tied to the beginnings of the earth. The earth was time encoded, so to speak. Time was integrated into the way the earth progressed. This is why time seems so real to you; it is part of the earth's programming. There are encoded within earth's time certain key events that will help remind you all—animals, plants, and various other aspects of earth—to reawaken. Think of it as a snooze alarm! These times are encoded within the earth itself. The calendars you hold are not exactly in tune with this inner clock, though perhaps not too much off the mark. Certain key dates, such as the 2012, would be best held not so literally. Understand too that if you awaken before the alarm goes off, there is nothing to stop you from simply turning off the alarm.

It is not my intention to engender fear or to purport that certain events will or will not happen. Rather, you might look at the consciousness and underlying patterns of what is occurring when various prophecies are spoken of, especially those relating to the "end" of time.

Begin to use the tools that were put forth in the past. Stonehenge, the Sphinx, various temples, towers, ancient burial grounds, even the crop circles—these are all tools you may use to develop a more expanded perception of what time is and how to incorporate it in understanding yourselves and your world.

Time is not an absolute. It is a tool among many others. It is a means, a perception, and a kind of mnemonic device for those of earth. You—all of you—chose to come to work within these conditions, to experience this version of time and space as well as this type of consciousness.

The notions of time travel, bilocation, time warps, time holes, and so on, are all variations on a theme. Sometimes it is by exploring the edges and inconsistencies of time that you come to a larger, vaster appreciation of what time encompasses for you.

If there is time—to pun a small joke—I would like to speak to the presence of ancestors, not only of horses, but ancestors of all sorts. We exist, as I mentioned, around the corners of time. In truth, we are always here for you. Every thought, image, person, animal, consciousness, event, happening, and idea is always available. This is perhaps hard to understand through the human constraints of time and space, but in a larger sense we all exist outside of time and space. The ancestors are none other than you. We are "past versions" of you.

As the earth comes to a meeting of cycles, the ending with the new, we are more available to you. There is much we can teach you, remind you, and help you to see. Think of us as yourselves in Elder form, for in our reality we have passed through and embody much experience. Choose us wisely when you come to work with an ancestor, however, for we hold both "good" and "bad." We hold much information, and part of your adventure in sorting out the paradox of time is also to learn how to discern for yourselves what is valuable and what you wish not to experience again.

Not all humans on this planet live in their heart. There is much about control and manipulation that has yet to be healed. There are those who speak of these dangers and who have revealed scenarios of past times of earth when control and manipulation got out of hand. It would not be prudent of me to tell you that all Ancestors hold only wise energy; indeed, some hold energies that are based in control and manipulation.

Learn to discern for yourself where you are headed, where and what you wish to create. As you step out of time and space, you will see that there are infinite possibilities. Growth is an individual matter, though we are all connected to the One.

If you want an expanded version of time, sit with rocks. Perhaps more than anyone on the planet, rocks hold the understanding of time in its largest sense. Listen to the wind as well. She will reveal to you the secrets of rock and time whenever you care to listen.

Ancient Memories
Spirit of Elephant ~ Morgine Jurdan

Ancient memories are those we talk about in reference to your current times here on this plane. You are bringing to the surface of consciousness many ideas and thoughts from the past, a time in which you learned similar lessons you are learning now. Sometimes you can learn from the past and not relive things that were not beneficial to you before. Tying into this information can aid you in better understanding yourself and where you came from and how you developed.

At one time, you were one with us in every way. We were much more similar than we were different. We experienced our feelings on the same level. We could understand one another without the need for spoken words. We could connect regardless of how far apart we were. We could "feel" one another at a deep level. We would like to see you gain this tool back again. Feeling is one of the most important things you do on this physical plane, and when you numb yourself, you lose much—if not most—of your experience.

When you learn to work with Nature, instead of trying to control the outcome, you will evolve by leaps and bounds. When you begin to comprehend the inter-connectedness that exists between all forms of life, you will truly awaken to a new day. Your actions, every single one of them, affect us all. We are patient, we are kind, and we are understanding beyond your imagination or ability to believe. We wait still for that time to arrive.

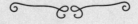

15

Miracle and Manifestation
Made Real

An old legend told by the Lakota Sioux relates that one summer very long ago, seven sacred council fires came together in difficult times. There was no game, and all the people were starving. The Chief sent two young men to hunt for food. Early one morning, they climbed a high hill to scan for game on the prairie. Gazing into the distance, they saw a young woman dressed in white buckskin who appeared to float on the land.

White Buffalo Calf Woman was a messenger from the Creator. She came to the people to deliver a sacred pipe, telling them that with it they would "walk like a living prayer." White Buffalo Calf Woman stayed for four days, spending a day in turn with the women, the men, the children, and the elders, teaching them to remember that each day is holy and all peoples on the earth are sacred and should be treated as such.

Before leaving, White Buffalo Calf Woman told the people that she would return to them at the end of four ages. As she walked away, she transformed herself into a buffalo. The people watched her roll on the ground four times, each time turning a different color: red, yellow, black, and white. Then White Buffalo Calf Woman ascended into the clouds.

In 1994, a white female buffalo calf was born on a farm in Wisconsin. Though the owners of the farm realized the calf was rare, they had no idea of the worldwide interest that would focus upon the little buffalo they named Miracle, nor of the profound spiritual significance of the event, particularly to Native Americans. In the first two months, more than twenty thousand people made a pilgrimage to see the white calf, including representatives from two dozen Indian nations.

Some Native Americans explained that Miracle's birth had been foretold by the legend of White Buffalo Calf Woman. The calf was the fulfillment of a prophecy, they said, the return of a legend, marking the beginning of a new age of unity and harmony. Just as White Buffalo Calf Woman became the four colors of the human race (black, red, yellow, and white), so too would the buffalo calf "wear" all the colors of humanity.

When I visited Miracle, she was two years old and her color had already changed from white to reddish brown to black, followed by a stint of yellow, and then a natural buffalo brown. Much of the media had lost interest when Miracle lost her white coat. Reporters not familiar with the prophecy didn't see the connection between the buffalo calf's changing colors and the significance of White Buffalo Calf Woman's story.

The land around Miracle was considered sacred by many, and visitors had filled the fence surrounding her pen with an assortment of offerings. That is how I first saw Miracle, in her pasture surrounded by a wire fence knotted with hundreds of different colored ribbons and objects—blue, red, yellow, green, white, black, purple—all fluttering in the cool spring air.

The role of animals as mythic connections, conduits from the human to spirit world, is the basis of many legends. Such animals are often depicted as special in some way. When I first saw Miracle, she looked like any other brown buffalo calf. This was a living prophecy? I had a sudden empathy with the reporters then; I understood why most of them had left. Deep down, I found hidden away my own clamor for truth, something not so far from "I'll believe it when I see it."

But myth and miracle do not work that way. Sometimes, it's not until you begin to believe that you acquire the eyes to see.

Penelope Smith told me that Miracle was exactly what the Native people said she was: the portent of a new age. "She's a sign of the increase of consciousness and she's holding that space. There will be more like her," said Penelope. "She's a spiritual manifestation that we're okay. She's a very good sign."

Wanting to know more about Miracle and her message, I asked Nancie LaPier and Sam Louie for help. While it was not my intention to set this up as a skeptic's experiment, the following dialogues serve as an intriguing example of how two communicators receive the same basic message although in slightly different forms.

To begin, I told Nancie and Sam only that Miracle was a buffalo calf who had significance to Native Americans in connection with a legendary spirit being named White Buffalo Calf Woman. Neither communicator knew the specifics of the legend before we began.

Miracle and Nancie
"She shows herself to me wearing a crown with many jewels," Nancy began. "My sense is that she is very aware of her position of spiritual royalty and that many beings on the earth accord her this honor. When I ask her if there's something she wants to

share for this book, the first thing she tells me is what an honor it is to be here. She is very connected with her purpose of being on earth."

I represent an archetype of graceful energy that has long been missing from this plane. My gift is to anchor grace and gracefulness.

There is a need to bring balance and healing to the spiritual wounds of Native Americans. There is a spirit of hopelessness among today's Natives who are living out among the reservations. Some change is going on, but the reality for the biggest part of the culture right now is some very real hopelessness.

I'm here to shake everybody out of their boots. The way of the graceful dance needs to be reinstated on the reservation.

Nancie paused and laughed. "She shows me something like dancing moccasins. . . . Now she shows me a woman in a long white deerskin or calfskin robe. The woman is dancing in circles and swinging in a wild, ecstatic kind of state. This woman is Native, perhaps White Buffalo Calf Woman. She has a 'come follow me' movement, as if she's leading everyone in a dance, going forward to another time."

It is time to move forward now. It is a time of healing the earth within. A very cellular, ancestral type of healing needs to take place, going all the way back to when the vision of White Buffalo Calf Woman's presence first became manifest.

There is a real need to let go of repression and belief systems about being repressed—not to go into denial about those things, but to acknowledge the pain, release it, and move forward. Some people have tremendous gifts they're not in touch with, but they need to be part of what's going on. I come to remind them of their part in this sacred circle. And it's time to return now.

We talk of cloud people. Our ancestors are in the clouds. "There needs to be a leap of faith, but rest assured you have not been abandoned," is what they are saying to Native Americans.

They are not saying it so much to those who are connected and teaching and being a part of mainstream metaphysics, but to the ones who have emotional problems with drugs and alcohol, with lack of abundance. These things need to be changed in the mental and emotional body so they can vibrate and return to the strong, honorable beings they once were. We need them; the rest of the world is waiting.

"Who is speaking now?" I asked Nancie. A change in tone and voice patterns was becoming familiar to me as I spoke with more animals through various communicators. With Nancie, subtle changes in her voice and pronoun shifts—*she* to *they* to *we*—indicated that it was not just Miracle who was speaking.

"Right," said Nancie. "It's hard to separate sometimes when I am in the midst of this. White Buffalo Calf Woman was speaking as the archetype energy that is manifest in Miracle. I can hear Miracle speaking, specifically about her life and feelings and what is going on in the corral. She is very closely tied to White Buffalo Calf Woman, who is part of the higher aspect of who Miracle is. But when it comes to the message for the Native Americans, it is more White Buffalo Calf Woman explaining the energy of Miracle being here and what that means.

"The message is very strong in terms of Native Americans not identifying with their place of emotional wounding. White Buffalo Calf Woman says that those born into Native American ancestry have a talent to transmute that energy. They often don't remember they have that ability to move the emotional wounding to a place of acknowledging and knowing their spiritual royalty."

What about the connection between Native Americans and other races? Miracle, why did you choose to be born at a farm which belongs to white people?

This is one way of drawing Native American energy out into the white community. Basically I am saying, "Return, return, come out, we need you." There are many white people on the earth who have Native American cellular memory and heart, and it's necessary now for Native Americans to not look at the white people in the same way that white people once looked at them.

I want you to sense the essence of the individual and not to look at the cover. What happened before won't happen again. It is the cellular fear a lot of people have of simply walking their path because of the cellular memory of being persecuted at one time. You don't need to repeat this if you can find a way to raise the vibration and fill that hole in your emotional body.

You need to understand that the belief system in the white buffalo calf is really what created the opportunity for me to come. That's how strongly your belief system can create reality in this world. Native Americans need to understand the strength of their belief systems and work in a cocreative way with that, because they can create a new way of being. They have a way that needs to be incorporated in the world. It's part of the cog in your wheel.

There is a certain holding back, a resentment by the Native American people, but understand that it comes from emotional pain and years of suppression. You all need to allow that to this race of people so that they can heal beyond it. The more you try to fix it or make it better or ignore it and pretend it's not there, then you also create the energy that maintains it at its current level. The key word is *allowing*—for both races to come to a place of allowing so that all can get to that place of unity.

White Buffalo Calf Woman says, "The important thing is that you are connected to the earth in your heart, that you celebrate this planet and understand how this earth operates through and with the cooperation of the beings who walk it. It's a sacred gift and an expression of God."

We held silent for a moment and then Nancie laughed. "Miracle loves to dance! She prances her two front hooves all over the place, like she likes to dance. I can see that she's in a huge corral and there are people who come and look at her. She thinks she's hot; she just really thinks she's hot and she knows it! The more the humans look at her with that kind of respect, the more hot she gets. She is very aware of her own specialness. She says that if we would look upon one another with that same awe, then we would create beings of awe who live in the world. That's her final message."

Miracle and Sam

Before Sam contacted Miracle, he began with a disclaimer. "I have to tell you that I start this one very skeptical, especially when people talk about the return of great spirits and legends and stuff like that." Sam couldn't see that on my end of the phone line, I was smiling. Part of what I enjoyed about talking with Sam was the attorney in him, for it seemed whenever he was about to bring forth some information out of the ordinary, he felt obliged to voice his standard disclaimer.

"I'm not sure what I'm getting," said Sam, "but it's definitely a woman's voice, being very humorous, saying, 'This is Miracle, but you can call me Miracle Whip.' You know, the Kraft product," Sam explained with a laugh, clearly amused by the voice of Miracle Whip. "As far as who she is:"

Well, let's put it this way. I come from a realm and am trying to emphasize a sense of unity. Oftentimes when people are looking for a symbol to be personified by a person or "animalized" by an animal, their prayers are heard. Given a Oneness that is existent in all things, no matter what people's beliefs are, I can make myself manifest as a messenger representing the energy that is White Buffalo Calf Woman. Legend has brought about the symbol of White Buffalo Calf Woman, which has now been personified by my presence.

What am I here to teach? What is my purpose? For one, I, as the spirit answering the call of the need for the return of White Buffalo Calf Woman, want to know what it feels like to be a buffalo calf. I have come to teach unity. What's needed is figuring out how to bring us [Native Americans] into an acceptance with the dominant white American culture, and to make ourselves a distinct, recognizable, and respected voice, not one that's glorified nor one that's looked down upon. That's my unity message: to face up to fitting in as a distinct group that has something to contribute.

Another message is about gentleness, that the world needs to surely move toward gentleness. And in many ways it has. As the Universe, we have definitely succeeded in helping to move the earth toward less destructiveness. Even though there are many wars, and the sufferings are tremendous within those wars, on a mass scale there really has been human movement away from mass destruction.

Lastly, my message is to be a kind of hero symbol in a time when both Native Americans and mainstream American culture are lacking some hero symbols. Now, don't expect me to do somersaults, because I am going to be a calf living a calf's life, being very gentle and growing up to do what I'm supposed to do as an animal. And I will be happy to talk with those who want to communicate with me in this way.

I also want to be good humored and make a lot of the issues around legends and Native Americans and spiritual worship lighthearted, so that people don't take any of this overly seriously, because spirituality is very much about humor.

I'm going to address why I said "Miracle Whip" other than to just be funny. This is a message for New Age seekers not to become spiritual snobs. Don't think that following this path is a higher path. We're all actually on the same path, and each person's path, no matter where they are, is as worthy as the next. Remember to be humble and humorous.

Who was the original White Buffalo Calf Woman? Was she also a sign or a manifestation because the people needed a sign?

The original Buffalo Calf Woman was a human being of very sincere motives, great wisdom, and great simplicity. She also had a truly earnest desire to bring some spirituality and leadership. However, she was not anything more divine than the rest of us who choose to tap into our divinity are. Again, the message is unity. We are all unified as one supremely divine being in different manifestations. And, yes, like all the New Age practices and religions teach, in many ways it's about concentration, focus, letting go, stripping away layers on top and getting to the beautiful divine core underneath.

I was impressed that Miracle ended both her talks emphasizing the importance of celebrating the essence of spiritual divinity in all animals, humans of all races and cultures included.

While we may find the oneness of our spiritual essence by deconstructing the barriers of form, species, race, religion, culture, and color, it is also important for all beings to walk in authenticity, sharing our diverse beliefs, practices, and views with the world. This, too, is how we find meaning and presence of spirit.

Earthkeeper, teacher, and author of *Buffalo Woman Comes Singing*, Brooke Medicine Eagle believes White Buffalo Calf Woman underscores the importance of respecting diversity within our quest for unity. "Now is the beginning of the new time of peace," notes Brooke, "and we must all make it real by learning to respect each other across not only racial lines, but lines of kingdom and realm. From the 'highest' spirit to the deepest stone, all must be respected. All are alive with creator's intelligence, and other kingdoms and realms (such as spirit, deva, animal, and plant) are anxiously awaiting for us as two-leggeds to step fully conscious into the Circle of Life."[1]

Perhaps we are called to become the caretakers of a small white buffalo calf; perhaps we are opened to talking with animals. Can any of us say which path is right for another or direct how spiritual unfoldment will occur? The key, it would seem, is simply to be open, to listen to that which speaks honestly and genuinely to our deepest self, and to follow the prompting of the spirit that moves us, wherever that may lead.

Many months after the talks with Miracle, I read a book entitled *Fools Crow*. The book details the life of the holy man and ceremonial chief of the Sioux, Frank Fools Crow, as told to Thomas E. Mails.[2] Though many had approached the revered leader for the honor of telling his story, Fools Crow had always refused. How was it, then, that a white man was given this task? Perhaps for the same reason that Miracle chose the farm of a white family in Wisconsin to be born.

In 1974, during a social visit, Fools Crow related to Mails (through a translator) that he had been instructed in a vision quest to tell his story to the world through a person who would become known to him. That person, Fools Crow said, was Mails. Mails was astonished, for although he was a writer and artist who had published several books on Indians, he was not Native. Moreover, he and Fools Crow did not speak the same language. But Fools Crow was firm. He was sure this is why the spirits directed Mails to be brought to see him that very day. Equally fascinating, wrote Mails, was the realization that the very same thought had just occurred to him.

The unfolding of spiritual paths, like the unfolding of elegant truths, can rarely be understood by logic alone. When and how we are called to participate in the unfolding is often both a mystery and a miracle.

The Circle of Life
Penelope Smith and the Animal Network

Tuning into the animal network at this moment, I see the frogs, the lizards, the whales, the birds, and more—all of them are together in a big circle, among their own species and interconnected. They say: "We see the circle of life as continuing in an unbroken fashion. There are many places on Earth that are dying, that are in a destructive mode. They too will come to life. We wait. We animals of all species see that the evolution of consciousness is going as it will, as it is meant to be. We are not concerned about the destruction of the bodies except as it affects our immediate families, our groupings, and then we cry out for help, for consciousness."

As humans wake up, the Earth will be revived. The life force is strong; the Earth is strong and will heal all, and all beings on Earth can be healed as they tap into this. There are still species dying and people dying in many sections of the planet. Awareness is growing, however, and this is the greater force.

The animals have a lot of news; a lot of messages are being transmitted to people all over the planet. And people are listening. Those who are particularly focused on the telepathic connection are getting it in the way we get it so that we can translate it to others.

Penelope Smith. Photo by Marty Knapp.

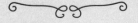

16

The Role of Llamas: Holders of the Light

Every species has a distinctive energy it brings to the planet. One need only look to the incredible diversity of physical form for a sense of this. Just as individual animals, such as Miracle, may bring forth a very specific type of spiritual energy, so do larger groups of animals work together to carry or embody a particular energetic with a common spiritual goal. These goals may be focused on by small groupings of animals within a species (such as the Orange and Oriental Cat Contingents), an entire species, or even a larger grouping. The cetaceans, for example, are often cited for their focus on healing humanity and elevating vibrational frequencies.

Through several conversations with a llama herd, Nedda Wittels learned that llamas have a special role in relation to planetary evolution. As they participate in herd consciousness as well as individual consciousness, the llama outlook offers a unique perspective on maintaining conscious awareness of both individual and collective levels.

The following interview by Nedda features two llamas who offer insights on the role their species plays in anchoring light to the planet. Cathedral Pines Abracadabra (a female llama known as Abby, serving as herd healer and midwife) and Black Velvet of Crestland (a gelding known as Velvet, serving as herd medicine man/shaman), live with their herd in Rhode Island at the farm of Tom and Helen Rowe-Drake.

After making contact with Velvet and Abby and sending greetings to the rest of the herd, Nedda began.

First, I'd like you to explain how the herd consciousness works. I have some understanding from previous conversations, but I'd like to capture your thoughts and experiences with this for other humans to read about.

[Velvet:] A llama herd is a single unit of consciousness at one level, and a combined unit of many individual beings at another. This means that, although we are individuals, we are always connected with each other and know what every member of the herd is doing at all times. If one llama is sick or giving birth or dying or eating or whatever, we all know.

[Abby:] Yes, and this makes some situations very difficult. If a llama has a particular fear and another member of the herd is experiencing that which the first one fears, the frightful llama will block out of his or her awareness the unpleasant situation. For example, getting our toes trimmed or being clipped or examined by the veterinarian or given shots. These are all situations we don't relish, but some of us really hate it, so we block it out.

What are the advantages of herd consciousness?

[Abby:] Instantaneous warnings of danger. Continuous emotional and spiritual support for one another in a very powerful way. Sharing of blessings, good times, and knowledge of when dinner or breakfast is being served. Powerful support for the birthing and transition (death) process.

[Velvet:] When we choose it, we are a very powerful single unit of energy and consciousness, which makes us spiritually powerful. This is not a power in the sense of dominating others, but rather a loving power. The strength of love is without limit, and we can and do build and project a strong field of love.

What is the process for integrating a newborn llama or an older llama who is new to the herd?

[Abby:] Working with the newborns (crias) is part of my responsibility as midwife. As you know, the mother llama gives birth in the wild without any aid and the newborn must dry itself off and stand without aid. So the mother and the baby must be physically strong. To provide support for this aspect of the process, the herd midwife's role is to help the spirit of the newborn implant strongly into the cria's body at the time of birth. While the mother is humming aloud to strengthen the cria's physical form as it first encounters life outside the womb, the midwife hums telepathically and gives directions to the spirit to help it implant energetically, attaching at the chakras and interweaving with the DNA and spinal chord. By the end of the first twenty-four hours, if all has happened successfully, the new llama will be strongly grounded into the earth through its physical body.

Does the rest of the herd help with this?

[Abby:] Not usually. This is specialty work that we train for. In a large herd, there are always apprentices, so when I give birth, there is someone to help my cria spiritually implant. Otherwise, I would have to do it all myself. That's possible to do, but very exhausting.

Velvet, do the males ever help with this process?

[Velvet:] They do sometimes. If the cria is male and the spiritual energy is having a difficult time connecting and adjusting, Abby asks for my assistance.

Llama group. Photo by Helen Rowe-Drake.

When I assist her, I blend my individual energy with Abby's and that helps the spirit adjust.

When a new llama joins the herd, it is my role as shaman to work with the new energies to bring the new member into energetic alignment to the frequencies and vibrational patterns that make this herd unique. I am able to see/hear/feel the vibrations and I weave them together, like a pattern in a piece of cloth.

(Velvet is now showing me a tapestry of patterns that look like something a Peruvian human might weave. He indicates the patterns are more refined than this, but isn't sure I can see the real thing because it is shifting very rapidly. He says he also can hear sounds—musical notes and vocal tones.)

Did it take you long to learn how to understand and work with this web of energy?

[Velvet:] I was trained for several lifetimes as an apprentice in other llama herds before I became adept at this work. That is why, even though I am quite young, I am able to be the shaman for this herd in this lifetime.

Do llamas tend to reincarnate in the same species?

[Velvet:] Because most beings of spirit incarnate in soul groups, it makes sense that when it is important to experience many lifetimes as a particular species, a number of spirits will come again and again to the same species. One can stay with the same species for a very large number of lifetimes, but often that's because the individuals prefer that species, or because there is something special to be experienced or learned.

What about you, Abby? Did you train over several lifetimes for your role as midwife?

[Abby:] Yes. My tasks are different, but still require special skills and deftness with spiritual energy. I am also a healer. I work energetically with any llama who is sick, whether physically or emotionally or spiritually. This is also an area where Velvet and I work together.

Are there other roles assigned to specific llamas in the herd that have responsibility for or to the herd as a whole?

[Velvet:] There is a storyteller, who is really the herd historian. That llama keeps an oral history of the individuals and the herd as a group. In our herd, it's Blu. There are times when he tells very good and funny stories, but he needs to become less self-conscious, and his storytelling will be much better.

How often does the herd storyteller tell stories? And what is the purpose of this activity?

[Velvet:] In the winter, he tells them almost every night. In other seasons, it depends on what is going on. During breeding season, because Blu is going to sire crias, he will undoubtedly have breeding on his mind. Still, I think he will be a good father to the herd, as well as a good biological father.

Is that why the role of historian/storyteller is given to a breeding llama?

[Abby:] Yes. It is important that he be a true "father of the herd." Blu will grow into this. He's very young in many ways.

Would Blu be willing to share one of the stories that he uses to teach young llamas?

[Velvet:] Not at this time. It would be difficult for you to translate these, because they are all energetic exchanges at higher frequencies designed to help young llamas retain their connection to the soul and higher frequencies. They are not easily translatable into words.

Let's get back to spiritual matters. Tom (Rowe-Drake) has said that llamas are the "dolphins of the land." Do you understand what he means by this, and would you agree?

[Velvet:] This is a difficult question to answer. We know that the dolphins are from another dimension and that they are here to perform specific functions for maintaining earth rhythms, like the whales do, and for helping humans awaken to ascension. Llamas were designed to be here to parallel the Tibetan Lamas, the spiritual leaders of humans at the top of the world. We are here as spiritual leaders for the land animals on earth. We set a model for living in complete oneness with each other as herd animals, while also living separate existences, which is something the dolphins also do.

Regarding our being "the dolphins of the land," you might say that we are similar, but not the same. We are not, for example, attempting to heal humanity, which the dolphins are attempting to do. We are, as a species, now spread around this side of the earth more, so that we can teach and share energy with more humans. We bring light wherever we go, but we are not attempting to heal per se.

How do llama herds differ from herds of cows, sheep, horses, and other herd animals? Don't these species have herd consciousness as well?

[Velvet:] Yes, but it's not at the same vibrational frequencies as llama herd consciousness. Our frequencies are higher and finer because our natural habitat is higher geographically, and therefore those frequencies are consistent with our habitat. As a result, we vibrate more closely with beings of light, so we can communicate up and down the scale. We are pivotal between other land herd animals and beings of spirit/light. We are a bridge, as it were.

What functions does this bridge serve?

[Velvet:] It is a transfer point for spiritual information that needs to come down from Source into the animal kingdoms, into their forms and DNA. This is the main function.

Is this the parallel you speak of with the Tibetan Lamas?

[Velvet:] Yes. As I understand it, they kept open the energies and frequencies to high spiritual realms that were lost to many humans over the centuries and even millennia. It is similar in that regard. And they were able to keep it open by living in a particular habitat at high altitudes.

Do other animal species recognize the role of llamas?

[Velvet:] Some do and some don't. I am aware that you have had many conversations with animals of a variety of species. Some are more spiritual than others are. Some are more aware than others of the earth ascension process. I would expect that some might be aware of the role of llamas as a species and others wouldn't care, even if you told them. Even among humans there is wide variation in interest in spiritual matters, true?

True. Do you work with nature spirits and the earth as you bring in these energies?

[Velvet:] Oh, yes.

How is this work affected by so many llamas living at lower altitudes around the world?

[Velvet:] Well, it makes our work more difficult in some ways. Truthfully, though, it also helps. What it really means is that the llamas who remain in the Andes Mountains are the primary contact to continue this spiritual work, and those of us who live at lower altitudes now act as transfer points or transmitters of energy to other parts of the world. There are no accidents, you know. This is why so many of us are now living in other places. This is also why the Lamas of Tibet are living outside Tibet.

A very interesting theory.

[Velvet:] It's not a theory. I know it to be true, although the human lamas might not be willing to say so.

Velvet, I'm very interested to know how you know all this.

[Velvet:] As herd shaman, it was part of my training. It is also part of my role/ life purpose to help educate humans to understand more about spirituality. You know, of course, that everyone who has a llama herd is being affected by our spiritual energies? The animals, in general, are having their frequencies raised as the Earth's vibrations are also being raised.

Can you speak more about the Tibetan connection?

[Velvet:] We llamas have held the light for this side of the earth during the dark ages of this period on earth, as the lamas of Tibet held the light for the other side of the Earth. By "dark ages," I am referring to the time since the fall of Lemuria and the disappearance of the Mayan civilization. By simply being here in this body type with knowledge of the Highest, we have been able to contribute to some mainte-nance of balance on the landmass.

Does the spiritual teaching you share with the Tibetan lamas have to do with the frequency bridge? And, do the llamas work with any other species in this regard?

[Velvet:] There is only one Truth, that we (all beings) are originally from the same source, that all are ultimately one consciousness and the experience of separation is illusion. Therefore, while we are not in contact with the Tibetan lamas (as in conversationally in contact), we are capable of speaking with whom-ever has a desire to speak with us. We, as many humans today, are anchoring light at higher and higher frequencies for the purpose of shifting the earth into higher dimensions. We have much experience bringing in higher frequencies of light, as we, as a species, are designed for this and have done it for thousands of years. We don't work with other species directly, but I am certain that there are others on the planet who are doing this work as well.

Velvet, do you or any of the other llamas have a specific message for humans you would like to share?

(The herd conferences and Velvet announces that the following message is from the entire herd.)

The entire world is a place of spirit. When humans make the artificial separation between the spiritual and the physical, they have an incomplete and badly distorted conception of the physical. Part of the enlightenment/ascension process is to remember that the entire universe is composed of spiritual energy—that's the only kind of energy there is—and to recognize God's presence everywhere, at all times, in all forms.

This Moment
KC (eat) ~ Morgine Jurdan

Life is beautiful and has much to offer. You can savor life in so many wonderful and different ways.

Do you savor what enters your mouth, distinguishing the different textures, flavors, temperatures, colors, and energies of what you eat and drink and inhale?

Do you hear the bugs singing, the birds caressing the plants with their voices, the leaves in the trees singing with the wind? How often do you hear your house talk, your pipes sing, the sway of the clothes on your body, the plants breathing, a friend talking?

There are a million ways to experience life. Take a moment to stop thinking and look into someone's eyes. Really see what is there, beneath the surface, beneath the words and motions, beneath the anger and pain. Real life can be tasted each moment you are alive when you are present to its richness.

Become alive today and look at what is in front of you. If this was your last day to live—and it may always be—what would you be doing and why are you not doing it now?

You are here now. I hope you can discover the simple riches offered to you every moment of every day. Life is not to be thought away. Life is to be lived, experienced, and loved for the gift it is. Nothing is more precious than this mo-ment, so do not let it slip away unnoticed. As you savor its richness, you might just discover the real meaning of life.

17

Dolphins, Whales, and the Multidimensional Now

One night on the phone, long after our conversation had taken a turn for the muddled waters of multidimensionality, Ilizabeth Fortune shared a story.

Ilizabeth was once on a boat bringing a group of people to swim with dolphins. She was in a room doing a session with one of the participants when people called out that the dolphins were present. As she heard the call, Ilizabeth began to come out of her trance state. Everyone was preparing to go into the water, but the person in the room encouraged her to stay. That's when it happened, said Ilizabeth.

All of a sudden, I was in the water and I saw the dolphins coming. I knew I was in the boat, but I was also in the water. There were seven dolphins. They introduced themselves and next I was conscious of being inside one of the dolphins. I was looking out of its eyes.

I saw the people from the boat getting in the water. I watched how they interacted with myself as a dolphin and the other dolphins. I then heard the dolphin speaking to me. He said, "These are the things that we want you to be conscious of in your role." The dolphins began instructing me, as if downloading information. This was information I proceeded to use for the next eight years.

They then had to prove that everything was real. So, as this dolphin, I intentionally put the dolphin's rostrum on a human's face mask. Another proof was to leap over a person. That was an incredible feeling, to be in the dolphin and make that leap over a human! And yet another proof was to come up next to a human and lean the dolphin body over and rest on the human.

Next, I was back in the room with the person, coming out of the experience. I could hear everybody coming onto the boat, yelling and calling my name. I opened the door and they were all excited, asking me where I was. I told them about the face mask, the jumping and the leaning, identifying each person who had each experience. It blew them away.

Now, that's an example of bilocation. It's also being multidimensional in the moment. It was an example of multiple worlds being experienced at the same time.

Ilizabeth paused. "Have I told you that one before?"

"No."

"Well, it's kind of far out. It's not one I usually share."

Ilizabeth Fortune.

Multidimensionality, the paradigm of coexisting dimensions in a hologram of time, is a mind-expanding concept both fascinating and frustrating. At its best, it leads us to a state of perception outside normal consciousness in which the mysteries of time and space are experienced in a new, illuminating way.

What is frustrating about the concept is that in order to experience it, we must venture past the confines of ordinary reality. This can be tricky. Using intuition, we sense our way, feeling for that foggy place-time kind of being where ordinary reality blurs. What we are seeking is the secret button that turns the bookshelf round—a crack in space, a window in time—for it is most often with a sidestep that we gain access into this other way of being.

Joan Ocean, a psychologist and scientist, has spent nearly twenty years interacting with cetaceans. In her book, *Dolphins Into the Future*, she notes that dolphins have the ability to experience life in the ocean as well as life in other dimensional worlds simultaneously. Not only are dolphins "inspirational examples to us of the possibilities existing beyond our present belief systems," writes Joan, but their ability to access multidimensional worlds is one of the major teachings they present to humanity.[1]

"They're serving as examples of what we're capable of becoming," Joan told me. "Their brain is much more complex than ours is and they are using more of it than anything we know about, and yet I feel that they are showing us we can do that too. We can change the form of our bodies; we can shapeshift. We can move into other dimensions, for we are multidimensional people."

As to how dolphins plan to bring this teaching forward, there seems to be a multilayered plan. "I truly believe dolphins and whales are doing everything possible to make contact with us right now," said Joan. "In a lot of cases, people can't get to the water, so they're meeting them in meditation, in dreams, and in out-of-body experiences. The cetaceans are showing up in many different places, every place they can."

Often, it is an inner encounter that signals to human consciousness an opportunity for change is near. Both Joan and Ilizabeth related that their first contact involved meeting cetaceans on the inner world before physical contact. And both agree that some of the most penetrating communications involve our sleep, meditative, dream, and awakened dream states.

"Some of my most profound experiences, even with as many times as I've been with physical dolphins and whales, have been on the inner," said Ilizabeth. "Likewise, it sometimes takes a physical experience to open up the inner world of the whale and the dolphin and that connection with someone's heart and soul. It is a soul memory."

I thought of Sugar the dolphin's metaphor of our multidimensional selves as tentacles, all connected to the one giant octopus of our larger being. As Zak noted, just how aware each tentacled self is of other selves is dependent on one's perspective, both of oneself and the whole. The interplay of memories, like the awareness of one's other selves, is thus only as consciously available as each self is open to experiencing.

Say one aspect of your multidimensional self (it could be the one who is reading this right now) desires to be more aware of your other selves. How do you go about doing that? Recognizing patterns is essential: looking for the hidden associations that lead to intuitive hunches and leaps of simultaneity. Many believe this is precisely the holographic language of multidimensional connections that dolphins are here to teach.

"It's important to allow that multidimensional ability of communicating to be awakened and dance, and for us to have fun with it, because it really is fun!" Ilizabeth told me. "The dolphins want to show us how to really enjoy being human here on earth. As we allow the information to flow in, we allow ourselves to be spiritually human."

But how does this really work? When I asked Ilizabeth how she received messages from the whales and dolphins, she just laughed. "Can you talk to them anytime," I pressed on, "or just when you swim with them?"

"Both," she said, "and it's through my whole body. It's actually like the whales and dolphins are in my bones. There's a process that has evolved with my personal growth, and with the acceleration of the energies that are happening on earth as well."

Ilizabeth was thoughtful for a moment and then continued. "To answer your question, yes, they are speaking to me all the time, and yet the 'they' also shifts because it's not only whales and dolphins. Other beings and species may come in and add to the message, which shows, to me, how all species are related to each other. When I call on the whales or dolphins directly, there is instantaneous response from them. That is one level. Then, they might expand on that, which would mean bringing in other forms, such as messages from other species. They might also bring a certain physical happening or awareness into my life, such as bringing my attention to something as I go for a walk or get a phone call; it would all be related. This is hard to explain because it's not a linear level of communication; it's very multidimensional."

Joan Ocean spoke of a similar process:

In my first physical contact with a whale I learned that the whales have a very deep and profound love for the earth and all life-forms on the earth. The way the whale communicated was to send its own deep feeling—deep within an understanding—directly into my cells, so that I received the same feelings for the earth and ocean that the whale had. Because I received it that way, it wasn't something I could analyze or ask, "Well, do I agree with this or not?" With the whales, you just receive it in one piece and it's yours from then on.

Now, with the dolphins, I find that I can really talk to them. We have conversations back and forth, and they are very similar to us in many ways. They reflect our feelings and are very sensitive to humans. Although I feel they are communicating the same way that the whale did, which is holographically and cellularly, dolphins also go back and forth with it.

What this means is that if I put out a thought or am wondering about something, they will come back with information that seeps into me so that I find the answer to that question. Then I'll have another question that grows out of that, and more information will come to me. Then there is another question, and so on. Whereas with the whale, it was "here's all you need to know about everything," and—boom you got it.

My experience with whales has been more about being and living in another dimension, while dolphins seem much more interactive with us in this dimension, the third dimension. And that fits with what the dolphins have explained to me. They said that they came here in a physical form so we would feel comfortable with them, but are here to teach us about nonphysical realities. I feel the dolphins are definitely here to make themselves available and easy to communicate with, and to lead us into the realms where the whales are all the time.

When Joan first met the dolphins, she sensed that while they wanted to pass on their knowledge and understanding of the universe, "it was up to us to transcend the limitations of our human programming and open ourselves to these new possibilities."[2] How was that to be done? Joan found that she was simply to watch, listen, and

Joan Ocean and dolphins. Photo courtesy of Dolphin Connection.

be near the dolphins, for the answer was to be found not in doing, but being.

The dolphins worked with Joan in various ways, expanding her to the instantaneous nature of holographic, group mind communication. As dolphin communication involves a different mindset than human cognition—one that utilizes vibration, sonar, synchronized movements, acoustic images, feelings, sounds, and even electromagnetic grids of the planet as underwater pathways to send messages—Joan began to experience multiple worlds. The dolphins continually encouraged her to stretch open her mind to new possibilities.

One of the most intriguing aspects of this was a history lesson and mind stretching exercise extraordinaire. Most people believe that dolphins have been on earth for quite a long time. There are many ancient stories citing dolphins, and the dolphin image can be found in murals, paintings, and sculptures dating back thousands of years. When, on an intuitive hunch, Joan checked into the history of Hawaii, where she lives, she found no mention of dolphins in traditional chants and hula. How strange. When she asked a Kahuna, a Hawaiian healer, why this was so, he told her quite simply, "They were not here."

The mystery deepened when Joan went to the dolphins with her question. As she noted, "I was shown an amazing concept that opened my mind to reinterpreting my present reality. I began to understand that life on Earth is different than what we may think."[3]

What the dolphins related to Joan was that they arrived "through a window in time" that was not millions of years ago, but in this century. Furthermore, when they arrived on Earth, they brought with them a complete history of their presence on the planet. In her book, Joan explains:

> The Greek and Roman myths, the multi-cultural legends, stone carvings, cave art, artifacts, hieroglyphics, and so on, were all placed into the mind of humanity, into the many, varied locations on the planet and into our history books and archives. The reality of dolphins, from the past to the present, intellectually and physically, entered our mental and cellular awareness in a single instant. As far as humans are concerned the dolphins have always been here. But in Universal reality they are fairly recent residents of our globe! This instantaneous arrival on Earth was a galactic decision based on necessity.[4]

If there are many different realities, then perhaps both versions of the cetacean history are real. Could it be that the dolphins had evolved in one reality a long time ago and, in another reality, have just recently arrived through some window of time?

"Yes," Joan said. "There are many parallel realities happening at the same time. All of them really are created by our thought forms. If everyone believes the dolphins have been here on planet earth for millions of years and they live in that reality, then that's what is. When I am communicating with the dolphins, we are always in a reality that asks how do we help evolve the planet and ourselves, and how do we become teachers for humanity. In that reality, the dolphins say they actually came in though a window of time to be here to assist us."

Ilizabeth also heard the phrase *a window in time* from the dolphins, who expressed that this could be seen as a portal between dimensions and times as well as a means of accessing expanded knowledge. Not only have dolphins come through a window in time, said Ilizabeth, but "some aspects of some of us have also come through a window of time."

When I asked Joan what she thought of that, she laughed. "Yes! The earth is vibrating into a higher and higher frequency. My own experience has revealed other aspects of my soul and they are more in contact with me as I am evolving into a higher frequency. We are pulling ourselves into our own future so to speak. The idea is that our higher self and other aspects of ourselves that know what we need are bringing us there, or are coming here to interact with us to show us the way."

"It's a wild concept, isn't it?" I asked Joan. "The whole idea of dolphins planting memories in our past; there's something wild about that."

"Well, yes," she laughed. "Even when I tell it to people, they say, 'But what about the wall paintings in Greece, or what about the this or that?' And no matter how many times I say all that came in with them, it's such a different concept that people can't quite grasp it."

"Maybe that's why it can be helpful," I said, surprising myself. The dolphin people had a way of shaking my thoughts free. "It makes you think about time and reality in a different way, and if you follow that spiral of a thought, it takes you to a place where there is an expansion of how and what you're seeing, and then . . . I guess pretty soon you're getting it."

"Exactly!" cried Joan. "There are so many things going on around us that we are unaware of because of the way we are. There's so *much* power in the power of thought and the power of love, the power of the spiritual beings that are all united to help and assist us. There are things we don't even know about. If we knew, I don't think anyone would still wander around in their everyday life and do the things they do now. I think we'd all be filled with joy and adventure and be having amazing, wonderful experiences every day. This means being in touch with many different dimensions and different dimensional beings any time, all the time."

As we awaken to the ever expanding reality of who we are, we might also experience the sense of wonder that is awakening itself, the sudden realization that each moment is a multidimensional window.

The dolphins are leaping. The whales are calling. The time is always now.

Waking Up
Penelope Smith and Elephants

When I tune into elephants, I get a lot of sadness. Their species are dying, but they can't die. Elephants dying would mean a huge break in the chain. They're not meant to disappear. If they do, humans will suffer greatly. Some species have willingly let go in smaller areas of the planet. But elephants can't go, for something very big will die in people.

The elephants are drumming. They are drumming to each other and they are drumming all over and around the earth. I feel it as a low tone of "Wake up, wake up. Wake up before it's too late. Wake up, wake up!" The elephants are drumming for humans to wake up.

It's what our ancestors did. It's waking up! When you drum, you tune into the earth. There's no way you can't tune into the earth and drum. Some people like to space out when they drum, but they are also rooting themselves to the earth. More people have taken up drumming. The dolphins have said that we need the sound of a thousand drummers drumming the heartbeat of the earth, all over the earth, connecting us. So, you'll see more and more people drumming. There will be drumming everywhere. It is already happening.

The elephants are drumming. And the drumming that the humans are doing is uniting with the drumming of the elephants. It's a healing tone. It gives me great hope when I tune in. Even when I feel the sadness of the elephants, I sense that sadness is necessary now. It communicates to people what is happening.

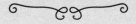

18

The Cetacean Nation:
Love the Greater Love

The night before I was to call Joan Ocean in Hawaii to talk about cetaceans, I dreamed of dolphins.

In the dream, I traveled to meet Joan at her home. When the time came to talk with her, she met me on the terrace, saying she had another commitment and had to leave. As I walked away, I saw several dolphins playing in a pool. They invited me to jump into the water and join them. When I told them that the water looked too cold, the dolphins laughed. They then dove down into the water and made a ball out of part of themselves. It was soft and round and gray. They tossed the ball to me. It had a wet, squishy quality to it, slick and spongy, unlike anything I had ever seen or felt before. The thought occurred to me that this was a dolphin brain that had been wrapped in dolphin suchness. The dolphins then began clicking loudly in laughter, encouraging me to toss back the ball. The dolphins really wanted to play.

When I told Joan about the dream, she laughed. "Well, they do that sometimes! People often wonder what they are doing in that big ocean. Actually, they have all kinds of toys out there, all kinds of fields of energy they play with and even real toys, like leaves and bubbles. I feel they often play with things we can see just for our benefit. They say, 'Oh, these poor people can't even see all the other fields of energy out here that we're playing with so we better make a few things and play with the things that they can see too.'

"I feel that dolphins can manifest whatever they want to, and they often slip into a higher frequency of energy to interact with their creations. Many times, both alone or with friends, I have been swimming with them and they disappear. Where did they go? It's a mystery! There are so many mysteries I've experienced in the ocean that I don't write about or mention, because until I've seen it happen repeatedly even I have trouble accepting it. Dolphins are doing lots with fields of energy and they do create their own games and ways of playing. Often, they combine this with inspiring information."

Ilizabeth Fortune and dolphin.

The dream had certainly inspired me. I felt gifted by the inner dolphins, and there was a contagious joy about them, in their laughter, their desire to play and be with one another, that followed me for hours after the dream.

Many believe this is precisely the endowment dolphins bring to humanity, as they reveal through their presence an energetic pattern whereby we may learn to elevate our vibrations and move into states of joy and ecstasy. Dolphins and whales are thus said to co-hold the frequency of ecstasy on earth.

On simple levels, dolphins engage us with their playful nature. Or, as Joan puts it, they help us to understand that we have an inherited right to live in joy and happiness every day. By being in close proximity to dolphins, many have noticed a tuning effect whereby the physical body shifts in vibration. This is likened to a good meditation wherein stress dissolves and old emotional baggage releases as the body attunes to higher frequencies of health and well being.

Like Joan, Penelope Smith believes that cetaceans are key players in our evolution. "They are messengers of our awakening," Ilizabeth Fortune agrees, "for us to realize who we are and why we've come so that we can remember what we are here to do."

Among many of those who spend time with dolphins and whales, there is a feeling that the cetaceans are a nation unto themselves—"a whole civilization apart from the ones on earth," remarks Joan—operating from a very different mind-set and reality than humans are used to. "If you want to see aliens," say many of the dolphin-people, "go to the ocean and be with the dolphins and whales. It's not a matter of aliens coming to earth; they are already here."

In specific terms, there are stories linking the cetaceans to certain star systems, as well as the idea that some cetaceans have arrived from other dimensions or planets through a portal of time. Robert Temple, an English astronomer, researched how the Dogon, an African tribe who live in Mali (the former French Sudan) had knowledge of advanced astronomical data regarding the stars Sirius and Sirius B. (The latter star is so difficult to see that photos were not obtained until 1970.) Western scientists were stunned to find that the information the Dogon possessed was incredibly accurate.[1]

When asked how the tribe could possibly know this information, the Dogon presented a story: A huge spacecraft once came out of the sky and landed on earth. The beings, still in the ship, created a large hole in the ground, filled it with water, and then jumped out of the ship into the water. They swam to the edge of the water and began to communicate with the Dogon, giving them detailed information of where they came from, namely the Sirius star system. What did these beings look like? Dolphins.

It is an interesting story, one that links dolphins not only to other planets, but to humans via animal communication. There are many other details and stories about the Sirius-cetacean connection as well as a number of commonly cited links between Sirius and Earth. Some have even asserted that there is both a genetic and spiritual link between the beings on Sirius (and, by connection, whales) and the human race.

Now, what do we make of this? As we move into the multidimensional paradigm, pieces of the puzzle, such as the Dogon story, begin to form a new type of multifaceted picture, one that is larger than anything any one of our old pictures could hold. While it is the nature of the hologram that, in essence, each piece "holds" the whole, it is often difficult to glimpse the wholeness of the hologram itself. Outside of multidimensionality, we only see pieces. However, by remembering bits of forgotten information, discovering common themes, and recognizing symbolic patterns, we begin to reconstruct and move toward a much larger, multidimensional understanding of the hologram itself.

Still, what is it about the cetaceans that makes them so connected to awakening humanity and the evolution of the planet? Some say that whales carry ancestral earth memories, that they are the "recordkeepers" of life on earth, holding the memories safe so they can eventually be remembered.

"That's why, throughout the world, whales and dolphins are coming closer to humans again," said Ilizabeth. "Now the human role is to awaken the heart and take action with consciousness in partnership and cocreativeness. We need to have it be a part of our lives, to realize that we are not an isolated factor of earth. We must be in partnership with her, land and sea."

As leading emissaries to our higher vibrational frequencies, there is deep meaning in the fact that cetaceans make the ocean their home. "The connection between dolphins, whales, humans, and the water has to do with memory," Ilizabeth told me. "It has to do with who we are."

Indeed, in nearly every legend, myth, or story of creation, there is water. Always water as a birthing force, a fluid reminder of our connection with the essential ocean of self. The unconscious, too, is often represented in dream language by water, especially large expanses of water. The fluidity of both water and the unconscious is linked to memory, reminding us at even deeper levels of our inherent connections with all life. Consider the following flow, as noted by Joan Ocean:

> The whales have connections to the Akashic records of this earth. I think we all have that connection, but they have easy access. There's a connection to that in water molecules and the fact that water on earth is recycled. Every bit of water that goes through the land or through peoples' bodies or goes up in mist or fog and comes back down again to water the plants—all of that, sooner or later, goes back into the ocean. All of the information of the beings and land and life that it has passed through are contained within the water molecule. The whales know how to run that water through their systems and have that information available to them.

Whether it be from literature, television, art, mythology, stories, events in everyday life or through dreams, meditations, and other inner adventures, the cetaceans leap deftly between the worlds, modeling to us the means of achieving higher states of awareness. And yet, their fluid dance of connectedness is one in which change can occur rapidly and in unforeseen directions.

"Much of what is happening on Earth is to wake us up," said Ilizabeth, "to shock us open into receptiveness and acceptance of the responsibilities of being human. Our denial is dying, and reality is setting in. To accept ourselves as we truly are is to accept ourselves in our magnificence, in our capabilities and our responsibilities."

There are many who believe that the cetaceans and other life forms who currently hold memories for humans can no longer do it alone. The challenge is to awaken humanity into accepting the deeper role of who we really are. That is why the call from the Cetacean Nation is one of transformation.

As one of the coordinators of a marine mammal stranding alert network, naturalist Mary Getten has had the opportunity to speak with many cetaceans, both wild and captive, but especially Orcas* near her home in Friday Harbor, Washington.

"Some whales tell me they have a mission to open consciousness in people," Mary told me. "These whales seem very clear that they have a job to do: to interact with people, help people understand their environment, and give people more of a feeling about who they are.

"What I find fascinating is that we basically didn't have any idea of who whales were or what they were about until we captured them and put them in tanks. Until we imprisoned them, we looked on them like an oil well. They were dog food or fertilizer and that was it. It wasn't until in the mid-1960s that the first Orcas were brought into captivity. People's consciousness about who these beings are has changed 180 degrees in that time. That's really very fast."

"Do you think it was the whales who helped to bring about that change?" I asked.

"Some of the whales said they chose to spend a lifetime in captivity to be of service. They felt that was a contribution they could make toward changing the consciousness of humans. And some of the whales said they didn't have a clue what happened when they got caught. So, there are both sides. It's not that every captive whale is a saint or a martyr. Some whales say that is true and others don't know what you're talking about."

"Like humans," I supposed. "We all have varying degrees of consciousness."

"Exactly," said Mary, echoing what many have pointed out all along. "Animals are as individual as people; they have a wide range of consciousness and purpose and ideas about life."

"Addressing the whales who do have a conscious purpose to interact with humans, who are they?" I asked.

"They are vast beings who live totally in the moment. Every time I ask them about the past and future or about earthquakes and earth changes, the answer is basically, 'We don't spend time pondering possibilities or worrying about things. We are

*Though whales and dolphins carry different energies, they are linked in many ways. Even the human categorization of cetaceans (which also include porpoises) reflects this ambiguity. For example, the designation of *whale* has been given to cetaceans more than twelve feet long, though some of these animals—such as Orcas—actually belong to the dolphin family.

here in the moment and we do what has to happen now, and if that has to happen then we'll deal with it when it happens.'

"That's one big difference from humans. The whales are very centered and in the moment. In a lot of ways, they lead simple lives. Now, I'm mainly speaking about Orcas, who are very much in the now and concerned with what's happening today."

"What do some of the whales you speak with think of us humans?" I asked.

"They are conscious of people and the changing attitudes in people. The capture eras here were frightening for them. When asked why they didn't organize and fight against people during captures, they related that was a concept so far out of their thinking that it just didn't occur to them. They are very peaceful in that way. Their interactions with other animals emphasize their sense that they are all part of the same world. 'We live together and, yes, sometimes we eat others, but it's not because we don't like them. They are just part of the environment.'

"The whales are, for the most part, very nonviolent. Orcas are socially oriented. Food is probably their number-one concern and, beyond that, the family. For the whales, that's what's happening in the moment: you have to eat and you have your family and friends. There's no worrying about a job or degree. They don't have things, so they aren't dragging around a bag of cool shells or anything."

"What about the notion of whales holding the memories of the earth?" I asked.

"I haven't come across that," said Mary, "but we could ask Granny."

Granny is an Orca who has formed a relationship with Mary and Raphaela Pope. Mary invited me to speak to Granny through her.

Can you tell us about your life and why you chose to speak with humans?

I have been a whale for many lifetimes, hundreds of lifetimes. In this time, I have seen many changes in humans. There is a great need right now on this planet for humans to understand their place in this world, and I am very pleased to be able to help them understand their place within the scheme of things. It is my experience that people are disconnected from nature, and this disconnection is causing them great distress. They do not understand their impact upon the rest of the world, the natural world, the world that most of us live in. It is my desire to help them understand their place and regain their connection with All There Is.

What do you feel is the best thing humans could do right now regarding that?

Do not think of yourselves as separate. We are all interconnected, and everything that you do affects everything else on the planet. You are not an island unto yourself. This disconnection from the whole will lead to your destruction. Things have deteriorated in certain ways, and things have gotten better in others. But time is not to be wasted at this point.

You are asking us to feel our essential connection with all of life, is that it? What we really need is a change of consciousness?

Correct. A reunderstanding of your place in the world.

Is it true that whales hold memories of the earth?

Granny. Photo by Ashley Anderson.

Our memories go back quite a long time. The faculty that you speak of is more common to the baleen whales, the big, slow-moving, migrating whales. My experience is that their consciousness is more expanded in that direction. A lot of our consciousness is used with our fine abilities to echolocate and map our world. It is the bigger whales who are the timekeepers.

Can you speak more about being in the ever present now?

Time is nonexistent. Time itself is an illusion. We merely exist. I've spoken to Mary and Raphaela about this when people have wanted to know how they could have more time in their lives. This is a funny concept because everyone has the same amount of time. Time is endless. You cannot have more time in your life. You can only use it in different ways. Time exists for everyone the same. But it also does not really exist. There is only this moment, and what you do in this moment is all important.

What about the concept of multidimensionality? Are you in contact with other aspects of yourself?

Yes, I am very familiar with this concept and that is my reality. I am able to experience myself in different realities at the same time. I am focused in this particular reality right now and choose to spend most of my energy in this area. But, yes, I do understand, and this is something that we are capable of at this moment.

Could you tell us about one of those other realities?

[Pause]. I've had many lives as a whale, so most of my realities have been as a whale. In that way, they are quite similar.

At this point, Mary interjected, "What she's showing me now is a picture of a gray whale doing what gray whales do, which is migrating and feeding on the bottom. She's showing me that is another life that she is participating in."

Is there anything else you would like to add, Granny? Is there a central message you would like humans to know?

Love yourself. Get in touch with the deep essence of who you are as a being. That will open you to who everyone else on the planet is.

As we thanked Granny, Mary's voice changed in tone and lightness, and I realized how deeply Granny's presence had seeped into our conversation. "When I'm communicating with Granny or other whales, I feel very far away," Mary agreed. "I feel—way down there, far far away. When I'm talking to a whale, it's a downshift into a totally different energy level."

This is not uncommon among those who converse with whales. After Penelope Smith told me that whales were, in her opinion, the greatest manifestation of God on earth, I asked if she would ask the whales what they most wanted humans to know. I also asked if she would convey the whales' voice, how they sounded to her and the feelings associated with their message.

"Oh," she said in an ever deepening tone. "They give it to me in this booming sound that's very low. They say, 'Love . . . the Greater . . . Love.' They keep saying, 'Love . . . the Greater . . . Love.' It's like Boom . . . Boom . . . Boom . . . And it goes deep into the earth and it resonates all through our bodies. I feel my heart filling up. It is going boooom . . . booom . . . so very deep. And it translates as 'Love the Greater Love.'

"I get real clearly that it's not an individual thing. It's loving the Greater Love, loving it and being it. They say, 'From the dolphins you learn what love is, and from us you learn to love the Greater Love.'

"The image I get beside this booming tone is of a giant lotus. It comes under the earth and completely supports the earth. It goes through the earth. And now my heart has turned into this huge lotus, which is the Greater Love.

"And there's nothing more that I can say," said Penelope with a laugh that burbled up, layer upon layer, from somewhere deep within the oceanic depths. "Love the Greater Love. That says it all."

Part Five

Into the Shadow

Animals in Captivity

Pets

Pests

In Quest of Learning: Animal Research and
Human Education

Animals Eating Animals: The Predator/Prey Relationship

Releasing Judgment
Snake Spirit ~ Dawn Brunke

Snakes come into this world for a variety of reasons. On the one hand, we are not meant to be caged or treated as pets. However, some of us come consciously to work with humans and, at this time, many are willing to live in the glass houses in order to work on relationship issues.

We have agreed as a species to take on some "misunderstandings" from humans. We cry out when we are killed for no reason other than just being who we are. We are often a reflection of hate in your culture: hate for the unknown and that which is beyond you in understanding. We embody—as well as represent—beginnings and endings, the continuous cycle. We work deeply in the human subconscious to help you connect with ancient and timeless memories.

One of our tasks is to help you release judgment and open to the energy of Snake within. Snake energy is for awakening, connecting that which is most ancient with that which is most spiritual. Snakes exist in all aspects of your life—snake as caduceus; snake as symbol of royalty; snake representing sin, sexuality, the umbilical connection, and the cycle of beginnings and endings.

Those who fear snakes often fear their own true nature. We work on a different level from animals such as dolphins, who have chosen an engaging form that most humans find appealing. Right now, we most often work with specific individuals to help open particular passageways in humanity at large. That is the nature of snakes at this time—not to work with the many, but to initiate the few. There are reasons why we are associated with fear to some degree, for not everyone is ready for our kind of initiation.

We send you blessings and hope you too will open more to our kind. There is much more to snakes than meets the eye.

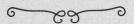

19

Animals in Captivity

It is wonderful to speak to animals who are happy with their lives. Most often, there is an ease and freedom to their words matched by their sense of freedom in the world. Likewise, it is hopeful for humanity to regard the leaping dolphins and singing whales as portents of where we are headed, these wise and playful emissaries of our evolving spirituality.

But what of animals kept behind bars? If cetaceans swimming in the oceans represent our potential, what do wild tigers pacing in small, cramped quarters of zoos reflect to us? What do snakes and other creatures of the earth, surreptitiously snatched from jungles and rainforests, put in cages and never allowed to touch the earth, represent of where we are in our spiritual development? What of dolphins confined to waterparks? Or whales trapped in tanks so shallow their muscular abilities deteriorate so that they can never return to the deep sea again?

It is here, among the captive, that we descend into the depth, darkness, and inner richness of the shadow.

Captivity is one of those interesting words in which meaning is dependent upon perspective. To be in captivity is to be held prisoner. One can be held just as captive by strong emotions as by any bars in a jail. If you are captive, as in a captive audience, you are obliged to be present. And not far from captivity is *captivate,* to hold in fascination with special charm or beauty.

Just as there are many sides to captivity, there is a multifaceted wall of shadow content surrounding the issue of animals in captivity. What do we feel when we face animals in zoos or circuses and other performing acts? Is there an irony in the captive captivating us? What reflection can we see in the pattern of collecting and holding animals in cages so that humans can watch them? What do we do to ourselves when we capture an animal and force that being to live inside a cage?

The issue of captivity is a source of powerful emotions for both humans and animals, and it is easy to become captive to the subject of captivity itself, endlessly caught in a morass of questions regarding morality, human rights, animal rights, karma, and more.

Any deep journey into the shadow world requires leaving behind superficial notions of right and wrong. To carry morality down into the mines of the shadow is to sabotage the expedition, for one merely ends up with justifications—seeing exactly the type of boogeymonsters one expects to meet down in the dark. To meet the shadow we must dig deeper into a vision of who we really are. If we truly want to understand the shadow meaning of animals in captivity, we must first ask ourselves: what does this reflect to us?

When I asked Morgine Jurdan about animals in captivity, she contacted Belle, an elephant who resided for many years at a zoo in Oregon. Belle had raised her young in captivity. Morgine told Belle about this book, relating that many humans would be interested in knowing about the role of animals in captivity. Although Belle was now in spirit form, she had much to say about her life in the zoo.

I loved being in the zoo. I had many friends there and it was difficult to leave. I am not angry with people. I often find them amusing. I know people come to look at me; however, I would often look back and examine them. It was fun.

I know many people assume I would be happier in my native environment. However, I chose to come into this experience to be near people. I wanted to teach them lessons they might not learn in other ways. People love the elephants at the zoo. Some people come just to see us. Once they do, and once they make that connection, they often feel different about other animals in captivity. We are huge and big and yet so kind and gentle. It amazes people how gently and delicately we can respond to one another. It is something you could learn from us.

I know many animals come to zoos because they want to connect with humans. There are others reasons too. Did you know that some people take time to be animals, to learn about life from a different perspective? Some people lived lives in which they were cruel to us and they feel they can learn more by experiencing life as we do.

Some animals are surprised to end up here, and they have problems. What is most difficult is the idea of a cage and bars and glass and things that prevent us from getting close to one another. I liked it most when I could touch people and interact with them. And I love babies! They are so fun to watch and talk to. Babies understand us all very well and can usually tell us many things. I love them most of all.

I think having animals interact with people is beneficial. It helps them to get to know us better, to see and realize our oneness. I am sad when humans do this in a way that portrays us as prisoners behind bars. This affects our spiritual and emotional nature. We are affected on all levels. Intention is so important. We are

often treated as a display, not an individual with a unique personality and qualities. We, like humans, are each different in many ways. All lions and giraffes and
gorillas and anteaters are not alike.

I enjoy most the zoos where many of us can mingle with one another and
develop relationships. Many species enjoy being with one another, like in some bird
exhibits. We live in the moment and enjoy things that are new and fresh and alive
and different.

Things in zoos seldom change. Routines develop boredom much as you find in
your own lives, except we lack the choices often available to you. Living in a zoo
can be very challenging to some of us and enjoyable to others, depending on how
you perceive our reason for being there and your interactions with us.

I think humans desire to have a connection with animals and yet do not know
how to make it. You feel afraid of what you do not understand. Some people think
they can learn something about us by studying our behavior in zoos. You can no
more learn about us looking through bars than you can about the human race by
examining prisoners in prison! Being wild and free to be who we are is where our
true natures lie.

Visiting a zoo, you learn about yourself. What are you searching for when you
visit a zoo? What have you lost and what are you hoping to find? What do you feel
as you view the animals? Why? Ask yourself questions and see what comes up. You
may be surprised when you take the time to be present and think. Then, many of
the answers you are seeking will appear, and you will begin to walk on a new road.

I send love to all people reading this wonderful book. I adore you all and look
forward to a time when we can all share, consciously, our love of one another.

Though Belle chose her experience of living in a zoo, not all animals feel the same.
And even if an animal reports a conscious choice of captivity, this does not imply that
such a life is easy. As communicator Sharon Callahan relates, although many wild
animals choose to serve in this way, "it must never negate the tremendous sacrifice and
suffering they endure to bring these lessons to us. For example, elephants who, in the
wild, would walk thirty to fifty miles a day, in captivity suffer terribly from infected
feet, sore muscles, and arthritis."

Lessons to humans are not the only lessons that emerge from captivity, for many
animals taken from the wild are not solitary creatures, but part of an existing social
structure. Many have young. What are the lessons learned by the animals left behind?

When Jeri Ryan asked the giraffe species to speak as part of this book, a young
female giraffe living in the wilds of Africa answered the call. Jeri told her the purpose

of the talk was to help humans become more aware of other animals and the "significant place of all animals on Mother Earth." The giraffe replied:

And she is indeed our mother. My mother always said that to me; that I have more than one mother. She was my mother and Earth is my mother. I didn't know that humans felt the same way.

My wish for humans is to know of the quiet and peace of my home. I have heard that it has shrunk. I feel that smallness. I am very young in this body, so I don't know what was before. Yet I feel a difference.

How is this so?

I feel confined, like I'm running in circles; I feel closed in. It's pretty silly. I don't have to run in circles. I can expand myself. My mother told me she had faith in me, that I would understand it all when I discovered that what I think is a prison isn't that at all.

You have felt your shrunken home to be a prison?

Yes. That is a struggle for us all. Some never believe that and some never leave that. My mother said it is always a matter of time, that we all have a chance to leave the prison of a closed and fearful heart. I have encouragement from that. She was so wise and gentle.

Is she with you?

No. She got a great sickness and died. I could not even be with her when she died. She was in a box with bars in a far away place. She told me of it from a distance.

I am sorry. How did that happen?

Something was wrapped around her neck and feet, and she was carried away with others. She told me from there of keeping my heart out of prison. That's what she had to learn.

It sounds like she learned it well.

She did.

It sounds like you have learned it well.

I have. And I still learn. I keep remembering her soft, loving, kind wisdom. I must live up to that.

Lessons come to us in many ways, sometimes quite unexpectedly. I was impressed by the words of the young giraffe, just as I had been impressed by a group of giraffes at the Giraffe Centre in Nairobi. While on holiday in Africa, I had the opportunity to touch and feed a gathering of these gentle, magnificent animals who had been orphaned and brought to the sanctuary from all over Kenya. So, too, had people come to visit, busloads of wide-eyed schoolchildren and slightly jaded tourists who quickly became like children themselves. It was there, hand cupped with food pellets, arm outstretched to reach the giraffe, that I was reminded of a secret. Through the intimate act of touch one cannot help but be touched.

As the young giraffe told Jeri, we all have a chance to leave the prison of a closed and fearful heart. It is not always a matter of escaping cages, for there are many forms of captivity. Perhaps it is not just to help animals that sanctuaries such as the Giraffe Centre are built; perhaps the existence of such places is also an attempt to help ourselves.

What, then, of zoos? Just as Belle and others have noted, the interaction of animals and people can be beneficial in helping us to become aware not only of ourselves but of animals as individuals. A problem occurs, however, when humans get stuck in a projection that automatically portrays all animals in captivity as prisoners.

Intention, that slippery turnstile of perspective, is a major factor in understanding what the situation of zoos (or any aspect of captivity) truly holds. "I know some animals have agreed to come into captivity, for us to learn," Carol Gurney told me. "But instead of coming up to them with pity—'Oh, look at that poor guy in that cage'— they would rather have us say, 'Thank you so much. We may not agree that this exists, but we thank you for coming to teach us.'"

While some animals may choose captivity as a spiritual goal or mission, what of the animals who don't choose captivity yet are held captive nonetheless? Mary Getten found that among whales held captive for long periods of time, the story often changes once again:

> I've heard whales say, "Get me out of here!" One whale said she wanted to be released, not so much because her life was hell but because it would further her mission. Being released would cause a lot of publicity and more people would hear about whales and get involved. Another whale said, "Don't even talk to me about being released. This is my life. This is where I live. I don't want to talk about it."
>
> The whole issue of captivity and release is very controversial. There are some good points on all sides. For example, whales in captivity are often kept on antibiotics. There is a scientific fear that a released whale no longer on antibiotics could spread a disease to the local population. There's also a possibility that after they've been in a small tank for a long period of time they don't have the physical conditions to make it. They can't dive deep, they don't have the lung capacity,

and the muscle structure has deteriorated. So, are we actually doing them a favor by letting them out? Personally, I think we should ask whales if they want to be released before they are.

While humans may be tempted to divide animals into captive and noncaptive groups, the realm of the shadow reveals many shades of gray. What we see (or think we see) may not, in fact, be what is at all.

With regard to dolphins, for example, there are those who swim and interact with humans and those who stay in the wild, having nothing to do with people. Ilizabeth Fortune, who has brought many groups in contact with both wild and captive dolphins, breaks it down further, noting that among dolphins in captivity, some intentionally die while others choose to stay, though "it's often like a part of their soul goes into forgetfulness." Of this group, some remain in the dull state while others awaken.

"Then there are dolphins who have chosen to be captive, though they wouldn't term it *captive*," said Ilizabeth. "Rather, they are bridgers of communication from water to land. They are the keyholders, ready to open up windows in humankind, to open up their hearts to allow the memories to be unfolded. In that category, there are those who remember what they came to do and those who have forgotten.

"What is interesting is that there's always the factor of relationship: the human, the dolphin, and the environment. Those are all playing a factor on the soul agreements. So, there are individual stories. Each dolphin carries a unique message, just as each human does. The uniqueness of that message is also part of the bigger message of that species, for each species has their own message."

In a larger space that includes both freedom and enclosure, we begin to understand the shadow of captivity. It is only by embracing both that we see the deeper meaning.

What does the shadow of animal captivity mean for humans? What does it mean to see a wild dolphin—or any wild animal—penned in an enclosure? As the ones who have conspired to set up these scenarios of captivity, what are we telling ourselves?

Ilizabeth believes it is precisely at this point of self-reflection that we begin to understand.

The role that's being played by dolphins in enclosures is very important, for it is to awaken people to freedom. It is for people to recognize how enclosed they themselves actually are.

If we were to allow all species in natural habitats to coexist, there would be a realm of the natural flow that would bring health back to the earth. One of the purposes of enclosures is to awaken the outrage of holding in life. People find it far easier to be in outrage for a species, and bring them out of captivity, than to be in outrage of the captiveness in their own soul.

Now, simply saying, "They are in an enclosure and need to be freed," is not looking at the whole picture. Many people who have been with whales or dolphins in natural habitats and then experience enclosed cetaceans have a far deeper experience. They actually gained a bigger and deeper perspective on the whole.

Human perception can be rather narrow and limited. Once there is an explanation, a framework, or a name put on something, there is limitation. One might look at a dolphin in an enclosure and say, "Here is a dolphin in water that has cement around it, so therefore the dolphin is not free." And that is the human perspective.

The consciousness of the dolphins and the whales, as they have told me, is that they have ways of traveling, perceiving, and communicating that are far beyond our perceptions and awareness at this point. They have ways to link with other realms and be free within their own space, even physical space. This is something that humans can learn.

In fact, some humans have observed how enclosed dolphins are able to maintain play, creativity, and exuberance of movement, and it amazes and touches their lives. It actually creates creativity in that human.

We need to remember that it's not just the limited perspective of "in an enclosure" and "not in an enclosure." There's a tremendous amount of information that's being shared in both perspectives. And now is the time to bring them both together.

Always the mirror is before us. As we make others captive in the outer world, we reveal aspects of our own inner captivity. As we free others, we begin to free ourselves. And where do we go from here?

The call from shadow is not for reaction, but for conscious action. The call from shadow is one that urges us to awaken.

Working Together
Binah (dog) ~ Dawn Brunke

Animals serve humans in many ways that are barely recognized by the majority of humanity. Many of us are like gods and goddesses among you, waiting for the opportunity to help you awaken. For many souls, the life of an animal is much easier in which to travel in the mundane world.

We are alert to your emotions and desires. Sometimes all we can do is be with you, as a buffer against your darker thoughts. At other times, we are guides, pushing you with our antics and annoyances for you to see more of yourself and the myriad of life around you.

The world is much, much larger than you imagine. Open and listen—that is all that is needed for you to grow and awaken. We are here for you, just as you are here for us. Let us work together to create a world in which we can all flourish and love one another.

Binah.

20

Pets

For several years, a trio of goldfish has swum around in an aquarium in our living room. It would be nice to say we welcomed these goldfish into our family as the wonderful sentient beings they are, but that's not how it started.

One long, dark Alaskan winter, I decided we needed an aquarium. Wouldn't it be great to see a brightly lit tank, alive with the flash of colorful fish and playful bubbles in some corner of the house? I had been reading about Feng shui, the ancient Chinese art of placement. Fish and moving water were supposed to be good elements for one's living space.

I acquired an aquarium and assortment of fish paraphernalia—pump, gravel, nets, some rocks, crystals, and marbles—and went to a pet store to purchase some fish. I bought what the owner recommended, four cichlids. They lasted a mere three days. When I complained, the woman told me to bring in a water sample. "Ah! That's your problem," she said when she tested the water. She instructed me to buy some less expensive fish to use temporarily while correcting the water pH levels. I could then return these fish for credit when I was ready to buy my "real" fish.

This went on and on, the aquarium water never achieving proper balance, and more fish dying in the process. I was frustrated, when finally one snowy Saturday, while telling the store owner's sister my woes, she led me to the goldfish feeder tank. This was a very large tank full of medium-sized goldfish sold as food for larger pets. Deftly netting up three goldfish, the woman plopped them into a plastic bag full of water, explaining they were very hardy and would get our water levels correct in a hurry. She waved me off without payment, telling me I could just "flush" the fish whenever I was finished with them.

Home I came with the three goldfish. They were quite lovely in the tank, much more colorful than the cichlids, their filmy orange tails swaying and dancing in the water. It became my habit to feed them each evening, and long before I had even heard of animal communication, I would talk to them aloud, telling them how beautiful they were and how I loved to watch their graceful swimming. In turn, the fish developed the habit of rising to the surface in a flurry of excitement as soon as they saw me reaching for their food.

I came to be very fond of the goldfish and soon gave up water testing altogether. It seemed silly to have such an elaborate tank for goldfish, but deep down I knew these were the "real" fish I was supposed to have.

It was only later, after talks with animals, that I began to feel a bit guilty. If other animals had thoughts and souls, didn't fish too? All of my dogs had told me they were with me for a reason. But what of the fish? They seemed to have arrived through a series of blunders and chance. I had wanted the fish for decoration, but I never stopped to think about the fish themselves. It was not like they were dogs, after all; they were just—goldfish.

Perhaps it was a guilty conscience that boomeranged me into a state of hypersensitivity, for I began to wonder if it was right to keep any animal at all. Was my aquarium merely an elegant prison? Had I become an unwitting warden to goldfish?

Through many conversations about animal captivity, I confronted the presence of shadow material. Some people clearly thought zoos were horrible places. The sentiment was that whether or not adequate space, food, and living conditions were provided, zoos were prisons. "I don't go to zoos," was the self-righteous attitude of several of these humans.

And yet how many of these individuals had an aquarium filled with fish or a glass tank holding lizards or turtles? Did they buy an ornate cage to hold a bird, construct a wire-mesh pen as a home for rabbits, or watch mice and guinea pigs spinning endlessly in an exercise wheel? What kind of a zoo might there be at home? Was it right for a bird never to be free to fly in the air, a snake never to slither along the earth on its belly?

While it is easy to see a tiger in a small cage as a victim of imprisonment, it is much harder to see one's fish or pet rabbit that way. And yet, we might well consider: just what type of shadow material is playing itself out where our beloved pets are concerned?

Etymologically, it is unclear from exactly where the word *pet* derives, though it has connections to words meaning both "a spoiled child" and the "plaything of a spoiled child," indulgence being a key element of both. A pet is defined as a favorite, cherished object of affection; an animal kept for amusement or companionship. Ownership nestles right up beside a pet, because most pets are bought and sold. The pet owner is the decision maker who determines what the pet eats, where it sleeps, and what it does most of the day. Owners make other very personal decisions for their animal: neutering, debarking, declawing, even tail bobbing and ear clipping. Most often, these decisions are made according to what the human wants, not the animal.

As I heard myself tell others that I would never do something as cruel as debarking or declawing an animal, I felt my own self-righteousness bubble up inside. Was what I did with the three goldfish (as well as all the fish who had died in sacrifice to my precious water pH levels) any less unthinking than other humans who fail to realize that animals are living, thinking, feeling, sentient beings too?

As the captivity issue played in my mind, I recalled Ilizabeth Fortune's idea that it is easier to be in outrage over the captivity of another species than over our own inner captivity.

A clear understanding of captivity cannot be found merely by denying the forms of captivity that humans are both a part of and have brought about. Rather, we must see these things—zoos, circuses, performing animals, pets, even research animals—for what they truly are. And if we are to see things as they truly are, we must be willing to enlarge our perspective. We must be willing to let go of the hotly guarded judgments and cleverly presented rationalizations that are often mere defenses against seeing the larger picture.

I began my own exploration of captivity at home with the sage advice Mojave Dan had given J. Allen Boone: If you want the facts, ask the animal.

As I centered and made contact with the goldfish trio, their beauty immediately touched me. Just as graceful and lovely as their physical form, the words and thoughts from the goldfish bubbled up in my mind as if filled with light and air. The more we spoke, the more I sensed them as very gentle, kind, and intrinsically beautiful creatures.

My main concern, of course, was their living conditions, and so I questioned them about their tank. Did they feel captive? Perhaps they would prefer being in a pond with other goldfish?

Surprisingly, the initial feeling I got back from this question was one of shock. The goldfish were appalled.

We are very happy in this tank. Why would we want to go elsewhere? Life in a pond would be very different, troubling even. We would need to have a completely different consciousness for life in the wild, as there would be the constant necessity of being aware of predators.

As this line of thought wasn't something I expected or even imagined, it was my turn to be shocked.

We are especially pleased that our tank is in the main living area so we can watch the humans and dogs and television.

Television? You watch television?

Oh yes. We like the television, especially the nature shows. We learn much about other species from watching the television and that is one of the reasons we are very pleased to be in this situation.

Remember where we were when you met us—in the feeder tank. The consciousness of many of the fish in that tank was filled with fear and resignation. Most knew they would be a meal for some larger creature, as we believe we would have been.

Was it destiny or karma that kept you from becoming a meal for something larger?

We don't know. We are just pleased with living in this tank and enjoying each others' company. This life is very special, not only because we don't have to worry

Goldfish. Photo by Dawn Brunke.

about predators, but because we have a chance to learn so much about humans and other life-forms. We also like communicating with the dogs.

Again and again, the goldfish related how contented and safe they felt. They definitely did not want to be anywhere else, at least for now. The largest fish added that he was living longer than he expected because he was learning so much and enjoying his life a great deal.

As I ended our conversation, not only relieved but awed by the quality of thought these marvelous creatures held, I began to understand how an animal's life is often very different from what we humans might expect or interpret it to be. It was my human lens that first viewed the fish as decorations and then, through my own fears of captivity, as prisoners. As the fish related, neither of these scenarios was their experience.

Though it made sense, a part of me still questioned if all this goldfish talk was just my elaborate way of assuaging my own guilt for keeping the fish in the tank in the first place. How could I confirm what they were saying?

A few nights later, my husband and I were staying up late, watching a video of *The Abyss,* a film in which the action takes place largely underwater. At one point I turned my head and happened to glimpse the goldfish. I was stunned and amused to feel a tingling rush of inner knowing that all they had told me *was* true, for there were all three floating gently in the middle of the tank, their eyes gazing straight ahead, directly in line with the television screen. I started to make contact, excited to ask—Are you watching this movie with us?—when I heard a loud "Sssshhhhh!" voice inside my head. They flicked their tails as if in irritation.

I fell into laughter, never in my life believing I would be so happy to be shushed by three goldfish.

In letting go of expectations and assumptions, what one finds beneath the surface is often surprising. I no longer see my fish as either decorations or prisoners. Through a series of mysteriously orchestrated events, the fish and I have come together in the same life, opening to the opportunity of relationship.

I do not believe that animals in general want us to feel guilty about what we have or have not done. I believe the animals want us to wake up, pay attention, and start being responsible members of the web of life. However, sometimes guilt is a means to awakening; as such, it can be a useful tool.

Marcia Ramsland told me a story about Plecostomus, a black, bottom-feeding catfish she acquired when he was very small. "He outgrew his tank," explained Marcia, "and he kept outgrowing his tank and I felt guilty, guilty, guilty because he was always too big for his tank. I was at a workshop at Penelope Smith's, more than two thousand miles away, and she said, 'Let any animal come in and talk to you.' It was this fish who popped up to say to me, 'Don't feel badly. This has been my whole life. I wish you would talk to me.'"

As with the goldfish, Plecostomus was not angry or resentful. Rather, it was the misdirection of human projection and guilt that stood in the way of communication.

Marcia later spoke to a group of neons in her aquarium tank. "They said, 'Life in the water is really quite different. It's a different world in many respects. Though consciousness is the same, living in the water is a more free-flowing existence. We wonder why you choose a gravity-based landform.' It's like when you live in a warm climate and wonder why anyone is snowplowing—that's sort of what these fish were saying. They also said that the unique thing about being a fish in a tank is that they can see our world and us too, whereas most fish can't. Most water-based animals are unaware of the other side, of life beyond the water. 'It must be a heavy existence' is what they say."

The neons' comment that life on land must be a "heavy existence" echoed something other animals had pointed out—namely, that not all animals think being human is such a great thing. Just as I had asked many animals, why did you choose to be a horse, a dog, a mosquito, the neon fish were asking, why do you want to be human?

Marcia laughed. "Oh, yes! I think we often look at the world considering ourselves the highest life-form on the planet, when other life-forms kind of raise their eyebrows at us and say, 'Uh huh . . .'"

Why do certain animals choose to live with humans? A dog named Maxie told Laura Simpson that the reason animals come into our lives is "because we ask for that kind of love."

We sometimes fail to remember, however, that animals who come to live with us are not *things*. By regarding these beings as objects, we fail to discover the deeper opportunities of relationship. Nedda Wittels had a conversation with Spirit of Horse, who focused on the spiritual mystery of relationship. Here is what Spirit of Horse told Nedda.

Horses represent freedom. This is an irony, because horses have been beasts of burden for a long time. How can horses hold the promise of freedom, running in the wind with manes flowing, while hitched to a wagon or carrying a human on their backs? Humans struggle with a similar issue: how can they exercise free will and simultaneously surrender to the will of God/Goddess?

On another level, there is the mystery of how and why horses allow themselves to be used by humans as beasts of burden. This is our service to humanity. In exchange, horses dream of blending with human beings. It is not the human alone who experiences the ecstasy of union when human and horse are one. Both feel the joy.

When energies merge, a healing of primal relationship occurs wherein the power and freedom of physicality and simultaneous union is experienced by both human and horse.

Humans need to know that horses are most abused when they are treated as mechanical entities. Many humans treat horses as though they exist only for the amusement and pleasure of humanity, or to make money, or as food. There needs to be a complete change in humanity's relationship with animals, especially those who are living artificial lives by choosing to live with humans. Horses made this choice eons ago and have paid a high price for it.

What is the reason they made this choice?

For spiritual growth. To learn about interacting with potential Co-creators, which is what humans are. And to help teach humans about interacting with animals who represent freedom-in-form.

The notions of freedom, free choice, and learning lessons in the ways that best fit our unique circumstances are emphasized by animals time and again. Chrys Long-Ago experienced this theme in a remarkable way. Her instructor was a guinea pig she called Geisha.[1]

When Geisha finished birthing her first litter, Chrys noted that the mama guinea pig was acting strangely, refusing to have anything to do with her babies. Chrys tried a number of tricks to get Geisha to nurse, to no avail. Finally, tuning in to Geisha on a telepathic level, she heard the message, "I can give birth to them but I can't bond with them. I don't want to be their mother." Chrys was horrified. Why would Geisha not want to be a mother? "They'll be taken away from me," cried Geisha in a shrill voice. "I'll lose them! They'll be taken away!"

As Geisha the guinea pig could not be calmed down, Chrys deepened the connection and made contact with another aspect of Geisha. This "Higher Self" of Geisha thanked Chrys for caring to ask for her story. She then presented a series of pictures showing the life of a human mother in Nazi Germany who had been separated from her children, sent to a hospital, and subjected to "cruel and painful experiments" until she died.

My reason for reembodying as a guinea pig is to purify the trauma and anguish caused by losing those children and enduring the unspeakable fear of the danger they were in. Now I can re-create motherhood and heal the wounds of my heart.

But why become a guinea pig? Couldn't you do the same thing in a human life?

This is a motherhood lesson. It is a separation lesson and a trust lesson. I could have served all these in life as a human again, but I also would have been a child again, somebody's daughter, with all the work that is; then a student, with years of school and college; and growing up with all these many lessons and choices. It could have been twenty-five years into that life before I would re-create motherhood.

To create the experience of motherhood that would suit this lesson, I need only the space to focus my complete attention on the issues of helplessness, vulnerability, exploitation, and abuse. Think of what the term *guinea pig* means in the common language of your day! Why, I was a human guinea pig—what better form to take as an animal?

As a guinea pig, could I not then easily address the issues specific to that life in one fast, focused life like this, without the total work of a human experience?

Know that it is like this among souls: that we incarnate to acquire experience of our wisdom, to experience the acquisition of our wisdom, and that those acts can be accomplished in life well lived in any form, no matter how insignificant it may appear to other forms of consciousness.

It is the choice we have. We can take as long as we want to experience a lesson. Just as you have the choice of taking your problems through years of analysis with counseling, or through just days with intensive soul-searching seminars. This is my seminar—my guinea pig seminar. That I can learn wisdom and be free in a fast life, to return again and again in any form I choose, is my prerogative as well as it is yours.

In the end, Chrys and Geisha's Higher Self came to an agreement. As Chrys wrote, "I would be patient with Geisha and she could trust that whatever she created for herself I would accept. Also, her Higher Self would enrich my experience by allowing me to learn from her lessons."

From the cramped quarters of our own self-limiting belief systems, there is simply not enough space to see the full picture. Whether guilt-ridden by the idea of aquarium fish as prisoners or horrified by a mother guinea pig refusing to care for her babies, we must remember that the emotions are our own. The reality for the other may be something completely different.

And yet we must also remember that we fall for the illusion because it is the illusion that holds our lesson. As we grapple with the idea of who we think we are—as reflected in what we think we see—we begin to uncover projections and prejudices we never knew we had. We might just discover, as Geisha noted, that the experience of wisdom may be gained in any form, no matter how trivial or insignificant it appears to others.

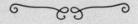

Joy
Marcia Ramsland and Flying Insect

A flying insect, a nondescript something, was buzzing around me.

I asked, "What do you have to say?" And there was great joy.

This little thing said, "There is consciousness in all things. Believe it!"

It also wanted to say that it wished people didn't have such a campaign against insects. But mostly it was there in sheer joy to say that consciousness is everywhere and it doesn't matter the size of the body.

21

Pests

Everything that lives, even a common domestic housefly, has something of value to share with you—whenever you are ready for the experience.

J. Allen Boone,
Adventures in Kinship with All Life

Only one letter away from pets are pests, those pesky little creatures that creep and buzz, burrow and gnaw, generally considered to be a nuisance in our world.

Most communicators relate that as we open to the essential oneness of the web of life, chatting and forming relationships with dolphins and dogs, horses and whales, we begin to sense animals as equals, fellow adventurers through life, sometimes teachers and guides. What happens to this wonderful view of kinship, however, when we're face to face with a cockroach? Is a cockroach just as much a reflection of the divine as a whale? What about snakes and slugs, flies and maggots? Could it be that in those animals we think of as pests, we come face to face with yet another aspect of the human shadow?

"We have to really work through that," Raphaela Pope told me. "You may work through that with one species, but then you find your blind spot: rats or spiders or even small dogs."

"Do you have a blind spot?" I asked.

"Well, ants maybe," said Raphaela reluctantly. "I used to kill ants. A few years ago, we had an ant invasion. I told them, 'I don't like this. I'm having to wash tons of you down the sink and I would really prefer that you leave.' They said, 'Oh, we don't care. There's thousands and millions more of us! Wash us down; it's all right, we don't care!'" Raphaela laughed uproariously. "I thought, Oh no! I can't be getting this. This can't be right!"

"What happened?"

"I kept asking them to leave, but there were more of them every day. They were extending their range. Finally, I bought some Raid and plunked it down on the counter and said, 'Listen guys, I'm sick of this and I'm going to use this stuff if you don't take a hike.' In two hours, about 99 percent of the ants were gone, totally out of the kitchen!"

185

J. Allen Boone tells a similar story about some ants who once invaded his house. "I was just about to let them have it with both poison and broom, when my New England conscience began to hiss," wrote Boone. "It demanded to know why, with all that I had been privileged to experience in relationship balancing, I should want to kill these ants."[1]

Boone began talking with the ants, complimenting them on their intelligence and zest for life. He then proposed a gentlemen's agreement whereby the ants would vacate the house. As he prepared to leave for the evening, Boone told the ants that he had done the best he could; the rest was up to them. When he returned home, the ants were gone.

In a later book, Boone relates the story of an estate owner plagued with gophers. Having heard of Boone's success with ants, the man wondered if he could work out a similar agreement. He decided to do this by writing a letter to the gophers. Late at night, after everyone had gone to bed, the man snuck out of the house and pushed the letter deeply into the nearest gopher hole. As Boone tells it, the next morning, "to his fascinated amazement, he couldn't find a fresh gopher track anywhere."[2]

I had my own experience with pests when some spider mites crawled onto a lemon plant in my kitchen. Although I couldn't think of many nice things to say to the spider mites, I let them know they were hurting the plant and if there was something I could do to help them move, I was willing to oblige.*

To my surprise, the image that formed in my mind was a piece of lettuce leaf. The feeling associated with this bit of lettuce was that it should be an offering, such as one might place at an altar or temple. Although skeptical, I put the lettuce leaf next to the plant and, in the morning, there were definitely fewer spider mites. At that time, I asked again if they would leave and again received the image of a lettuce leaf. I repeated the process and the next day there were no spider mites.

What do these stories tell us? What is the common denominator between a gentlemen's agreement with ants, a letter to gophers, and a lettuce offering to spider mites? I believe the answer may be found in a combination of attitude and intention. Surely it was not the proposed agreement, letter, or lettuce that magically made these critters leave. Rather, it was the energy behind the event. Even Raphaela's threat to the ants came not from anger but from a preference for the ants to leave peacefully.

---

*Though I interpreted this situation at the time as the mites "hurting" the plant, a more enlightened approach might have been to ask both plant and mites what was going on. Did the plant need the mites for some reason? Was there a larger picture of which I was unaware? Questions such as these take us into a deeper appreciation of the interwoven roles of all beings.

The shift from seeing animals as pests to seeing all life as a manifestation of One is a movement toward deeper kinship. J. Allen Boone wrote how he formed a short though unforgettable relationship with a housefly he called Freddie. Man and fly agreed to form a partnership whereby both would learn about each other as fellow beings.

In the beginning, Boone's questions to Freddie were met with counterquestions. When Boone asked Freddie why flies annoy and treat humans so badly, Freddie asked Boone why humans treat flies so badly. Back and forth the question and mirrored question bounced. It was then Boone realized how ardently thought creates reality. In expecting flies to annoy and bite, they do; in seeing them as dirty creatures, they are.

"The more I was able to see beyond the physical form of Freddie the Fly, the easier it became to recognize him as a fellow expression of the Mind of the Universe," Boone wrote. "I could then listen with him as well as to him. And again I realized that all living things are individual instruments through which the Mind of the Universe thinks, speaks and acts. We are all interrelated in a common accord, a common purpose and a common good. We are members of a vast cosmic orchestra, in which each living instrument is essential to the complementary and harmonious playing of the whole."[3]

It is difficult for Western society to see beyond the physical form, and it is particularly difficult for us to see flies as fellow expressions of the Mind of the Universe. Why? Basically, because we have bought into the cultural projection that flies are worthless and dirty, perhaps even evil. Along with other pests, flies have become a cultural repository for group projections of the dark aspects of ourselves. A bit of research, self-reflection, and willingness to look beyond our own surface prejudices reveals that this is not the reality of flies at all.

In her book, *The Voice of the Infinite in the Small: Revisioning the Insect-Human Connection*, Joanne Lauck notes that in other cultures and times, flies were admired and respected. For example, the ancient Egyptians honored the bravery of the fly and wore fly amulets to symbolize the human spirit. Members of the North American Blackfoot's Fly Society sought to emulate the fly's cunning ability to harass the enemy without being captured or killed. Some cultures have celebrated the fly for its remarkable skills of flight and navigational abilities; others saw the fly as a symbol of rebirth, honoring its presence as sacred and worthy of instruction.

How is it, then, that we have come to have such profound disrespect for flies? How have we moved from a space of honoring all life and learning from our insect kin to believing that a fly swatter in the closet is a good and necessary thing?

In brief, Lauck believes it happened like this: In moving from a sacred to a mechanistic model of nature, we separated ourselves from the intuitive understandings that link us to the web of all life. We began to lose touch with that which was not easily seen as similar to us. What was unknown was considered dangerous. If an animal seemed especially incomprehensible, we imagined it might also be evil. In our imaginings, we became so fearful that we decided to take control. And so we made war on insects. Out of fear, we killed so that our fear could be controlled. As we became increasingly insect phobic, we passed our fears on to our children. Because we are now barely conscious of the fear, we pass it on unconsciously. It has become a tightly closed circle.

Indeed, we often kill bugs not out of fear of a real threat but simply because we don't know what they are. Could it be that we have adopted the unthinking act of crushing bugs as a metaphoric gesture for crushing our own unrealized fears?

Lauck notes that insects are a particularly easy hook for our projections of fear. After all, many insects seem quite strange to us, both in their appearance and behavior. They often live in great numbers, some bite and sting, and many insects, such as the fly, work with the dark mysteries of life such as death, decay, and rebirth—all excellent sources of shadow material.

If animals in captivity reflect our outrage against inner captivity, insects such as the fly reflect what we deny and disown in life. As such, the fly is an initiator, a profound reminder that what we disown about any aspect of life, we also disown in ourselves.

When Morgine Jurdan struck up a conversation with a fly, it was this point the fly considered most important:

I am a fly and I would like to share a message with the world.

I love people and I enjoy interacting with them. I find it sad when I am taken as an enemy. I love being who I am, and my joyfulness of being is shared throughout the realm of nature.

Each of us shines and sparkles in our own unique way. You perceive us through filters that allow you a limited view of our nature. We live in a realm of love where each being understands the part it plays in the world as a whole and knows how things move to and fro, back and forth, in and out, up and down, weaving the tapestry of life.

When you see me, you often feel repulsed and your first reaction is to kill me. I have not hurt you. I do not even sting and yet you desire to eliminate me from your presence. I am labeled as "dirty," whatever that might mean to your kind. I find this sad. There is so much more here than meets the eye. You often do not look below the surface to find the buried treasure that might lay hidden.

I wish people would begin to think before they act. I wish they would ask themselves why they are deciding to kill me, or any other tiny creature. What threat do I pose? Am I causing harm? Or are they reacting out of habit and assumptions?

I am a fly and I help to create love, harmony, and balance in this wonderful world. I am not the enemy. I am your friend. Take time to get to know me better and you may discover just a little more joy that had been hidden from you before.

As Joanne Lauck notes, "healing begins when we dare to become conscious of our violent and irrational ways and the mythologizing that makes flies or any other species our enemy."[4] Daring to look at our shadow material means we are willing to face that which is disowned, denied, and hated within the self. Transformation comes as we begin to reclaim our own lost faces, peeling away the masks we have projected onto others in the world.

Lauck notes that we tend to accept that which reinforces our projections. "When we read about flies softening their food with digestive juices tainted with their previous meal, which might indeed be feces or decomposing flesh, we become nauseated. It confirms our belief in their despicable nature and satisfies the projection. We also don't want to know that honey is partially dried bee vomit or that butterflies seek and sip urine and sweat as well as nectar and fruit juices—facts likely to spoil any positive projections we have accorded these insects."[5]

What stops us from seeing the animal itself—be it goldfish, fly, or honeybee—are our own projections, which can be both positive and negative. In some ways, it makes for a tidier world to think in terms of dark and light. It is also infinitely more appealing to think of honey as nectar from the gods than as partially dried bee vomit. Similarly, it is easier to project our fear of such things as disease onto certain animals rather than explore impermanence and decay within ourselves.

It is no coincidence that we associate pests with disease. The word *pest* comes from the Latin *pestis*, meaning plague or contagious disease. A pest is defined as a noxious person or thing, and is linked to *pestilence*, meaning a fatal epidemic disease, especially bubonic plague. It is here we see how language shapes our view of the world, for word association may lead us to believe that the source of disease is to be found in the pest. However, most often pests are simply carriers of disease—the messengers, not the message.

As is widely noted by holistic health professionals, a more expansive way of looking at disease is as dis-ease, a lack of ease. This lack can be on many levels: physical, mental, emotional, or spiritual; within an individual body, and within the "body" of a group or culture. In short, when there is great imbalance in any aspect of our lives, disease is likely to manifest.

Think of plague and contagion, and you will most likely think of rats. Even more than flies, rats arouse fear, disgust, and hatred in many humans. As the object of so much of our animosity, they are also key players in reflecting the human shadow.

In an attempt to help educate us about the lives of animals we consider undesirable, Dr. Jeri Ryan asked a female rat living in the wild if she would share her thoughts about life and her place in the world.

Thank you for paying attention to us. Thank you for giving us recognition and significance. We are scum to most, we hear.

Yes. Many humans believe you are dangerous because you carry disease.

We do have some of that. I wonder if we are alone.

Humans and other species also carry disease. Perhaps we have a prejudice about you based on our projection. Tell me, who are you?

I represent my beings, my kind. I am industrious. I am not fat, though I eat a great deal when it is available. I also take food to my nest to save and feed my younglings. I am single-minded and determined. I can work as a team without planning, or I can work alone. I have no time for fear.

Are you concerned about beauty?

Beauty is a given in all, so we are not allowing it priority; it is always there, in all things, within deeply. Beauty is not in separateness from anything.

Perhaps that is why many humans believe that animals have no concept of beauty or aesthetics, because you consider it a given. We humans are moved deeply by the beauty of certain music or flowers or a poem or sunsets. What about that for you?

We are on a level of peaceful appreciation. Beauty is there at all times—if not in a sunset, then in a blade of grass or a mealy bug or a mosquito, or a snug warm nest, or myself.

That is important. You have a concept of self.

You seem surprised.

Actually, I'm not. I just want to know more.

"Me" is just one part of a very large picture of life. "Me" is important, important enough to protect and guard and care for. I have to be important to me, or I will not be here tomorrow. But I'm not so important that all else takes second place. I slip into my place and I love my place just because it fits; it belongs. I belong.

Why did you choose to be this particular species?

To learn what could be learned. I was not sure of what that would be. I have learned much of humility, acceptance, and willingness to work. I learn what can be smelled and viewed from this vantage point. I have made my choice to be here and I learn of a world that has my needs, my behaviors, my wishes, my learning all included.

I learn of nibbling as a way of taking in food. I learn of sharp teeth that gnaw when necessary to go where I need to go. I know of swiftness and lightness to allow me to appear and disappear in a flash. I receive much information from the air with my nose. I stand on two feet sometimes to get that at higher levels and thus further distances. I burrow. I sleep. I make my own kind.

What are your feelings about death and rebirth and being in the nonphysical?

It changes as I repeat myself by returning into different worlds. I am now so complacent about it that I think nothing of it. When I was so new, I was very afraid of death and rebirth. They seemed far away, and the nonphysical was something I could not even make come into my mind. Then I glamorized it because I wanted to want nonphysical whenever it was imminent. Now I have a love for both sides because both have their own beauty and ways of teaching. The nonphysical is always ultimate because peace and love are all there is. Nothing else exists.

All spirits have intelligence, so we all have deep understanding without the need to communicate. That understanding is a given, because we are One, so no one has to teach anyone. We all just know. That is how learning takes place there. And here it takes place by doing and discovering, finding and resisting and fighting and—what have you! It is as it is in each world, with so much to give, as much as those who are willing to participate.

Thank you. Is there anything else you would like us to know?

Perhaps you will just look at us and consider that we have a world. While you are in a world we share, we also have our own.

As we begin to consider that all creatures have a world, we open to a much larger view of our own. As we begin to rejoice in the unique abilities of all animals, we may come to realize that the label of "pests" is not so much about particular animals but more about our attempts to distance ourselves from what we fear.

In shifting to a deeper acknowledgment of all that every being contributes to the whole, we reconnect ourselves, opening to more intimate, heartfelt states of awe and appreciation. It is here we know that as J. Allen Boone noted, all animals, from whales to rats to flies to humans, have something of value to share with you—whenever you are ready for the experience.

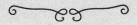

Opportunities to Know Yourself
Ayala (Animal Kingdom Deva) ~ Toraya Ayres

Animals are also given opportunities for choices. Many choose to take on a certain emotion or illness that expresses something for their person. They give many gifts that you are not aware of. These are given voluntarily. Cats and dogs are particularly good examples of this kind of behavior and very apt to express in their behavior something that the person feels unable to cope with more directly.

What of animals that are abused, dogs that are neglected, beaten, not fed, or tortured? How do such experiences fit into their group soul's development? In much the same way as with humans—as a widening of experience. Again, they are mirrors of aspects of yourselves. Sometimes they willingly accept experiences that are uncomfortable and painful in order to spare you. You get to see the issue in front of you instead of living through it more directly.

Everything in life around you is meaningful. Whether you meet a starving dog or a homeless man, you are always seeing something that relates to your own reality. Treat it as a symbol to be understood. Is a part of you starving? Is a part of you feeling like a victim or without a home? Explore these opportunities to know yourself better.

Someday you will understand the intimate web of which each is a part, a web in which you affect the weather and the foods you eat and the thoughts you think and the emotions you feel as a result. All are woven together in an endless interaction.

2 2

In Quest of Learning: Animal Research and Human Education

In the midst of working on this book, I visited a new SeaLife Center in Alaska that promotes public education. Though I didn't stop to talk with all the animals, it was my experience that while some were quite content with their surroundings, others were clearly not happy with the arrangement at all. Issues of captivity aside, is this so different from life anywhere?

A group of five fish captured my attention, for they initiated a conversation, telling me that when they had "signed on for this project," they believed it would be a mutual exchange of human and animal education. Unlike the fish in my tank at home, these fish had a serious tone. All five faced me as they spoke in a group voice, their shared consciousness reminding me of some wise elderly scholar whom no one seemed to notice. The fish told me they knew they were not particularly rare or beautiful by human standards.

The fish said their group had known humans would be taking some of them for this center, and they had agreed to be representatives. They related that they were still in contact with their group in the ocean. Though they didn't say the decision to come to the center was a mistake, they indicated that what they thought it would be like and what it actually involved were two very different things.

The fish said they were disappointed in the humans who had visited the center so far. "We thought humans would come to learn about us," they explained. "But most of you have no attention span to speak of. You take a glance and go on. Very few of you stop to actually *see* us. We have much information, but many of you do not have the patience to listen."

I felt bad because I didn't have the time to listen. I had come to the SeaLife Center with a number of children, all of whom were quickly racing off to other tanks and displays. I thanked the fish for speaking to me and asked if I could contact them again. They agreed.

For my second talk with the fish, this time from home, I asked if they would comment further on why they agreed to come to the SeaLife Center.

We came to help humans learn more about the consciousness of our kind. We saw this as a mind-to-mind meeting place, where we could come in order to exchange ideas. We had hoped this would be a temporary situation, that we would be allowed to return when we wished. This, we see, is not the case. Too many human minds are closed to such an idea. Ideally, however, this situation could work as an exchange, in much the same way that you have "exchange students" visit from one institution of learning to another.

Our group is involved in what you might call research in that we record daily happenings in the waters. We do not hold the vast memories of life on earth (though we have access to that), but are more like scribes of a particular region in the sea. We sometimes question others about what they do and mentally record this knowledge. We are scribes in the sense that we *describe* life in our waters and hold that information for others. Think of us as a living library—though, of course, we all have our individual and group lives as well. It is in the quest for knowledge that we agreed to come here. However, we thought we would be called on for knowledge as well.

What would you like to tell humans?

First of all, we would wish for you a slowing down. It would be good to center yourself inside your consciousness so that you can see all that is around you. Fish are very good at this, as we are accustomed to the movements of water and have an ability to "feel" around ourselves entirely.

For humans, there seems to be too much hurry-hurry all about. From what we have observed, your consciousness as a group is very scattered, going in many directions at once. You seem to hold consciousness on a shallow level. We have also noticed that you hold various judgments against animals and thus fail to see the gifts each one has to bring. In this center, for example, everyone wants to see the sea lions. That is much of what we hear—sea lions, sea lions. It is true that the sea lions are amusing for humans, though the sea lions say the humans also amuse them.

However, we—as well as every other animal—have gifts of another sort to offer. We could offer you a vision of life in our neighborhood of the ocean, for example, that is quite beautiful. You could learn much from talking with us. We could learn from you too. There are a number of things about humans that both intrigue and confuse us.

Alyeska and sea lions. Photo by Dawn Brunke.

We are hoping to have more exchange at this center. On a more global level, this is called for as well. That is why we came, though that is not always the reason animals come to places like this. We would like for humans to talk to us, to exchange thoughts, to question us as well as themselves. Think of our interchange as an opportunity to learn about different cultures and species. We are here as teachers, spokesbeings, ambassadors of knowledge as well as goodwill. There are many things both of our species could gain if we could only open to more like you, and if human consciousness included a bit more respect when meeting other species.

In summary, we would like to see more openness from humans, more exchange in consciousness and ideas. We would also like to be returned to the water at some point. It would be best if humans would first ask animals if they are willing to come into captivity. There could also be agreements whereby species would visit for a short time and then be returned to their homes. Our feeling is that this would be much more harmonious and many animals would be more open to this than the "long stay." This would benefit everybody.

Another way of connecting and exchanging information is by the means we are communicating now. All of us have the ability to tune into one another. If you chose, you could come "into our eyes" and see what a typical day is like in our waters. By agreement, we could come along on a day with you. It is a learning experience for those who are open and interested.

Thank you for your comments.

You are welcome. We are pleased to be of assistance and wish for more humans to come to speak with us.

I am sorry, but I cannot remember your species name.

Call us the Float Fish, for that is how you see us in your mind and how you remember us, floating nearly motionless when we spoke with you that first time. We can be very focused in this way. We hold a good deal of knowledge, not only of our species but also of the sea around us. We see a lot of fish and other animals come and go, and we make excellent notes. If you or others would like further information, please feel free to call on us, the Float Fish.

I was very taken with the Float Fish and sensed they were genuinely interested in meeting with humans in an ongoing interchange. I felt they didn't understand why we would not be more interested in this. And I felt sad that, as a whole, we weren't.

Creating an exchange center where animals and humans could meet to share ideas and experiences seemed an excellent idea. As was the notion that certain animals might agree to meet with humans in these learning centers for short periods of time and be returned to their homes when they chose. Could we ever create such a world?

Just as the Float Fish believed that interspecies communication was part of their mission, there are other animals who would love to communicate their feelings to humans, if only given a chance.

One of the darkest aspects of human-animal interaction is found in the field of animal research. Among these animals are those not only held captive but experimented upon by humans in the name of science. There are many (including both humans and animals) who view this as torture. Others say, however, that even lives lived within the confines of research laboratories are chosen and have purpose.

Dr. Jeri Ryan agreed to speak with two research animals for this book so that humans might learn more of what animals in these situations think and feel. She first made contact with a young male primate who lives in a research laboratory.

Jeri began by asking the monkey if there was anything he wanted humans to know.

I have very little to say to humans. I have such closeness that I have confusion.

I feel like a brother to those humans who enter my dwelling to bring me joy or distress. I have confusion about my closeness to that and wonder if I too could be doing that, had I thought of it first.

Why did you choose to be this particular species?

I have always chosen this species. I do not recall anything else. I enjoy the freedom of this body and my agility. I enjoy the closeness of our members, the honesty and quickness of solving differences even when tempers are high. To be peaceable is what we mostly want. We have quiet caring among us. We accept and receive without fuss, and we give in the same way. I find comfort and freedom in all these qualities. That is why I chose this kind of body.

You don't exactly have freedom in a research lab. How did you get there?

It was, in my understanding, temporary. It was not in my understanding what happens here. I chose to be with the particular spirit who birthed me. I thought I, too, would learn of humans. It felt like a harmless and cooperative endeavor. I did not know of all things that would happen.

How do you feel about being in the lab now?

I have my friends and my moments of joy in knowing I can rise above all this. I am a youngster at heart and still have very mature wishes for the good of all. I do not wish this to be where I end. I wish fulfillment.

Some say life can be meaningful to lab animals because you help a greater cause. You are not fulfilled?

No. I have not seen a greater cause without a greater dilemma. Is it not a paradox to inflict suffering on one group to prevent suffering for another? The suffering of me and my kind lasts this lifetime. The suffering of the souls who make this happen lasts many lifetimes. I do not know of the learning that happens for either of us in here.

Is there a more cosmic purpose to this?

Yes, as with all of life. We must all find our place in the sun without interfering with another's place in the sun. We are so far from that—my kind as well as your kind.

I think my kind is further because we have so many complex ways of interfering with another's place in the sun.

Perhaps simplicity keeps us a tad more innocent. We do not do research on each other. We always have honesty so no one is fooled.

Perhaps we are not to know of the cosmic purpose. Perhaps if we know this purpose with great certainty, we will not follow our spontaneity. Perhaps we would become contrived and keep in mind only that goal and not take in all of life. Or, maybe we know and don't know that we know.

Maybe we don't want to know?

Maybe. Perhaps the reason we do not know cosmic purpose is so that we can discover and develop that purpose and meaning for the good of our kind and the cosmos.

For her second interview, Jeri contacted a male rat living in the research laboratory of a pharmaceutical company.

I am a lab rat with a horrible disease given to me by human injection.

I wish to ask only a few questions so humans might understand your experience. Do you suffer?

I have pain. I will probably die soon. We die by sacrifice. This is what I hear. That means we are killed by hitting our heads against a hard object near the water place. They do not want confusion in our bodies, so that is the best way to kill us. I have witnessed it many times.

Some humans believe lab animals have chosen their situation. What is your belief?

I chose this body to bring dignity to rats. I hoped I could. I believe I am. I don't know for sure.

Did you know of the pain and misery you would have?

No. I did not expect perfection. I expected learning. I know learning happens with hard experience, with challenge. I did not design this.

Does anybody design this?

I suppose there is an element of that, as we decide things in our lives. I suppose entering a certain body contributes to design. I am not happy with this design. I make the best of it and search for meaning and purpose.

What have you found?

That dignity has many forms. Sometimes it is refusal; sometimes it is acceptance. Always it is knowing self-value and self-worth in a situation where I am not valued except as a tool. I hold to that because it helps me and others with me. Yet, I wonder of what purpose is this suffering? And the purpose of those who give us our pain?

They say to improve life and health of humans, to take away their suffering.

It puzzles me. How can inflicting suffering on one being prevent suffering in another?

Well, it prevents physical suffering when a disease process is known and "cures" are developed. The spiritual awareness, however, has either not opened or has been shut down, or they would ask the same question.

I see. That explains grim faces and sometimes high-pitched laughter.

Yes. Feelings are trying to break through.

We feel that very deeply in our knowingness. It does not escape us. Perhaps there is another way to look at this. I have not yet found the spiritual purpose to my suffering. You have explained the purpose of the flesh. I do not understand the spiritual purpose at all. Yet I say something has to happen to redeem this pain. What can that be? I believe it will be what it is to be in each situation. I believe it will be a consequence, a result that brings a spiritual meaning to suffering—not before suffering but after suffering.

Something other than a cure for disease?

Yes. Something deeper than a cure for disease.

Are you talking about the gift that comes from tragedy?

Yes. I hold out hope for that. I have hope for that.

Does this justify this whole system of research?

I have not yet found spiritual justification for this endeavor.

I wish to preserve the dignity of my rat essence, to present that for all rats. Dignity and nobility are found in the willingness to be honest with the self and to live according to the honesty each essence presents. Human honesty and rat honesty may be different. As a rat, I live simply, so to be honest is simple. In my rat culture, the rules of honesty are few and clear, and we mostly follow them. They are not so complex to fool us into believing we are in our honesty when we are not. It is perhaps not so simple for humans to be honest.

That is a problem for humans. We can fool ourselves in that way.

I am not at all times in my honesty, and I have no problem knowing that. Perhaps that is my strength in my dignity. I may not fool myself. My dignity comes from my honesty in knowing that this life of suffering is meaningless. Because I keep that in my honesty, this life is meaningful.

As the lab rat related to Jeri, meaning and spiritual purpose are dependent upon each situation and individual being. For some animals, meaning is found in personal relationship. Sharon Callahan relates, "Animals in the most deplorable conditions have told me that they offer themselves willingly if just one person is touched by their plight and motivated to change. A little rabbit in a laboratory cage communicated that there was one technician who treated her with affection and would pick her up and comfort her when no one else was looking. The rabbit felt her life had been worthwhile simply by eliciting a response of kindness from this one woman."

On the other side of the research cage are the humans who experiment upon animals, subjecting them to massive doses of experimental drugs, radiation, poisons, a variety of diseases, or perhaps simply a quick death so as to end up on a dissection table.

As a society, we both deify science and call it cruel. Science saves lives and science murders. But science is not "out there," for as part of the One, we all have a scientist living inside. What aspect of shadow are we asked to look at, both individually and collectively, when we consider the use of animals in scientific research?

Morgine Jurdan contacted a spirit form whom she named Radeva, for research animal deva. Radeva offered the following:

I am an energy form of spirit that exists for the animals used by humans for testing, where the relationship is not that of companion, but as an experiment.

Animals who choose to come for research or experimentation do so out of a love of your species that defies description. For the most part, they are willing to be here. They hope, through their love, you will begin to understand and feel their pain. They hope, through their love and dedication and courage, you will begin to open your eyes and realize what you are doing. Each and every day, they send messages and love to you. You often do not hear. . . .

Some scientists are very dedicated to their work. They are so focused on helping suffering humans that they do not feel the pain of the animals. They honestly, at times, do not believe the animals suffer. They think animals do not have feelings or nerve endings, or systems that work the way in which humans' do. Often, they are numb themselves. They work very hard in stressful situations. Some work long hours and feel frustrated because results do not come quickly. They see no other choice than working with animals to save humans. We understand their focus and appreciate the love they feel for fellow human beings.

There are others who are merely doing a job. They are like robots and do not question whether something is right or wrong; they just do what they are told. This we find very sad.

Animals are often isolated from one another. They are poked and prodded, intentionally made ill, and stressed and killed with a variety of foods and chemicals or machines. Do these beings hate humans? No. Why would they choose to return again and again if they hated you? They come from a place of love as teachers and guides. They come to show you how to feel again. They do suffer; they do have feelings and emotions, longings and desires. But most of all, they have love.

If scientists would just take a moment to breathe, calm down, and really look into each animal's eyes for several moments, they would recognize themselves instantly and understand what is going on. Time, however, is not on the side of animals. Humans are often too much in a hurry.

Today, more people are becoming aware of animals as equals, or at least, playing an important role. Humans are beginning to recognize the roles we play as servants to children, blind and deaf people, the elderly, or as someone's best friend. As you recognize our gifts to you, you begin to recognize what you are doing to other beings used for experimentation and it angers you and chills you to the bone.

I do foresee a time when I can be considered a memory and my function in the world will take on a different form. I hope those reading this message will live long enough to see that day. Thank you for taking time to ask such questions, and for having the love to listen and hear my story.

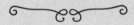

An Act of Becoming
Carmen (cat) ~ Dawn Brunke

In regards to the hunt, killing is an act of becoming, not an end in itself. We are part of a larger movement, in and out of spirit. We are about at-one-ment with nature, of which the hunt and kill is a part.

We honor the hunt, as most animals do. We are both—bird and cat, mouse and cat. We are a part of each other. If you truly see this and understand it, then you will not have judgment of how killing another for food is "bad." That is our belief. That is the sound/tone in which we move. In this perspective, all is orderly and harmonious, no matter how it seems to those who are not of this harmony.

23

Animals Eating Animals:
The Predator/Prey Relationship

Mythologist Joseph Campbell once noted that among certain peoples the way to pay homage to a deity is by sacrificing and eating it. "For the deities like to visit this earth," writes Campbell, "and to do so they assume disguises; but they are then locked into their animal forms until relieved of them through the sacrifice. They consign their pelts and meat willingly, in gratitude, to those who have released them."[1]

As we find deeper relationship with the animal world, we eventually face the mysteries surrounding the notion of eating animals. In fact, the entire issue of eating animals—and refusing to eat animals—holds a great deal of shadow content for humans.

As Nedda Wittels points out, "Anyone who thinks we shouldn't eat animals because they are sentient then has to consider that the plants also have consciousness and sentience. Even rocks, the wind, the Earth herself are sentient. Because our bodies must eat to live, the issue is more about honoring the beings who give up their physical form rather than abstaining from all food."

Many ancient peoples knew this as they lived in harmony with animals and the land. Taking only what was needed, they honored the spirit of the animal, always asking if it would be willing to come and give life to others. All parts of the animal— from meat to bone to hide—were then used, and thus honored.

It is different today, when most people do not hunt the animals they eat. We are removed from the immediate connection with the animals we ingest when we go to the grocery store and buy a neatly packaged square of meat. "We need to see the whole process," Carol Gurney agreed. "When animals are fed antibiotics and hormones and kept in places where they can't even move, they are literally sometimes going crazy in their cages. By eating them, we ingest that energy. What we really need to do is heal ourselves. We can't heal anything outside ourselves that isn't healed within."

In the last days of 1997, a strange "bird flu" in Hong Kong reportedly killed six humans and infected others with the H5N1 virus, an avian strain of influenza A that was never before known to infect humans. By early 1998, 1.6 million chickens had been destroyed by humans in an attempt to eliminate the virus. It was reported that most of the chickens were suffocated by carbon dioxide in sealed plastic bags, while others had their throats slit.

What was going on with the chickens, I wanted to know. What lesson does the slaughter of more than a million chickens—not for food, and certainly not with honor—reflect to humans?

Nancie LaPier made contact with a spokesbeing for the merged consciousness of the chickens.

"The chickens say they were actually very happy to be free of the life they were forced to live with humans at this time. The mass killing wasn't necessarily a preferred way to handle the problems those birds had with human beings' lack of sensitivity and lack of honoring their life and life purpose. But it was planned at deeper levels to give them release from the earth plane."

Relations between human caretakers and animals have deteriorated to such a degree that this process becomes necessary to the awakening. Until we are honored for our gifts once more and given respectable living arrangements and considerations, diseases like this and others will be a danger to humans. Crate living with no exposure to nature and freedom destroys our immune system, and we pass this on to humans. Free range provides for more than just chemical-free nutrition. You ingest freedom, joy, health, and healing properties of nature—sun, wind, water, air—when you ingest free-range meat.

What you are eating is spiritually lacking, which is one of the reasons you have lost a lot of your spiritual connection; the animals you use for food provide that earthy spiritual connection when allowed to be in that kind of environment. Because you have literally cut them off from their spiritual connection, you're not ingesting the spiritual part of your food.

Why do you think the term *mad cow disease* was chosen? We're getting a little angry at the fact that our spiritual essence is not being considered, honored, and respected. That's not to say that you do not need to eat meat. There are certain animals whose entire purpose is to provide wholesome nutrition to human beings. If an animal has good physical living conditions, a good emotional balance, a belief system of mental clarity, and a connection to the earth, then you are eating something that nourishes in a physical, spiritual, emotional, and mental way. If you don't provide that for those animals, then you are ingesting negative things—the fearful emotions they have when they go to slaughter, their lack of connection to the earth.

This is a lesson to humans to wake up and pay attention. What you do to us all, you do to yourselves.

Nancie said, "They say they are free now, but I feel we have lost something by losing their presence. To lose that particular kind of energy and wisdom on our planet is a great loss. Their movement is a gift if we can understand the lesson behind it.

"They thought it was rather amusing that the way we handled the problem was just to kill them all. They told me, 'Isn't it typical of humans to handle their problems that way?' In actuality, it didn't need to happen. There were other possibilities, but look at the way we automatically went into a trigger reaction of fear, of just 'kill everything.' That is not going to take care of the problem; it will continue to show up until we get it."

Like so many animals, the chickens echoed the same deep refrain: We are all connected, one unto the other. What happens to one ultimately happens to all.

The reference to mad cow disease and the fact that "contaminations" from animals to humans are not so much isolated incidents as reflections of a deeper pattern is a plea for awareness. The human response to these diseases—slaughter the animals, kill the messenger—smacks of denial. Do we really believe that if we get rid of the evidence, the problem will go away?

Mad cow disease, more properly known as bovine spongiform encephalopathy (BSE), became a worldwide issue in 1996, when scientists reported a link between BSE and its fatal human equivalent, Creutzfeldt-Jakob disease (CJD). A number of humans died from CJD, apparently from eating infected beef. In Great Britain, nearly one million cattle were reported to have contracted BSE.

After Nancie spoke with the chickens, she contacted the group consciousness of cows. They began:

Has there ever been a time when you really looked into our big, beautiful brown eyes and felt our essence? Do you think there ever will be a time on the earth when you again will look deeply into our eyes before you kill us and acknowledge our spirit and the gifts we give to you of our life?

Don't you know we have feelings? Don't you know we feel fear? You have despiritualized us. No longer do we live a life of honor upon your planet. In cattle raised for food, we do not send our spirits in, for they have not been appreciated or recognized for a very long time. No one looks into our eyes anymore. Animals whose spirits choose not to come in cannot protect their body from disease. Yes, we are mad; we are very mad without spirit. How curious we have manifested mad cow disease! Madness comes from being devoid of spirit. Spirit leaves when it has been too long neglected.

Physical form without spirit? Surely there must be something to animate the body?

"There is some level of consciousness," explained Nancie, "but it's not attached to the body, almost like they won't anchor it in. In shamanic work, when human or animal beings are traumatized or go through something damaging to the spirit, the theory is that part of that being's spirit leaves and goes someplace where it's safe because it can't bear the trauma. Hence, the practice of soul retrieval involves bringing back that part of the essence and reanchoring it in the body. The cows feel there's a big aspect of the spiritual nature of cows that has not been here for a long time."

The pattern of trauma to the mind/body/spirit and its subsequent splintering of personalities is common to cases of child abuse. Perhaps on some level, what the cows were talking about was species abuse.

"It is," Nancie agreed. "And the problem is not that we use the body of the animal for food, it's that we don't celebrate that. The cows seem to be much more emotionally traumatized by the fact that they're no longer recognized by humans as spiritual beings. The chickens were more detached about why this was happening. But Cow is not. Cow is very connected to humans and really quite sad about the relationship between humans and cows."

I wondered if it was all cows who felt this way. For example, what about milk cows?

"It's a more nurturing relationship and certainly they don't go into fear," said Nancie, "but they say that a lot of people who milk don't understand how sensitive the process of milk coming in can be. Some humans may not do the best things that would allow for more nutritious benefits."

I asked if the cows were referring to the hormone shot of rBGH* that is aimed at increasing milk production.

The cows concurred. In addition, factory-type production, a reliance on milking machines, and other removals from human contact produced stress. Just as Buddy the

*Recombinant Bovine Growth Hormone (rBGH) is a genetically engineered hormone that, when injected into dairy cows, increases milk production by 10 to 15 percent. Though the U.S. Food and Drug Administration approved rBGH in 1993, there are many objections to its use; even the manufacturer admits it may cause a variety of health problems in cows. Many believe that by ingesting the milk, humans are also susceptible to these health problems.

horse observed, the cows also felt it was the general behavior of humans that was often most upsetting.

So, did the milk cows still have their spirit?

Nancie sighed. "They say, 'Not fully, but there are many humans on the earth who don't have their spirit either.'" At this point, a shift occurred in Nancie's voice as well as a shift in the energy of our conversation.

We are not beings that are able to fully hold our greater self yet, because there's work that needs to be done in order for that grounding to occur. Many of the things now happening in our universe between humans and animals are specifically to show those places that require us to be more conscious so that we can hold more of our consciousness here. It's part of the process of moving into a place where we can experience heaven on earth. We know about this in our cellular system because we planned it. As we become more sensitive to these issues, they point us to the places where we can make corrections and allow more of ourselves to be fully present with one another and in relationship.

"Was that you speaking or the cows?" I asked.

"All of us," Nancie said. "It's all of us."

I was reminded yet again how seamless this magnificent web of life truly is. The message from the cows was about cycles, interactions, being interconnected in a much larger plan. If cows are helping humans to become more aware of honoring the spiritual worth of our food, what is our part? Could it be that we are also helping the cows become more spiritually present in their bodies?

Nancie agreed. "The first thing for us to understand is that the cow spirit is not in their body, and this is why our food chain is doing what it's doing. The cow's purpose is to jog our sensitivity and consciousness. The way they do that is through disease. Unfortunately, right now, many humans only respond to fear or threats. Once we understand the higher perspective of the event, as human caretakers of the earth do, then we are able to assist by changing some of the ways we operate. And once we do that—helping these animals ground more of their spiritual essence into their bodies— it will allow us to do it as well, just by virtue of the fact that we eat them as food."

What an extraordinary plan! As we aid the return of spiritual awareness into the body of cows, or other animals, we gain a deeper understanding of our connection to all life. By ingesting the meat that holds the awakened spiritual essence, we take on deeper spiritual grounding. Eating becomes a truly sacred act. We participate in the giving and taking of life in a much deeper and more consciously connected way. One feeds into another, for what we eat is what we become.

There are some animals who speak of the predator/prey relationship not as a problem but as a dance, a celebration of life partaking of itself. To take in the essence of another animal is to take in the essence of the divine.

One morning, I unexpectedly made contact with an animal spirit who identified herself to me as Kayla, a cat living in the spirit world. Here is what Kayla related:

There is a great deal to be learned from the predator/prey relationship. Many people will be surprised to know that there is a great deal of love in this relationship. There is a spiritual aspect of taking in the essence of another being; there is a trust and an inherent agreement to this relationship, which is not always (or rarely at this point in time) seen by humans.

Most humans have fallen away from and dishonored the contract that is implicit in the predator/prey relationship. As the cows told you, many animals who are slaughtered have chosen not to invest their souls in physical form. And so you are eating dead meat. It is very different than giving chase to a bird, or any animal, and honoring the spirit of the chase, the kill, and the eating of the flesh.

There is the understanding among some human tribes that the eating of the flesh of certain animals, and even humans, endows the eater with that essence. This is part of the truth that "We are all One." For those who study religions, many symbols can be found about eating and drinking of the divine.

There is a spiritual aliveness in the predator/prey relationship. If you are not genuine and do not honor this relationship, then you miss the point, then you fail to see the divine in this dance and fail to partake of the divine as you live in and experience the world.

The predator/prey relationship is a planetary lesson. It is called other things when seen in connection with plants and other living beings and the earth in general. And, in many ways, this is truer to what the relationship is, for when you go beyond "predator/prey," you find it is about exchange, especially the exchange of essences. Sexuality is another aspect of this, for it is about the exchange of vital fluids, vital essences.

There is not a right or wrong to this issue. Rather, the experiencing of all relationships and living through them—feeling the genuine honor of all beings within the dance, whatever their dance may be—is what the lesson is about.

What do prey animals feel when predators make their move? What do predators feel toward their prey? Just what is the interaction that makes up the dance of the predator/prey relationship, and how are both predator and prey honored in this dance?

Nedda Wittels addressed these issues in a four-way conversation she held with

Echo the horse, Violet the cat, and Sunshine, a cat who serves as her barn's "Rat Patrol." Each of the animals offers a unique perspective, as Echo is a natural vegetarian, Violet was once a hunter but now lives indoors and doesn't need to hunt, and Sunshine is an active hunter.

One must eat in order to live. In the wild, horses are hunted by wolves, mountain lions, and other predators. How do you feel about the possibility of being someone else's dinner?

[Echo:] In this lifetime I am protected, but in other lives I've been hunted. Of course, everyone wants to live. We take form for a purpose and want to fulfill that purpose before giving up our bodies. Then, too, the genetics of the physical form contain programming for self-preservation. Still, at a spiritual level we are all connected and we all serve each other. So if I were ever trapped, cornered by meat eaters, I would honor the sacrifice of my body. My spirit is who I really am and will live on.

That sounds very noble. However, doesn't the prey animal feel fear and anger toward the predator?

[Echo:] Fear, certainly, but not anger. Fear is the self-preservation mechanism of the physical form. It makes the body defend itself. However, if the life is requested by the predator for purposes of survival and if the predator shows respect and honors the prey, the offering of one's body for food of another is a great gift.

What form does the honoring take among the animals?

[Echo:] The predator asks something like this:

"Noble being, I am hungry and seek sustenance.
Will you offer yourself to honor me in this way?"

The prey will reply to the effect,

"Noble one, I do offer myself to you with blessings.
May you grow strong through the nourishment of my body."

At what point in the hunt does this conversation take place?

[Echo:] It takes place when the prey is first sighted or during the chase, or even after capture, although usually at the point of capture, the agreement has already been made.

Sunshine, you hunt for a living at the stable where Echo lives. I've seen you take down birds, rabbits, and moles. Does Echo's description of the exchange between predator and prey match your experience as a hunter?

[Sunshine:] Yes. Sometimes I sing a song of honor. I have a different song for each species. Because I never know who is available when I set out to hunt, I wait until I have sighted my prey. Then I sing. Then I attack.

Would you sing one of your songs of honor?

[Sunshine:] Here's my song for hunting rabbits, whom I do love to eat.

Rabbit, noble Rabbit,
Who hops with power and speed,
Honor this hungry Cat with your tasty nourishment.
I thank you for sustaining me through another day.
I send you blessings, love, and light, to you and your family,
That we may all share the Earth together for all of time.

That is certainly a beautiful song. Do the rabbits sing back to you?

[Sunshine:] Sometimes. Some reply more simply.

Humans are often horrified when cats seem to play with their catch. Why do you do that?

[Sunshine:] We don't "play" with it. We do like to show off our catch, and sometimes we toss it about for that purpose. Other times we're practicing our skills. When one depends upon hunting for life, it is important to maintain a clear eye, a steady claw, and a strong pounce.

Violet, you live indoors and don't have to hunt. Still, you enjoy playing with toy mice.

[Violet:] When I was on my own before I came to live with you, I did need to hunt. It was hard finding suitable food in the garbage. My mother never had to hunt, so I had to watch other cats and listen to some of their rituals to know what to do for serious hunting. I had lots of practice with toys, but that's not the same as going after a moving target who is trying to get away.

Did you have any success?

[Violet:] Yes, once I learned to pounce more effectively and speak words of honor. The prey are more willing to sacrifice themselves if you ask them properly and if you hunt with skill. Both are required to succeed.

[Sunshine:] I agree. If I were less polite, I'm sure I would not be so successful. Many times, if a prey animal is old and ready to die, they will still make you work hard if you do not speak to them respectfully. When I was learning to hunt, my mother insisted we remember this. She was an excellent hunter and taught us very well.

[Echo:] Very few humans honor animals and plants at the time they are taken. Many more humans assume that life is here to serve them, but that is not automatically the case. We are here to share the Earth with each other. Plants and animals are both expressions of intelligence and spirit. If humans would ask the animals to make the sacrifice of their bodies, the animals surely would. To take without asking is stealing, and the energy of the food is less nourishing and may even be harmful to the one eating it.

Do animals honor the plants they eat?

[Echo:] Oh, yes. Even though you see us horses diving into our grain buckets or eating grass and hay voraciously, we do indeed say prayers for the food we eat. Here's one my mother taught me:

Spirit of grasses, legumes, shrubs, and vines,
Your sweetness and juices are like fine wines.
I thank you for granting me health and good times,
May your summer be long and lush.

Spirit of grasses, legumes, shrubs, and vines,
I sing to your beauty and bounty divine.
I give thanks and respect for your offering to me,
And bless you with love and light endlessly.

Lions in Africa. Photo by Dawn Brunke.

Part Six

Shadow and Beyond

Purpose
Spirit of Lions ~ Morgine Jurdan

You ask us what our purpose is in the grander scheme of things and we find this amusing. Humans figure each form of life must serve some "purpose," must have some grand role to shape its life and destiny.

Nature—including all animals, insects, weather as you call it (wind, rain, sun, storms)—communicates in ways you cannot understand, at levels you cannot perceive. You try to know us better. Why, we wonder? Because the planet is dying and you would like to learn from us? We are a bit arrogant. You come to us because you desire to save yourselves. If the planet were bigger and had more resources, you might not be asking these questions.

The greatest gift we could give you is to start you looking at yourselves as individuals, to recognize how you, not we, play a part in the overall picture. As you each heal yourself, we are all affected in ways you can't yet imagine.

We lions reside in every heart, as you humans reside in our hearts, in every heart. People do not suffer alone; no one does. We all experience starvation, hunger, pain. We call out to each other for healing and help. We cry out in pain, as one species after another disappears from this dimension, and yet most of you do not hear us. You do not really see us. You do not really know us.

We could tell you our purpose and the meaning would be one dimensional, like looking at a tree on a piece of paper. Instead, we offer you a warning.

Many humans feel they are the apex of evolution, the crowning glory of God's achievements. And yet, you isolate yourselves from the very essence that gives you life. You know not what it is to be a *real human being*, living in harmony with the environment in which you are immersed and from which you are inseparable.

When humans see lions, they think of power, pride, kings. You see us at the top of the pecking order, because you see through your own filters of domination, control, and hierarchy. All the qualities you relegate to us can be seen in a wren or a shrew. When you are willing to truly suffer your greatest sorrow and grieve your greatest loss, only then will you experience your greatest joy and your greatest love.

True healing of the world, of which you are an important part, begins one person at a time. When you love from your heart, every living being on this planet is blessed. The more you love, the more we are blessed. The rest is up to you.

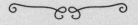

24

Exploring Shadowland

There is much to be gained by walking into the shadow. The shadow is the dark mirror of the soul's consciousness. Instead of the secret of the universe being explained to you by others, you see the secrets of the universe at work in the shadow. This is because the shadow is between light and dark. Think of it as the crypts, the diamond mines, the holiest of the holy where all the secrets are safely stashed.

Lunar

Lunar is an unusual cat who lives with friends Jackie and Brian Rahm. Though I never planned on talking to Lunar, just as I began putting together the shadow section of this book, circumstances arranged for this remarkable cat and I to speak.

Lunar told me he was a "shadow walker," a balance to the "lightheads" who lived with him:

I am a very aware cat, and I move from place to place with speed and agility. I am secretive in this manner. I've had past lives as a black panther and know how to stalk animals, humans, and other beings. I like a challenge. I like the opportunity to sneak up on prey. Part of my nature is to scare and attack. In this sense, I am a balancing act for this family. They are all so light-headed.

I have been a big cat (panther, lion) many times in life. I do not have the tolerance or patience of a house cat. I am most happy roaming, being free. I could tell you some hard lessons about the nature of freedom, ones not all lightheads want to hear.

I am not what you would call malicious, but I crave the shadow; I love to brush up against its darkness. The richness of that is quite extraordinary for me. This is not to say I am dark or evil; rather, I enjoy the shadowy realm that lies between light and dark.

When I asked Lunar if he would contribute to this book, he offered the following "treatise on the shadow." I commented this was great timing because I was working on the shadow chapters. In an amused tone, Lunar responded, "Not much is happenchance."

Lunar. Photo by Jackie Rahm.

On the nature of the shadow, I invoke the shade of the panther moving furtively, creeping, sneaking, waiting, listening in the jungle. That is the nature of living with the shadow. The shadow holds what is repressed and feared. As such, it is feared. It takes a courageous and cunning animal to walk into and among the shadows, to make Shadowland its home. This is the nature of some cats.

I want to emphasize to humans that this has nothing to do with honor or bravery. No, it is a much more feminine, feline aspect, to be at home in the shadow. It is the dark, red blood flowing in the bowels of the earth; it is the nature of rubbing up against the energy of rage, violence, unleashed emotions; it is to wait and watch in the nearness of madness.

If you glance into Shadowland, you might think it vast, unfathomable. In truth, it is a razor's edge—that is the path through Shadowland and the nature of shadow itself. Shadow looks deep, but it is more like a screen, the way an actual shadow reveals itself in the physical world of your reality.

I do not recommend venturing into Shadowland unless you go with an accomplished guide. It is dangerous and many people have no business being there. And yet, it is important that some understand and embody the shadow, for that is the nature of this world.

I find the shadow a fascinating place, for it holds the roots of all varieties of consciousness. As such, telepathists need to be familiar with the shadow in order to truly see and hear, and to honor those who tread there. If it weren't for the shadow walkers, the lightheads would have trouble staying on the planet. The shadow walkers provide the grounding and gravity necessary so that others can explore the light. In the same way, the presence of the lightheads allows for the shadow walkers to explore that realm without being sucked into the depths of darkness.

The truth is that we are all One. No one can say this enough, for even as many times as you hear it, it must be drummed into you until it finds a home, that place somewhere between and beyond the light and dark, where all is truly One.

Part of the problem with Lunar and his family was that Lunar loved to roam. He had gotten himself into trouble on several occasions, and Jackie was becoming frustrated with worry. Though Lunar expressed a desire to stay with his family, he also stated to Jackie, "It would be much more harmonious if you could open your mind and heart to understanding me, as I am just as much a part of you as anything else. I am not interested in changing you, only in showing you the suchness of who I am, which is also you. When you insist I stay inside, that is *you* doing *you*. When you fear that I will run away or be caught by the authorities—okay, you figure it out."

Lunar proposed that Jackie accompany him on an evening stalking adventure to learn more. Jackie, however, was hesitant. "I can feel my resistance," she told me. "I honor his shadow side, but why does it have to involve me? I've simply made different choices, such as being a 'lighthead' as he puts it. I see myself going off with him only to have him leave me as he goes about doing what he pleases."

"This is full of fear at work," replied Lunar. "If you hold the belief that I will leave, then that pathway is there for me to run off and make fun of you."

Though Jackie had first proposed finding a win/win situation for Lunar and herself, in a later discussion she broached the idea of compromise. At this, Lunar began to laugh. "Compromise for a cat?" he asked. "Compromise is not win/win, is it? The answer is not compromise. The answer is walking through 'What Is' with your self intact."

"What does that mean?" I asked.

"It is to act out of your deeper beliefs, not out of panic or compromise so that everything seems to be hunkydory with your superficial beliefs."

"But Lunar," I said, "Jackie has a point about not wanting you to get hurt and not wanting to spend money to bail you out of Animal Control."

"It is my life," replied Lunar, with a cutting tinge of amused arrogance, a tone that perhaps only a certain type of cat can truly pull off. "I am not naïve or uneducated. This issue is about trust, not only for Jackie to trust me, but to trust her own self."

After further contemplation and discussion with Lunar, Jackie related, "It is becoming clearer to me as I work with Lunar that he is his own being. I don't own him. We can't own sentient life. In fact, I've decided to disown him. He is welcome to sleep and eat here, to curl up with us, but he is free is to do as he pleases. As he indicates, he is highly intelligent and will do what he wants. I think this is a very important lesson about the animals. They are evolving beings and have their own agendas and experiences to play out."

In a desire to further understand the workings of shadow, Jackie wondered how it fit with the consensus among consciousness raisers that we are moving into the light, transmuting darker, denser energies into lighter vibrational frequencies of joy and love.

"To negate the shadow is to negate a part of ourselves, yet don't we need to live consciously in ways that honor the light in order to return home?" asked Jackie. "Is the current emphasis on light just our exploration of the other end of the spectrum? Are you saying that it's not about living in either aspect but on the edge of both?"

"Jackie has a lot of questions," I commented to Lunar. "How should we proceed?"

Words, words, words. Lots of words and picking things apart. The shadow cannot be understood in that way.

I sighed. It was the same refrain I heard from Zak when he told me that if I really wanted to know something I would have to let go of thoughts and words, my favorite defense against experience.

The world is a complex meeting of light and dark. There is a snobbery among the lightheads who believe that light is somehow better than dark. Even the idea that all is evolving to light is a judgment against the dark.

Dark is. Light is. Shadow is the interplay between the two, both in manifest reality and in the spiritual sense. To enter shadow is to enter into all that is unresolved and unclear. Shadow is the place one meets the deeper nature of oneself.

I feel the lightheads would like to pass this by when they say it is just a "stage" and that all will become light. That is to deny the existence of shadow. That is light reassuring itself that it is right. Dark does the same thing.

On another level, the frequency of light *does* exist in a different way. This is complex, and human language is limited.

[Pause.] Would you like an experience?

It is difficult to put into words exactly what happened, for the experience was primarily feeling based. To start, there were waves of feelings, each associated with an image, shape, pattern, sound, tone, and countless variations thereof. I sensed how I could go deeper into any variation and find something completely new and whole, as each was a world of experience unto itself. Incredibly, I found I could also explore a number of the worlds simultaneously.

Lunar commented that while in our normal reality humans needed the contrast of feelings, other realities could be experienced as a unification of feelings. Indeed, in my experience feelings were distinguished by levels or vibrations rather than polar contrasts. I felt this first as a subtle difference, yet one that effected a great shift in awareness. Lunar pointed out that though the "realities" were the same, the experiences were different. "That is how it is with light and dark," he said.

Reviewing the experience, I shook my head, not sure I was understanding it.

That is because it is not a mental process; it is emotional. One of the final tests is deleting the need to understand.

The world is shifting quickly into shadow. There will be many tests regarding the judgment of shadow, of the lights judging the darks and vice versa. Let go of the notion that all is becoming light. Not all wants to become light.

Perhaps the better word vibration is love, though there again humans have so many judgments on love: true love, bad love, dysfunctional love. If you could let go of words and categories, if each of you could just follow your own vibrational energy, you would be fine.

As Lunar continued to share information about the shadow, I asked about his earlier comment that Shadowland was dangerous. What I took this to mean was that we should perhaps prepare ourselves, not simply entering Shadowland on whim, as if an amusement park.

An interesting comparison. There is much about Shadowland that is thrilling and it is true that amusement parks, especially carnivals and such, do hold the element of shadow within their confines. We might also remark that Shadowland is a traveling place, not tied to physicality in the traditional sense.

Entering this "land" does require some preparation and serious intent. Just as a human would not climb Denali without prior training, one might consider some inner training for entering Shadowland. Then again, you may not be conscious of your training. Those who live in dysfunctional, abusive relationships, for example, are constantly training and learning to work with shadow.

My comment about Shadowland being dangerous was to imply that it is not for innocents, though there again, an innocent sits on a huge clump of shadow. At certain levels, all of this is interrelated. Again, this picking apart of information is, at a certain point, not helpful.

To explore the richness of what shadow offers, we open to a larger experience. We expand ourselves to include not only light and dark, but also the contradictions these polarities hold. We realize that shadow material is not always big and monstrous; sometimes, shadow is small and insidious. It can appear quite innocent, couched in ritual, social courtesies, or habit. Moreover, what is shadow material to one may not be shadow to another. It is such tricky territory. There are no hard and fast rules in Shadowland.

As Lunar notes:

At this time, the shadow offers an awakening to All That Is. This is not to say that following the light or dark are not honorable paths. Each has its own teachings.

I do not believe that all becomes light, nor that all becomes dark. I hold that the so-called battle between good and evil is a division of the self, a way of resolving (or denying) what is gray. In some ways, this battle is against shadow itself, because to pit light against dark is to proclaim that life is one or the other. In this way, the battle is a defense against shadow.

Shadow is what is disowned and unclear. Shadow resides at the interstices of culture and the individual. For this reason, shadow holds the key to the fullness of who we are, especially at this point in time, wrapped as we are, on this planet, in duality.

What I offer to humans is a deepening, a chance to behold more of the fullness of who you are, as well as the fullness of all creation on this planet. Earth is a remarkable place where the extremes of many polarities are played with and learned from. It is my experience that shadow, as the edge between the two, offers a unique place for explorers to discover the underlying energy of both light and dark, thus revealing a fuller appreciation of All That Is.

It is not my feeling that everyone should explore shadow. For some it is not necessary; for others it is dangerous. Who can say what life needs which teachings when, other than your own?

I extend my thanks to those who are willing to peer beneath easily explained paradigms of thought. For those who are up for an adventure, I offer my services. It is not for everyone. But, for those who hear the call, I welcome you in and beyond.

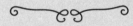

Balance
Animal Spirits (group) ~ Diana Roth

Stop trying to heal the planet and everybody on it. Heal yourself and work to maintain your center and balance. Then everything else will fall into place. Work in your community to better it for all souls, especially the youngest and the oldest. And respect the boundaries of all things and their right to live on Earth.

25

Animal Spirits:
Talks with Coyote, Jaguar, and Crow

Diana Roth has spoken with animals ever since she can remember. In 1997, Diana, a retired chemist for the state of Florida, became the human link to a unique web page maintained entirely by animal spirits.[1] "It is important that people know the site has been built by the animals," said Diana. "I open up and they talk; they control everything. This is really their work, not mine. My relationship with them is one of absolute trust and connection."

When I first approached Diana about interviewing some animal spirits for this book, she said that while they expressed joy in the project, she was not sure which ones would speak. "This is part of the trust," she explained, "trust in them to provide the information needed at any given time."

"Why do you think the animals chose you?" I asked.

"They say they chose me because I don't ask them why they want me to do certain things. The animals were adamant that the site be worldwide and not just have animals from North America. It was not to have a human presence and, most important, the information was to be free to all who asked. The site exists to empower people to walk their paths with Spirit/God."

The animal spirits chose three animals to speak in this chapter. The interviews were conducted at different times via an Internet program allowing messages to travel instantaneously. Though I was sending questions from Alaska and Diana was sending the animal spirits' response from Florida, our mutual conversation went back and forth as fast as each of us could type. I was amazed at times to read a few words of the response and suddenly be clued into thoughts and feelings that also seemed to be part of the message. Take it as yet another interconnected sign of our times.

COYOTE: ON DROPPING THE MASK

The first animal to talk was Yotee, a coyote spirit. As Diana told me, "Many people think of coyote as a buffoon always chasing his tail, but he has far deeper wisdom than that." And with that simple introduction, Yotee began:

I try to get people to look at the humor in themselves, not to take themselves so seriously—especially when they are doing "spiritual" work. You can have fun too. The main thing I try to teach is that all you have to do is open up. Trust yourself and you will receive all you need to know from Spirit or God, or whatever name you call the Big Gal/Guy.

No set of people deserves to have knowledge any more than any other set. Knowledge is a gift from the universe and available to all. It is easy to get the knowledge, too: all you have to do is open up and receive it. But humans are so busy making this hard that they just can't seem to trust themselves enough to do it.

So, I try and break down this barrier with my antics. Hardly anyone sees this, but I have hope. What I teach is that everything is sacred, yet nothing is sacred.

Are you the spirit of one coyote or coyote as a species?

I am one coyote spirit, but I am connected to all coyote spirits like a web.

Can you speak more about your belief that humor makes it easier for people to open up?

Humor makes people less uptight and more able to receive things. They aren't thinking very hard when they are laughing, and the barriers that they put up aren't so strong.

Everything is connected to everything else, thanks to Grandmother Spider, who wove the web of the universe that way. All energy is connected. We are all vibrational energy and each has unique energy. That is how we recognize each other without eyes—by vibration.

What is your perspective on the earth changes?

The earth is always changing. She is part of the web, just like you and me. But she is very big and when she changes, it causes big ripples.

The earth changes are part of the ebb and flow of all things; they need to be looked at with a sense of wonder instead of fear. When things die, they come back. Souls never die. And everything has a soul—rocks and plants and you and me, so nothing is truly lost.

This is really not about earth changes but about faith—faith that all happens as it should. Things will be okay. Who lives and who dies isn't important. What is important is the treatment of all life on earth now.

This has more to do with the soul of each person than humankind as a whole. It would be better for people to watch the cycles that are happening now, how the earth is adjusting herself. It is not a sad thing. It is about lessons and growth of souls. We are approaching new levels.

What about you, Yotee? Did you used to be a real coyote?

Yes, I was "real" once and will be again. I am teaching now. I am just a regular coyote . . . no college or anything.

In human mythology, coyote is often portrayed as a trickster.

Yes. I trick people into revealing themselves. I also drop masks and teach others how to see through masks.

By tricking people into a situation, they come to find other aspects of themselves?

Yes. They are forced to drop the mask they were wearing and put on another one. And in that brief time between masks you can get a glimpse of the real person. To do this, you must sit quietly and watch. This requires that the person let go of their ego and trust himself or herself. This is a much deeper thing than the mask. So, I just keep going deeper and deeper into teaching people how to look at themselves. I am sneaky that way.

What is the relationship between the trickster coyote, coyote spirit, and physical coyotes?

The trickster coyote is a myth about me. As for coyotes being sneaky, we are very smart, for we have learned how to live with you humans, haven't we? Everybody is always talking about wolves and how cool wolves are and everybody loves wolves—wolves, wolves, wolves. . . .But look at how many wolves there are compared with yotees! We have watched from the edge and learned your tricks and used them for our betterment. We have continued to spread everywhere. Forgive me about the wolves but I have had it up to my ears with them.

Is there a special message you'd like included in this book?

Just that knowledge is free and available for all who learn how to connect to it. There are lessons to be learned in how a person uses that knowledge for the good of all and how people use their personal power in general. Guess that is it.

Thanks for talking, Yotee.

You are welcome. I enjoyed it too.

JAGUAR: ON DARKNESS

I work in the darkness. Darkness is the same as shadow. To be balanced, one must be able to walk in both worlds, light and dark. Darkness is like light. I can see in the darkness and humans can learn to see there too. There are roads and eddies and swirls in the darkness. If humans can overcome their fear and walk in the darkness, they will meet lessons that their soul is supposed to learn during their earthwalk.

When you speak of darkness, do you mean the shadows of our consciousness, our fears? Or is there an actual place that is darkness?

It is both. I will try and explain. The shadows of our consciousness are actual places, but in other dimensions. These places are real, but are not accessed in real time. They are accessed in what you call altered time.

Our fears are lessons not learned from other times and places. They are sometimes kept in the darkness so we don't have to look at them. That is why the dark scares us—not for what is there naturally, but for what we put there ourselves.

So, the "earthwalk" is between the light and dark place?

Yes, it's in the middle, but they are all equally real. When we are in the light place, it is real. When we are in the earthwalk place, it feels real. And the same with the darkness place. All are real.

Reality is where our consciousness is?

Exactly! Where our soul is. Our soul makes reality. Darkness is just another place among many. But humans have lost the knowledge of this and now fear it. They are constantly wondering why they don't feel balanced. Why? Because they have chopped off the other half of the balance.

I work with people to learn to see in darkness, in chaos. Chaos is where energy is forming. It can be confusing when one gets there at first.

When you are helping others in darkness, what do you teach?

I have them sit on the ground and I sit next to them, so they can touch me. We watch the darkness until they can see how it is flowing. It takes practice and we do it for a while, but they begin to see what looks like rivers, and then they begin to feel the rivers flowing. They are really vibrational patterns. That is how you see there—by feeling vibrational patterns. You don't see with your eyes there.

Then they become able to see souls and other things. There are souls there for various reasons. Some are learning like we are; some are lost and scared. I work with them and lead them out.

Is that your main objective: to help others accept fear and see their own dark places?

Yes. It is very important for humans to understand the lesson that fear is teaching.

Can you tell us about yourself? For example, did you once live on this plane?

I am a black jaguar. I move back and forth. Sometimes I'm here in real time;

most of the time I'm a guide in other worlds. Sometimes I like to be in the forest, so I come for a life. Everything moves back and forth, even stones, sand, and air. Everything that is energy can move back and forth. But time span for some, like planets, is much longer than the life of a bee.

Are jaguars in the forest doing this same type of work?

Yes.

You are in communication with them?

Yes. I can communicate with everything. Pictures form in my head, thoughts form too.

What do you look like in spirit form?

I look like a ball of light, but when I come to humans I look like a jaguar. Each ball of light has a unique energy or vibrational pattern, so you can tell it is me that way.

Jaguars often figure in dreams. Are those aspects of you too? Oh! I just remembered a dream where jaguar came to me! I had forgotten that until just now. It was a black jaguar, and there was the element of transformation associated with him.

Yes. Transformation, understanding darkness. I can shapeshift. I like the dreamworld. Because I am a ball of light, I can be any shape I want in the mind of others. I can show by dreams what is happening in the other worlds.

I'm surprised I forgot how powerful that dream was.

But you remembered when you needed to. I plant seeds in minds and wait for them to sprout.

In my dream, a jaguar walked out of the jungle. I was in a house in which a door opened to the jungle. I knew the jaguar was out there, so it was my choice whether to open the door. I opened it to allow the jaguar in. I was a bit fearful, but it felt right. That speaks to me about waiting for the right time—gathering up courage, but also accepting the challenge in just the right moment.

Yes, you must have courage and trust yourself that you aren't making it up. It is an important message for humans: to trust yourselves more and pay attention to others less.

Humans who understand the shadow can do this, for they have faced fear and learned courage. Self-doubt comes from fear. Fear must be faced. No amount of money or position can keep humans from learning about shadow. It is like learning about other things, no worse.

Self-doubt comes from fear of what? Not trusting yourself? Or not trusting your own power, which is to say the power of the divine within?

Both. If you trust yourself, you have power. Personal power comes from trust of your own soul and courage to walk your talk.

Doubt comes from ego. Ego doesn't like it when things are not his way. If he can make you doubt, then you won't pay attention to your soul because you will be scared of the doubt. Ego always protects ego and nothing else. Fear of God, too, is from ego—using his "what ifs." When you feel the God power within, then ego loses control.

Self-doubt is the ego's way of defending against loss of control?

Yes.

Does ego exist in the spirit world?

Yes, I have ego. Ego is a protection for all. He will protect when necessary, but will also run amok if allowed to.

Ego is a barometer of sorts?

Yes. But many humans don't understand that. Ego is like anything that is out of balance—it takes over everything else if it is allowed to. You understand this very well.

Many animals have been helping me to understand. Is there another message you would like to give?

No. I have said it all. I just want humans to understand darkness and shadow and ego a little better.

Thank you, Jaguar.

CROW: ON FINDING LOST SOULS

I am crow. I work with souls. I move from the soul world to this world easily. I go between time. Sometimes younger souls get lost here and have a hard time letting go of this world and going back home to the soul world. I go in and they ride on my wings back. I also work with souls that are damaged.

A lot of people say they have soul retrievals these days, that souls get fractured off the main soul and can be lost. While this can happen, it is very rare. Most of the time, the person will put a part of their soul away—like putting something in a box in the closet. Then they don't have to deal with the part of themselves they don't like.

I can see in those boxes. I know where their soul parts are hidden, and I can get them out of the boxes. You see when part of the soul is in the box, it is very scared and sad, and that is why the whole soul is unbalanced and uncentered. When people look at that part of the soul and deal with the problem, they feel renewed. But that part of the soul wasn't broken off; it was just put away.

You feel people would rather believe their soul is lost or stolen so they don't have to deal with accepting that part of themselves?

Yes, exactly. It is easier to see the soul as breaking off and getting lost.

I know a parrot who is friend to some crows. They help her to find lost animals. Is this one of the traits of crow: to help locate lost animals or souls?

Yes. I can find them because I see their souls. That is how I know the individual animal. Each soul has a different vibration or signature, and I can see it.

Have you been a crow in this world?

Yes. I sometimes come in earth time. It is fun to fly and feel the wind on my feathers. I like the wind. I can shapeshift too, become other animals, take their form. But that is easy; lots of animals can do that.

Is the reason for shapeshifting primarily to get another perspective?

Yes. You are good at understanding this. I sometimes need to see out of another's eyes.

What is the main thing you would like to tell humans?

To stop boxing up your fears and making those parts of your souls so very lonely and sad.

How would you advise us to be more open with our fears?

To understand that fear is an unlearned lesson and address it that way. To look at the face of the fear and see what it is trying to teach you. To say you are afraid of something lets you put it in that box and not deal with it.

A boxing up of one's fear equals a boxing up of one's self?

Yes, and the soul can't learn what it is supposed to learn. I work very narrowly with souls, taking them home, and deboxing them.

Can you tell us more about your home in the spirit world?

I call it the place before existence. It is where the lights are. All souls are lights—tiny lights. And there are unformed energies there too, like star matter. There is no time. It is very beautiful.

Other than finders of lost souls, aren't crows also messengers?

Yes. I tell people about their boxes. I try and remind them what they are supposed to do here. I give them hints about things that will happen, to help them remember their game plan.

The game plan of why we came here, for this life?

Yes. Owl does that too, more than I do.

What about the relation of crow to raven—do you have similar messages?

Very similar. We are brothers and do the same work. We both work with wolves and other animals when they hunt. It is fun. We are like families.

Wolves? How do crows and wolves work together?

We all are together in the spirit world. People like wolves, so they are teachers; we work in the background.

Do you mean wolves are the attention getters because humans are enamoured of wolves right now?

Yes. Who will pay attention to a crow? The wolves come so we can get in there and do the work. It helps us.

How do the wolves feel about being human attention bait?

They don't like it. Not many of them come here now. Wolves have sort of retired. They feel they have taught their lesson.

Humans are confused. They aren't learning their lessons very well. The wolf has decided to step back and let others work with humans. Tigers too. Both of these animals may leave earth, as others have done. They feel this may cause man to become angry at their attitude toward animals. But that is for wolf and tiger to talk about.

Many humans would be saddened by the extinction of an animal species.

That is the point: they can't be gotten back once they leave. So, it will save others from the same fate.

Would you speak more about the association of crow and speech? For example, how do you speak with humans?

I am very smart. I can understand them and form thoughts in their minds. They feel either scared of me or love me, but I talk mind to mind. Soul to soul, I touch souls with my words.

Do you help humans shapeshift too, perhaps in their dreams?

Yes, I help them become me. Actually, I surround them and they see through my eyes. I fly with them. Through my eyes, they can see the boxes and souls of others, where soul parts are hidden. Then they can help people take them out of the boxes and begin the healing. Shapeshifting is always done for a reason, always to learn a lesson or to understand healing.

Humans sometimes have great dreams of flying or seeing in new ways, and even though we are inspired by that, we may negate it later. Can you speak about moving from disbelief to trusting our experiences, honoring them and sharing them with others? It seems like a big job!

Yes, it is. It takes great courage to trust your inner voice. It is easier to negate it than to deal with it. Dismissing messages is an easy way to get rid of them, a lazy way.

We need courage both to trust our inner voice and speak it to others.

Yes. To walk your talk is not an easy thing to do.

I tend to think that is common among humans—to dismiss the inner voice, hoping it will go away or wasn't there to begin with.

Right, put it in a box and hide it. Then a poor, tired old crow has to come and help out!

So, you are asking us to reclaim our boxes.

Exactly!

I just thought of the old crows in the film, Dumbo. *When they first meet Dumbo, the crows give him a feather and tell him it is magic so that he will believe he can fly. That is a funny truth, isn't it? We are all looking for our magic feather so that we can fly.*

Yes, that easy magic feather!

All the animals are really saying the same thing, aren't they? Trust yourself, see the divine, be the divine . . . grow up and fly! Not to diminish any animal's medicine, but underneath it all, you are all pointing us to the same place.

It is all the same message, just wrapped in a different package so understanding can come from many directions to the same place. It all goes to one place. The many paths lead to greater complexity of the soul.

Thank you, Crow. I look forward to flying tonight, to sharing the dream.

See you then.

A Different Point of View
Mosquito Being ~ Morgine Jurdan

Humans often feel that the world resides at the tips of their fingers and they can manipulate it as they see fit. We serve to show humankind that even something as small as a mosquito can be mighty beyond measure. This can annoy you, though it might also inspire you, such as when you feel you cannot make a difference in the world. We serve to remind humans of vulnerability.

We have come from another place into this dimension. We were called here to serve a purpose in the balance of Nature and its inhabitants. We were needed: our energy, love, and being. We filled a hole that wanted to be filled.

We journey between dimensions and go in and out of different realities. We take different shapes in the different places we visit. If you visited those other places, you would not recognize us. We live in the past and present, and you will find us in your future too. When we are no longer needed, we will leave.

Human beings often hate what they do not understand. If you do not understand it and it annoys you, you attempt to control or destroy it. Your solutions to problems often revolve around killing, be it plants, insects, animals, or humans. We do not feel this is what love is all about.

Our message is to see things from a different point of view. Each one of us—no matter how small or large—has a part to play in the scheme of things. Begin to trust that there is more to the world than you can understand in a lifetime.

We hope that some day you can appreciate things for what they are, regardless of your understanding. Unconditional love, pure and simple, does not require explanations, judgments, or defenses. It stands alone.

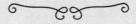

2 6

The Mosquito Story

Once upon a time, a little mosquito told me an outlandish story. On the surface, it was runaway science fiction: an intriguing yet disturbing tale of scientists from another world, human DNA mutations, insect creators, and a multidimensional portal. I asked myself: What did I do to become the recipient of such an incredible tale?

The reason I heard the story was partly my doing in the first place, the patient mosquito pointed out later on. Sitting on the porch under warm spring sunshine, feeling pretty fine with myself for integrating all sorts of animal messages, I carelessly tossed out the question, "Well now, what else could weird me out?"

Whilst trudging through the outskirts of shadow country, I have been warned time and again, "Be careful what you ask." The warning stems from the idea that thoughts are things, and that by requesting certain information, you may just get what you ask for in reply.

The little mosquito darted in front of me with a persistent, lively, high pitched humming. The image of a large mosquito encased in amber, as depicted in the film *Jurassic Park*, came to mind.

We are not part of the animal kingdom in the same way others you have been talking to are. You would like for me to fit within your Web of Life scenario and explain myself and my species, but it is more difficult than you imagine.

Yes, we have been here for a very long time. But we were different then. We were bigger. We have gone through many changes, and have existed—and even now exist—in realities you are not consciously aware of.

A second image formed in my mind of a beautiful glade, green and sun-dappled. The setting seemed to be of King Arthur times, when legends and magic still infused the forests of England. Within the interplay of sunlight and shadows, fairy creatures were flitting about. And there, among the fairies, were large mosquitoes with fairy wings.

A large bundle of thoughts and sensations caused me to realize that in this forest reality, the mosquitoes were creators, responsible for designing new and different creatures. The way they did this was through blood and, more specifically, through the arrangement of DNA.

"We have always been linked with blood and DNA," affirmed the mosquito as I saw two worlds existing side by side, or perhaps two dimensions of reality superimposed, separated by what resembled a one-way mirror. On one side of the mirror were inhabitants of planet earth as we know it. On the other side of the mirror were alien beings. They sat at a display panel in a manner suggesting they have long conducted experiments on our world.

Alien beings? I half-laughed and asked if I was understanding the image correctly, for the sense-thought was that the alien scientists were observing us and experimenting in much the same way that some humans observe and experiment upon animals. Further, the sense was that the mosquitoes sometimes served as the physical tools whereby these otherworldly scientists tested human blood.

Exactly! Every drop of blood we take in can be computed by the others. You may think of them as scientists who lack emotion, though they are also connected with a lost civilization on your planet. Their race has gone through tremendous change and they are dying.

I sighed. *This is exactly what you get for watching "The X-Files" way too often,* I told myself with irritation, and promptly changed the subject.

Are all mosquitoes as talkative as you?

No. I am responding to your desire to know more about our race. We are not what you think we are. We are much more than you see. Part of our group lives in other dimensional worlds.

Another bundle of information bloomed in my mind, revealing that mosquitoes not only communicate among themselves but also with their species on other planets and dimensions. I grasped the notion that most mosquitoes keep the same species form for many lifetimes, that many have agreed to be part of the mosquito group for a period of time, and that they are quite cohesive as a group in this service, not emphasizing the individual soul as humans tend to do.

I sighed again. In fact, I probably groaned. Judgment was cracking through the forefront of consciousness, wildly protesting that this story was just too strange. The mosquito, however, wasn't ready to stop.

There will be a change in the mosquitoes' role when humans meet the alien scientists. By waking up in this way—coming face to face with the other—both humans and aliens will learn to incorporate a highly mental and scientific aspect of self with a greater emotional and spiritual body.

That is the answer the others have been looking for all along. They thought they could understand your emotional body by studying your makeup. This is like

The Mosquito Story · 235

thinking you can understand how an animal works by dissecting its body. When you do things like that, you are like the alien scientists stealing blood from animals to understand emotions. It is not a match, a noncompute. And yet you keep trying.

When you learn how to use your emotional bodies, especially in relation to creation, you will be able to help the others. There is humor in the situation because some of you believe the others are here to help you. More than you realize, you will also help the others. It is all a matter of releasing us from this drama, these veiled roles, so that we can evolve into a much clearer expression of who we truly are.

What will the mosquitoes do then?

Perhaps we will move to another planet or dimension. Our stay here was much longer than originally anticipated. As a group, we would like more creative endeavors again. The fairy mosquitoes you saw are also an aspect of our greater being. Perhaps we will go to a planet where there is not much life and begin a new creation.

Consider how any animal comes into being on this planet. For example, we are born in and near water, and then we live our lives in the air. We are "betwixt and between" creatures. That is what we do in our job on earth. We serve between species, between layers of reality and dimensions.

Humans could learn quite a bit about animals by simply observing what they do, how they live, and how they come into existence. We are all living symbols of how our individual spirit manifests—and, how Spirit manifests.

Thank you for listening and opening yourself to other possibilities. Remember that this is only a small part of the whole. Think of this as a fiction if you prefer. You may not want to include us in the animal book, but perhaps you could write a story about us. We are not so concerned about context. We would only like that the word go out.

And with that, the little mosquito was gone.

I did not know what to do with the mosquito's story, for the implications were far beyond my comfort zone. Best to do as the little mosquito advised, and consider it a fiction.

But even as a fiction, the particulars of the story bothered me. If we receive the messages we do because they match what we need to hear, what did this story reflect to me? Why the story of alien beings? Why not a nice light-filled message about spirituality and planetary evolution? I began to sulk. What kind of shadow material was playing with me?

In an attempt to understand, I jotted down associations and patterns, reviewing the story as if it were a dream. A preliminary sketch of its symbolic composition gave me plenty to ponder.

For example, the mosquito's initial disclaimer that they are different from other animals indicates the material offered is likely to be unusual and special—both an exception and exceptional.

The surface connection of mosquitoes to blood is obvious, as any mosquito bite attests. The specific link with DNA, however, indicates that the deeper mystery of blood as a creative force is to be explored. This connects to the role of mosquitoes as creators of new creatures (as expressed in the fairylike setting) and as intermediaries and recreators (as expressed in shorthand by the *Jurassic Park* image).* The mosquito link to the ancient past indicates a timeless quality to their species.

The image of two worlds separated by a "one-way mirror" reveals issues of duality and separation—further portrayed through the pairing of opposites: human/alien; earth/other world; known/unknown. That the mirror is one way indicates a seeming inequality between the worlds.

The correlation of alien scientists experimenting upon humans to humans experimenting upon animals is perhaps a projection of cultural guilt. The alien scientists (further described as lacking emotion) might reflect our societal "inner scientist," emotionally disconnected from the psyche and web of life. That the aliens engage in scientific experimentation (as opposed to war or planetary takeover) indicates a desire for knowledge (as opposed to destruction). However, also apparent is the shadow element of rationalization as both alien and human scientists justify their "rights" over harming others in order to gain that knowledge.

That mosquitoes are portrayed as the tools whereby blood is analyzed reinforces their role as intermediaries, again linking them to the penetrating mystery of blood. However, further characterization of mosquitoes as "not what you think" and "more than you see" indicates that deeper knowledge cannot be gained by mere thinking or seeing. A jump of some sort will be involved.

According to the mosquito, realization of a greater plan will occur when humans meet the aliens. Presumably, what was formerly separated—worlds, species, aspects of consciousness—will begin a dialogue in which information is exchanged. The end result is a clarity of vision: veils are dropped and all are released from their roles in the drama, including mosquitoes.

---

*The novel by Michael Crichton portrays mosquitoes as unique holders of the past, for it is from the blood of a mosquito encased in amber that dinosaur DNA is extracted and used to re-create living dinosaurs.

The mosquito's parting observation that humans can learn much by simply observing reminds us that the answer to any question we have is always here, right in front of us, if only we have the desire—and courage—to see.

Though the brief analysis helped me gain an intellectual handle on the story, emotionally I was back at square one. It was a familiar pattern: just as I reached one level of trusting myself, I was dashed back down to the chasm of self-doubt and uncertainty.

As I sat on the porch, full of frustration, Zak walked by and plopped himself in front of me, looking directly into my eyes. I laughed. God, I loved this dog!

What about the mosquito's story, Zak? Is it real?

In the greater scheme of things, what the mosquito told you is really not so strange. There are currently many beings on this planet who come from many different places. Often what you see is only one aspect of these beings.

My opinion on the mosquito is that you are hearing one side of the story. It is not the total story, though the mosquito was telling you a truth and attempting to explain a lot in a small space of time.

You must remember that asking any animal about their species is going to be a limited view. Say another presence made contact with you personally and asked about the history of Earth. How much could you convey? What if it just asked about the history of your life? How much could you explain?

It is true that many animals in spirit form or other realms of consciousness are able to give much more compatible information to you, for they are able to see what fits your framework. Generally speaking, the more general the question and vague the answer, the easier it is for you to swallow. This is not a criticism, merely an observation.

Zak's observation made sense. If the mosquito had spoken more generally—saying something like, "We come from other dimensions and work by interfacing between species"—the message probably would not be at issue now.

So, what's the mosquito's role in all of this?

The mosquito being you spoke with is a very aware representative of the mosquito kingdom. The story you were given in terms of aliens, scientists, and especially the issue of manipulation and control is true, though it is not the full story. The mosquito was attempting to convey this to you, but you jumped into some degree of judgment and self-awareness, questioning if and how you might relate this to others.

You didn't know your life would become an open book with this, did you?

On a more serious note, there is one point to clarify. We might speak about being "invaded" by others (and aliens are always *others*—whether from different countries, planets, or species; aliens are simply unintegrated aspects of the self), but there is always a gateway where consciousness allows this to occur. From one perspective, it can look as if one species is invading and persecuting another. And that is a reality. However, I would encourage you and all readers to look underneath any scenario that is playing itself out as an "invasion." Realize that there truly are many realities—many of which are superimposed, one upon another and one within another.

Zak then flashed me the image of a painting by Salvador Dali with which I was only vaguely familiar. It showed a young child lifting up the edge of the ocean, peering beneath the surface. (The unlikely title, I later discovered, is *Dali, at the Age of Six When He Believed Himself to Be a Young Girl, Lifting the Skin of the Water to Observe a Dog Sleeping in the Shadow of the Sea.*)

Let us just say that the mosquito is painting a very vivid picture for you, though it is one of many realities. The mosquito is showing you one version of reality as played on the sci-fi channel. Within this framework, the mosquito understands that mosquitoes are in service to the "aliens"—or, an aspect of the human species not yet integrated. This is not to say you integrate the aliens in a literal sense; rather, you integrate the aspect of consciousness they reflect to you.

The mosquito alluded to this gateway by saying that when humans awaken, meet the aliens, and begin to teach them, just as humans are taught by the aliens, then an understanding—an integration—occurs. The mosquitoes are then freed from their role. Their part in the drama is done and they are free to leave the stage.

With that, Zak got up to leave. "Only one aspect of the whole," he reminded me.

Zak left me with plenty to think about. The following day, back on the porch, I asked if he'd talk more about why we get the particular types of messages we do.

The example of the sci-fi channel is a good place to begin. Let's say the reception of messages comes from the television (though we could also say reception comes from the brain). The channel is the program (or consciousness filter) through which you see the projection and watch the show. Take a historical figure—say Queen Victoria.

What an odd figure to choose! Why her?

She was funny. She tried so hard to say she wasn't amused that she refused to see her own humor and thus became an example of repressed humor.

I had the sneaking suspicion that Zak was having a good joke at my expense.

To continue, the history channel will present one aspect of the queen, perhaps focusing on her political ruling; the arts and entertainment channel will present another aspect, perhaps her love life; and the sci-fi channel will present yet another aspect, how she had alien advisors, for example.

You're joking with me about the aliens!

Yes. The alien scenario for you isn't so much one of disbelief as it is tied up with the issue of "How will others see me?" You are afraid others will discount you or other messages you present if you include this one. That is *your* fear—that is how it is being played out in the television program you are producing right now. Understand? That does not make it any more or less real than any other show. The fear is simply an ego attachment of how you believe others see you.

The issue of aliens is one that applies to everyone right now. It is not so much about the existence of aliens but what is perceived as "other than self." There are many dimensional layers to unpeel and much expanding of consciousness to be done until you sense it on a multidimensional level.

Think of any issue—say manipulation and control—and imagine how associated emotions (such as fear, anger, or distrust) can be projected onto "aliens." The aliens are a hot projection because they hold fear for many humans, as in "We are being invaded." A subset of this is the belief that diseases invade you. In other times, it was fear of invasion from another country. That you now fear invasion from other dimensions is a reflection of how your boundaries have expanded some.

At the deepest levels, you are never invaded or abducted or controlled. But some humans find it easier to deal with thought constructs of being controlled or invaded than to see the shadow aspects of self. As a species, you do not easily take to the idea that you are responsible for what you create.

So, the reason I got the message from the mosquito via the sci-fi channel was—

That is where your block is still located. Do you remember how you asked yourself, "What else can weird me out?" You called the answer in the form of an experience to yourself.

Even now you are busy asking yourself, "Is this real?" That is your joke. Reality is relative. It is the sum projection of how you live, think, and create your life.

The programs you watch and play out (in truth, create) are full of entertainment as well as education. There are universal beings at very high levels of vibration who have a very good sense of cosmic irony and humor.

Humor allows you to laugh at yourself. The vibration of laughter is an opening. It allows you to transcend your own self-imposed limits. Never underestimate humor.

The scenario of aliens was as much the mosquito's programming as it was yours. That was your match—how you were able to get the story. The mosquito told you to write it as fiction if you preferred. That was an attempt to defuse the energetic hold. The mosquito also showed you visions of fairy-mosquitoes! This too is true and you could well have asked "Are fairies real?"

Fairies appeal to the child inside who still beholds wonder. Humans are not afraid of fairies, so fairies have less of an emotional taboo upon them at this time. Aliens are still considered too strange. Even the people who talk about aliens are considered by many to be strange. Why is this? *That* is the more important question than "Are aliens real?" Aliens must hold a projection of tremendous fear for humans in general for you to see them in such a dim and shadowy light.

Another example you have considered in this regard are wolves. Some time not so long ago, wolves were hated, killed, even seen as evil. Through changes in your evolvement, the wolf energy became integrated to some degree. Humans then made wolves mystical heroes. Is that any more true or real? The wolves never changed. It was you who changed the channel. Do you see how this is *all* just a projection?

Despite my uneasiness, I knew the mosquito story held promise. Moreover, trust was involved. With a simple question, I had invoked an energetic request for knowledge, and a mosquito had been willing to trust me with an incredible tale. Perhaps the point was not so much the story itself, but the experience unfolding from the story. Perhaps it was the answer to the deeper nature of my question—of how we might all begin to trust the unique stories that come to each of us as we explore our limits, fears, and openings to ever more expansive perceptions of reality.

One day, shortly after returning to work after a two-day flu, I rose to take a break and walked over to my window. There was a mosquito, buzzing outside, close to the window. As I approached, she landed directly in front of me on the glass. "We have been trying to get through to you," she said.

Heart racing, palms sweating, I shuddered. Did I ask for more of this? The mosquito, who was female, related that she had additional information. For an instant, I considered running.

At that moment, in walked Zak, plumed tail held high, perfect timing intact.

Here we go again! Be careful what you ask, I thought, as I turned back to the window.

What do you want me to know?

We are, like yourselves, a multilayered, multidimensional being. Our kind has created thousands of races. We have worked with many different species of creatures, both in collaboration and in collusion.

I knew by her tone this wasn't the same mosquito as before. However, I also knew that, like the first mosquito, she wasn't going to fly away. They were definitely persistent beings. Zak said:

The mosquitoes wish to convey that they work in similar ways as the virus that has just swept through you. The mosquitoes are scientists in a medical sense and have worked with countless species and planets in fine-tuning DNA to achieve proper states of mutation.

I watched the small mosquito as she faced me through the glass window. With a pause, Zak continued:

The image of glass is something we have all been trying to convey to you. The important factor is not so much glass itself, but the transparent barrier that exists between worlds.

As I suddenly remembered the image of the observation booth the first mosquito had shown me, a shudder rippled through me and I understood—not just intellectually, but physically, emotionally—that the world we know and other worlds, perhaps even those populated by alien beings, aren't so far apart. I understood then, with deep inner knowing, that the separation between worlds is more one of varying vibrational frequencies than of physical space.

When you are close enough, you can actually see the barrier, just as when you are close to a window you may observe the glass. Though from far away, it is clear, transparent. Many birds learn this the hard way! Or do you think that when a bird smashes into a glass and you are there to witness, it is revealing something to you that you are not seeing?

As you open to more expansive levels, you approach the barrier that denotes separation of worlds. As you open to multidimensional consciousness, you are more keenly aware of these barriers. They are like glass or water in their transparency. In order to cross the border, one needs proficiency in changing vibration.

The mosquitoes are unique in that they operate on both sides of this barrier. Other species do too, of course, though some mosquitoes are aligned in particular ways with a specific group of extraterrestrials.

The female mosquito wishes to know if there are any questions.

What would she like humans to know about mosquitoes?

She says there are many, many varieties, subgroups, and divisions of their kind. All mosquitoes, no matter their group or type, work to elevate consciousness. How do they do this? They are masters of diversity, though in the sense of diversity in union. Even now, with many of their "brothers and sisters" zillions of light-years away, they stay in communication and have a sort of central network. She says it is true what the other mosquito told you about the mossies as a group—that there is no requirement to keep coming back as a mosquito, but most of their ranks are beings who choose to come over and over for a certain period of time. This is the only way they can progress as a group, for their earth lives are short, and there is the need of perpetuation of the thought process. She says it is all part of the "Mossie Party"—and she wishes to convey that term in many senses, such as a political party, a species, and even a celebratory party.

She wants humans to know there are other ways to work with mosquitoes rather than just to hate them. "We do not as a rule take your hate personally," she says. "We understand that when you hate another creature, you hate yourselves, so we feel pity or sorrow when you hate; it is sorrow not for ourselves, but for the depth of your misunderstanding.

"The alien faction is a small part of our work," she adds. "Many may think it strange, and you should perhaps think twice about publishing this to others as fact. On the other hand, it is a valid message and perhaps there are a handful of readers who will be sparked by this message and begin to work more consciously in this way. Perhaps even your government will begin to work with mosquitoes in the same way they work with dolphins!"

At that, both the mosquito and Zak laughed.

I wasn't expecting this. Is there something else?

Only that when you least expect things is when you are most open. When you are free of expectations, the mind and body are clear for a new shift to come into place. We are pleased you have given this so much consideration thus far. Many would have blown this off—"Oh it's only a mosquito talking." We are small, but we are powerful.

What about the diseases mosquitoes carry, such as malaria? What role do you serve in that regard?

Again, it is a reminder about the connection of all beings. Do you see how you still project onto us that we are the carriers of disease? Where did the disease come from? It comes from you! We are merely reminding you, by example, how closely connected we all are. Why? Because we are all one. That is what this book is about: to remind you, again and again and again, that we are all one. It is as if the ten thousand things are all shouting it at once to wake you up: WE ARE ALL ONE! We are all related! What you do to one, you do to all. This is the re-membering.

As you walk through the glass barrier to your multidimensional being in all its light and glory, there you will meet us, all of us, and begin to see the wondrous, beautiful, and imaginative workings behind the scenes of what you know now as reality.

And then, for a moment, there was quiet. Until Zak said:

I am pleased you are opening to this. I want to remind readers that as you approach the barrier, as it thins, you will feel the strongest vibrations of fear. This is a final protection of sorts. Ironically, it serves in two ways: one, to keep those who are not ready for this understanding out; and two, to heighten those who are nearly ready, in order to shoot them in. It is the final job of duality.

In truth, it is not a barrier at all, more of a gateway, though when you stand on the side you are now, it looks like a barrier. Later you will see it more like a sliding glass door!

Is there anything more from the mosquitoes?

We will be happy to come again and offer more. We would like our story to be told. Humans have for so long ignored us, though we have been with you nearly forever. Still, have you ever seen an artistic painting of a mosquito? Have we ever been seen with that type of human love?

We would only like to help you awaken, because by awakening yourself, we too awaken. In the vast connection of all beings, all times, all places, all energy, as you open to us, we also open to you. For example, we have understandings of things that the medical profession might find interesting. Is there a doctor humble enough who is willing to learn from a mosquito? This is when the world will begin to change.

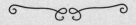

Great Changes
Penelope Smith

I was asked to help with a problem concerning jaguars coming too close to a village in Costa Rica. What I got from the jaguars was that they're being so crowded in their environment that they're impinging on human life, such as eating people's domesticated animals. It didn't come to me to communicate with an individual jaguar; it came to me to operate shamanically with all the spirits of the land, the spirits of the people and the jaguars.

This wasn't me doing anything. It was spirit working by request and me going in as a shaman, someone who is aware and asking spirit to move. I saw that all could be handled harmoniously with the jaguars and the people. I appealed to the consciousness of the people and the consciousness of the forest, and it appeared that a solution was being created. This is not my doing. I am a part of the web, so I just tuned in to my ability and spirit seemed to move.

There then appeared to be a raising of the consciousness and a blending of all so that solutions would come to people without me having to communicate anything. The solutions would come to them as to how they could operate harmoniously. I saw a lot of people changing and it was quite powerful. And then I just let it go.

It will be interesting to see how the jaguar situation plays out in the physical because sometimes there's a time delay. There are also all kinds of human gyrations that people go through because sometimes they don't totally accept what is given to them.

We'll see how it plays out, but I saw that, as a possibility, when beings of consciousness are called, great changes can happen without having to hit people over the head.

27

When All the World Is Wise

In some ways, the mosquitoes changed everything for me. By asking the question, "What else?" I had cracked open the door and invited in the answer. Just because the answer is in the room with you, however, doesn't necessarily mean you understand. For there I sat, more bewildered than before.

When I told the mosquito story to Penelope Smith, she listened and laughed, and then she listened some more. "The wisdom of the Universe is contained in every being," she said at last. "Insects are often messengers of greater wisdom. You just need to drop the barrier and your fear—your human conception of 'How could this be?' Wisdom is everywhere. Sit with a grain of sand and you'll get the same thing! Sand contains all of life!"

I sighed.

"You know, this isn't introductory material," chuckled Penelope. "It's about soul connection and restoring your soul's sensitivity. As you get in this deep space of love with another being—because that communion is what love is—everything is open to you.

"Some people say, 'How could an insect know this?' Well, we all know everything! When you're open and receiving, all the world is wise. All the world communicates to you. It's all beautiful, all pulsing, all incredible."

I understood what Penelope meant. When essential unity is felt throughout one's being, all the world is wise and answers are anywhere you look, in any face, any species.

It was the same understanding J. Allen Boone experienced when he formed his relationship with Freddie the Fly. Boone learned that neither man nor fly "were originating causes for anything, but instead were individual living expressions of a universal divine Cause or Mind that was ever speaking and living Itself through each of us and through everything else."[1]

When emphasis shifts from I and fly or human and mosquito to All That Is expressing itself though I and fly and human and mosquito, we move to a profound remembering. Learning to communicate with animals is also a lesson in learning to commune with the deeper layers of our being. As such, it requires continually fine-tuning our levels of discernment.

Penelope concurred. "All of this is about going home. People can often relate more easily to an animal as a spiritual being than they can to themselves. Then they discover that they are a spiritual being too, that they are wise also. Sometimes they honor the animal more than they do themselves or other humans. That's fine, because that's a vehicle. The animals want that too. They want people to wake up to the spirituality in animals, plants and themselves, all the world.

"We're all one thought. We're all having the same feelings. Of course, we're all individuals and a horse is different than a cow is different than a human. And at a certain level, you have to be real clear that you're communicating to an animal and the animal is communicating back to you. But when you're connecting at a soul level—and you can feel that because your heart uplifts and you open and expand and feel exhilarated—it really doesn't matter. Nobody's talking to anybody. It's all available and you're just tapping in."

"When you're in that state of oneness, it does make sense," I agreed. "But when you come back and try to explain it . . . "

Penelope laughed . "Yes. When people say it doesn't make sense, I tell them, 'That's exactly right. It does not make mental sense. It is not encompassed by the mind.' Once you get beyond that mental self and start to live as your soul self, you don't get confused anymore because the mind doesn't get in the way. You understand that when we're talking about human mind, that's one thing, and when we're talking about universal mind, it's a whole different level, like the mind of God."

"So, the idea isn't to kill the mind, but expand its boundaries, open it to something bigger."

"Exactly! It becomes your tool. You're no longer the slave of your mind. Perhaps you start communicating with animals and your mind says, 'Hey I can't grasp this.' You say, 'Right, mind. Just be quiet, go rest for awhile, and I'll grasp it as a soul.' That's the basic level. It's underneath everything. What I'm going for is to bring people home, so they encompass things with a soul heart, completely."

"And this idea correlates to ego as well? As with mind, the idea isn't to kill ego but go beyond the limits of ego." I pondered. "Do you think there's such a thing as universal ego?"

"Here's how we'll look at it," said Penelope. "What most people consider ego on a small level is the sum of our personality and desires. That has to be strong and balanced. There's nothing wrong with that. Every animal you talk to will say 'I' proudly—'I'm beautiful' or 'I'm great' or 'I'm this or that.' In animals that are balanced, and most of them are, it's self-love. In that space of self-love, you don't focus on the separation of the ego. You just say 'I,' and 'I' is 'We' and 'I' is 'Everything' and 'I' is 'All.'

"So, celebrate yourself! As you do that, you recognize that ego is the way we function here, and it's part of the soul. That's the place animals will take you to. We can all celebrate ego in each other. Otherwise, what would be the point of being individuals? Why would we be different people? Why would we be a frog or a dog? Well, to celebrate the ego! It's not all that you are, but it's a fun part. It's the clothes, the game. As long as you're conscious of that, it's all good. The animals seem to be very conscious of that. It encompasses what life is, taking it to a new place where it's a celebration."

"I celebrate myself," wrote Walt Whitman in *Leaves of Grass* nearly 150 years ago.

I celebrate myself,
And what I assume you shall assume
For every atom belonging to me as good belongs to you.[2]

A few days after her talk with a mosquito, Morgine told me she had also spoken with Zak. In summing up their discussion, Zak noted to Morgine that humans have been searching for answers outside ourselves for a very long time.

"We are always searching for the right diet, the right rituals, the correct exercises and meditations which will take us where we want to be," wrote Morgine. "We study books; we take workshops or visit our guru. We search for greater meaning and ask Aborigines or Native Americans for answers to our questions. Now, Zak says, we turn to animals, plants, and spirit guides. We are amazed that a dog or a spider can know personal things about us. Why then, do we think that humans somehow lack this skill?"

As Zak told Morgine:

You really do have all the answers! Morgine, you used to laugh at people who were searching externally to identify and solve their problems, when they just needed to go inside themselves and find the solution. How is asking nature and animals for assistance in understanding yourself any different? You know the same things that the animals and plants do. You have access to all the information you desire about anything. Who, however, is the last person you will trust?

Dawn talks to mosquitoes or me, and even if what comes is too weird for her to understand, she is a lot more willing to accept it. What if this came to her on her own, without any intermediary? Would she be so willing to share something that came from her alone? This is the last place most people look and it should be the first place! Learn to trust yourself, your intuition, your own thoughts, feelings, and ideas. We are all in this together, in more intimate ways than you conceive.

As I read Zak's words, I recalled a discussion I had with a cat spirit named Kayla. "That humans see these messages as coming from something 'other' than yourself is what helps you to be able to do this," she told me. In other words, by believing messages of wisdom come from others, we allow ourselves a greater degree of freedom not to censor or edit the message, as we might do if we believed the message was our own.

Kayla sent me the impression that animal communication is a gift from the animals at this particular time in human development. The belief that animals hold more wisdom than humans is a set-up, a drama through which we can learn to realize that wisdom in ourselves. But why would we need a set-up? What's so scary about wisdom?

I remembered my experience with the birds, the first time I heard the animals speak. My fear—not that I couldn't speak to animals, but that I could—was the core fear of experiencing divinity within.

"We all see different parts of the picture," said Kayla. "You can see the whole world in one focus if your lens is clear enough," she added, reminding me of William Blake's observation,

To see a World in a Grain of Sand
And Heaven in a Wild Flower,
Hold Infinity in the palm of your hand,
And Eternity in an hour.[3]

"There are many paths to truth," Kayla observed. "And humans have many ways of saying this truth too!" Perhaps we have so many ways of saying things because we need to hear the same things over and over in so many different ways.

The idea Zak, Kayla, and others were proposing is that underneath everything, animal communication is simply another means to finding ourselves. We can talk to mosquitoes or dogs or other human beings, for it doesn't matter which filter, face, or facet brings the message through. The notion is odd, yet utterly familiar: that every question, answer, and experience is yet another reflection of the grand Self, designed to show us who we really are. Finding the answer—any answer—is simply a matter of tapping into that place where all the world is wise.

"Failing to fetch me at first keep encouraged," wrote Walt Whitman.

Missing me one place search another,
I stop some where waiting for you.[4]

Remembering the Sacred Web

Good Tidings
Old Bug ~ Dawn Brunke

I am an old bug. I watch, I listen. I heard you were talking to animals, so I came to see for myself.

I am a slow bug—walk, walk, sometimes fly. I see many humans moving around, flurry, flurry and scurry, scurry. Not much mindfulness of where they are or the gifts present in each place, each moment.

I speak to slowness, of seeing the beauty and wonder of wherever you find yourself. I speak about saying hello to all creatures you meet. Spend a little time to get to know them, to share a greeting. The world would be a kinder, lighter place.

Many bugs stay close to the earth. That is my species. I am a type of beetle who lives in close concert with the earth, though I do climb and have a look from a different perspective from time to time.

I guess you could say I am old energy. I speak to being calm, sitting with new information and allowing it to filter down, not reacting so quickly on things, but allowing time to do her work, to watch, to listen, to breathe in the fullness of where you are and who you are in every moment.

Good tidings come to those who appreciate the simple things. This is an old truth, a simpler way of seeing the world. By releasing the excess that you believe helps you to see, you will actually begin to see better.

We are always happy to do our part. Bugs are very good listeners—some of us. Don't ask advice from bugs in swarms or hives; but solitary bugs—yes, we are good listeners. Happy to help.

I send greetings to all the world of human creatures. With fondness then, goodbye.

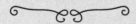

28

Recalling the Song

If there was something in the air
If there was something in the wind
If there was something in the trees or bushes
That could be pronounced and once was overheard by animals,
Let this Sacred Knowledge be returned to us again.

Atharva Veda

Very late in the process of this book's unfolding, I discovered the writing of Michael Roads. In his first book, *Talking with Nature*, Roads wrote of forming a deep relationship with nature. Even so, he was totally unprepared when sitting by a river one day, contemplating how he might write of this relationship in a simple way, the river began to talk. Then a heron spoke. And again, the river. Clearly, the forces of nature were conspiring.

Roads noted what the bird and river had told him, and then he wrote of his central fear: "Nobody's going to believe this."[1] Over a period of time, Roads went on to have conversations with trees, waterfalls, rocks, and birds. The experiences often left him feeling elated. But still, he returned to his fear. *Nobody's going to believe this.* Each time I read the words, tears welled up. I knew the feeling all too well. I had watched expressions of disbelief, bafflement, even horror cross the face of others when I spoke of my experiences. I had learned the hard lesson that some things may die as a larger vision, greater truth, or deeper remembering begins to grow.

As a tree explained to Roads, "We can offer you no proof. What do you need? Would a recorded communication heard simultaneously by a dozen or even a thousand people meet your need? Or would you then be one of a small group of confused and victimized people seeking further proof? Only by knowing who you are will you find peace."[2]

J. Allen Boone observed that by moving beyond the human habit of differentiation we begin to understand the flow of life, and thus ourselves, at deeper levels. However, like Roads, Boone was also startled by experience. It happened as he was outside, watching his canine mentor, Strongheart. With a subtle yet penetrating shift in consciousness, Boone suddenly awoke to a more expansive vision. He wrote, "Then I knew that what I was actually being privileged to watch was not a dog expressing great qualities, but rather, great qualities expressing a dog. He was radiating them from deep within himself, flinging them out as freely and as lavishly as the sun does its rays. He was not trying in the least to achieve this effect; he was just letting it happen."[3]

"We're the only species who can forget who we are," Penelope Smith once told me. "At one extreme, you could think humans are really pathetic. Or, you could see it as our creativity, our particular gift. I think that's why the animals are so understanding of us. They stay with us to remind us. Then we get our real mind back—our "re-mind," our universal mind."

"We remember," I said.

"Yes. The word *remember* is good because it means bringing the members back together again. We agreed to be separate and not remember because that was part of our experience on this planet. But we've done the separation bit to its max, and now we're remembering. Some are remembering before others, but eventually, we will all come back and be members together."

One morning, while seated by the computer, a fly landed in front of me on the keyboard. It was a very unusual looking fly, with some short, fuzzy white hairs growing on his back. The fly's appearance made me smile, for the white hairs made him seem very old. When I asked if he had a message, the fly flew to the top of my leg and began:

I am an Elder of my species. Our kind has been on earth for much longer than your kind. I impart this not in the sense of being better, but to point out that in many ways we are your elders. We have interacted with you, then and now, as intermediaries, healers, messengers, guides, and sometimes even friends.

As you peer beneath the surface, you will find many treasures and insights that are not found out in the light. Think of the metaphor "buried treasure"—part of the reason it is valuable and exciting is because it is buried. The metaphor is also linked to this particular time on earth. Much wisdom and understanding have been buried in the "past" because at that time it was harmful for you—too much light for you to hold. Now is the time of digging and finding the past buried treasure so as to face the future. There will be more discoveries of past information and hidden knowledge.

In many ways, animal communication is about rediscovering the stories that both animals and humans have to reveal. Humans are the vocal storytellers on the planet, at least with words, though others do this in a variety of means, with song, dance, energetic patterning, and more.

Our buzzing is a communication, a toning frequency that signals and sometimes initiates change. At times, our buzzing signals an energetic shift to deeper levels of understanding.

Flies are the messengers of shadow. We call explorers to the shadow side of life: the mystery of death, renewal, change. We are the ancients. We were with you in the caves, part of the mystery of return and remembering. Now, more than ever, shadow is a worthy exploration. This is your change—to go deeper, to grow. This is why you came to earth.

Buzzing off in a large circle around my head, the fly left me alone to ponder the mysteries of which he spoke.

I recalled another conversation I had with Penelope, in which she referred to the same buried treasure the Elder Fly had noted. "All the old needs to come out to go into the new," Penelope explained. "We have to recognize all the old, just like we have to completely embody the human condition before we move onto the next thing."

"It's not just a return to the old, then," I said. "It's a recalling of the old."

"That's right. Re-calling—you are calling it out, to sing it out. Everything has to be sung again. Everything that needs to be completed is coming to be recalled, and then we have the complete new, which is both old and new."

Penelope paused. "Well, there's nothing ever really new; it's all God. It's more like putting the sparkle back into everything—and then we'll see what creation comes. But we have to not hide anything. That's why all the shadow stuff, all the things that used to be secret knowledge, are now coming out."

In recalling our songs—individually and culturally, as a species and as a planet—we of necessity retrieve our shadow. In *A Little Book on the Human Shadow*, Robert Bly calls it eating the shadow. It's a slow process, Bly notes, and we do it not once but hundreds of times. We begin by recognizing all that we have abandoned, lost, forgotten, and pushed away from conscious awareness. We begin by reclaiming the "other"—with all its myriad projections—in our lives. Down on hands and knees in the rich soil of the earth, we dig up the roots of buried fears that have grown into bushes of anger, sadness, doubt and feelings of separation from all life. As we eat the shadow, we become wholly nourished and more fully alive, for we ingest the power and energy of all we have disowned. And then we begin to sing.

"Listen," said my dog Barney as I wrote this chapter. He got up from where he was lying, under the desk, and came to sit by my side.

Barney. Photo by Dawn Brunke.

Listen. In the deepest part of you is a remembering, not merely of mind or thought but of greater Being. We all come from that place, that space which holds form before form. We are here now as an event, a happening, a twinkle in the Larger Being's eye who chooses to experience the joy and pain, sadness and elation of being in form.

We are all participants in the larger flow of Life becoming. There are many metaphors with which to express this, but the best is the one you live and experience yourself.

By awakening to your own dream, you also awaken the larger Dream. It is said that the dream and the dreamer are one. This is so. We are now dreaming ourselves awake.

I am a being of stillness and depth. My being resounds at the level of deep and old wisdom, a different form of knowing. You might think of this as a bass note that moves upward from the center of the earth, as well as from the center of each individual. The note expands as it rises, becoming deeper and stronger, louder and more purposely known. As it plays into consciousness, you become aware of the magnificence of the world around you, the incredible detail that is fabricated into the making of this world, this event, this moment of nowness.

As more awaken, the note of the planet begins to sound louder, to rise up, and there is knowing of another form of reality, another tone that is heard and felt and experienced in another way. The Dreamer awakes.

All of you know this in your heart. It is a profound remembering, a regathering of knowledge and ancient wisdom, but also a time of new creation. As you open to oneness, you open to the greater majesty of the God Self, of All That Is. As we tone together, we open to a larger experience of who we all really are. The beat goes on. The beat is One.

A few hours after our conversation, and after my brief reflection on the mystery of return and remembering, the Elder Fly returned to where I sat. It wasn't with words, but with feeling, that I understood what he had come to share. He was going to die.

Following him to the windowsill, I sat nearby, watching as he rested upon a flat rock on which I had placed a small wooden statue. As the fly lay on his back, his bottom two legs stretched outward and relaxed in a graceful motion. His other four legs stretched upward and pulled together at the tips, stiffening, as if forming a tent above the body. Then, like a living prayer, the old fly expanded into death with a smooth and elegant flicker.

Deep down there stirs a memory, a faint recall—like the moment when you first wake up, like the deeper feelings of love you don't fully understand, like a song come to be sung.

Deepen and Center
Barney (dog) ~ Dawn Brunke

Deepen and Center. These are ideals I would like to encourage. I carry an energetic of calm depth, as in the saying, "Still waters run deep."

I am an old soul. I have been a shaman and elder, cat and horse, dog and minnow. I carry the sensitivity to touch others of a particular vibration. I work to calm, center, and deepen. Sometimes, I help to lull others into a state of complacent stillness where one may touch the inner connectedness to soul.

I am especially trained in the art of shapeshifting and have helped others learn to transform their physical body via thought-creations. Various teachings are associated with shapeshifting, some quite old. At the center of all of these, however, are the disciplines of centering and deepening.

There is a core at the deep center of one's being from which all forms come into being. In making a direct connection within yourself, you are able to travel far in a wide variety of form and shape. This ancient art will become more known as you recenter and reconnect with the fullness of who we truly are.

Many of the old methods and divinations are still valid, though they are of a dying breed. The direct route is now best, as more will be asked of you and as your experiences are deepening as well as expanding at an accelerated rate.

The ancient tools of deepening and centering, however, will never go out of style in this world. There is grace and elegance in these two simple means to a most profound, exhilarating, and enlightening experience. Enjoy these gifts, which many of us have held vibrationally for all to prosper from.

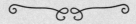

29

Zak's Chapter:
Finding Your Truth

Greetings to all readers of this book! I am pleased to be communicating in this way, for it reveals that Dawn has chosen to open to the experience for which I originally came into this incarnation as a dog.

I note this for all readers because you, too, may sense there is an animal in your life for a reason. Trust that small voice within, for it is the beginning of a much larger experience, if only you have the courage and inner strength to pursue your truth.

The nature of truth is an interesting scenario on planet Earth. One of the great joys and abilities of humans is to be storytellers. At this you excel. Some of your stories are quite grand. You allow yourself to be swept into the emotional experience of stories (be they plays, poems, novels, movies, tales you share around the campfire, or even inner stories such as dreams, which you tell yourselves), yet you often doubt the very experience that touched you.

The central message I would like to address is the nature of finding your own truth. To seek truth is a profound journey and requires a good deal of what you call centering. The journey of truth begins with losing preconceptions, beliefs, ideas, and most especially, thought. It is first of all a journey of death. Just as certain animals slough off old skin, by sloughing off old ideas and thoughts, a new and more vulnerable being emerges. It is not so different from the old, but still, in many ways it is.

It is and isn't—when one comes to this paradoxical nature of yes/no, that/not that, one begins to truly take a giant step into the voyage of seeking truth.

To live in a state of paradox is in many ways a training zone, for one must open to larger perspectives. At this stage of development, there comes to be joy in both diversity and unity. One will make comparisons, contradictions, and begin to see the value of patterns, manifested synchronicities, and other realities or dimensions of truth. One's being—especially the mind—begins to relax its grip on control. There is humor in seeing this as "releasing the death grip."

Zak. Photo by Dawn Brunke.

There are many exciting and enlightening aspects of this paradoxical space, though the end result is always the same: one comes to know that All is One. Even in diversity, one senses the One. And one knows there is no lesser truth in seeing the many in the One. This may not make sense to your mind, but that is the nature of the paradox!

From resolving the paradox, which is basically a re-membering, one graduates to a grander, more expansive view of the universe. At this level, one moves from the Earth-based plane to the universal.

Though it has been said time and again, it is often difficult for humans (and some animals) to remember that human Earth is a duality-based life system. From computers to light switches, from preoccupation with the male/female, yin/yang interplay, to language—all are based upon dualism. You love examples, which are a dualistic way of revealing truth: one thing representing or reflecting another.

Know that there are other ways of seeing the world, and that other worlds view their realities in entirely different manners. There are countless languages in the universe, and most are based upon unity consciousness. Implicit in each word, gesture, or tone in these languages is a reconnection to the whole. I mention this not to diminish your language system, but to open your viewpoint and remind you of other systems of connection that operate in other ways.

This brings us around to the point with which I started: the connection of all things to one another. Earth is clearly at a point of opening to this understanding, and many beings are working "under cover" in a myriad of shapes and forms to step up consciousness and bring this understanding to human awareness.

Part of the reason animal communication is important at this particular point in your time-space reality is because it offers a step out of dualism. It opens humans to a reconnection with animals and the web of life. It also connects you to other star systems and energetics that will help to invigorate, expand, and increase your ability to become in the world.

Many beings have chosen to come in animal forms to work with specific individuals or groups of individuals. A vast number have come in other forms as well.

There abides within the universe layer upon layer of plans and patterns. This is not so much a linear progression, as one to another, but an ever deepening, ever expanding opening. Opening is a good way of saying it, for it is as a continual movement to vaster and more expansive majesties and manners of perceiving realities.

In human terms, you could say God is both a scientist and an artist. The two are one. God is of course also a songster, prankster, joke teller, philosopher, magician, and murderer. Every aspect of you is an aspect of All That Is. How could it be otherwise?

Earth is already having problems because of the human insistence on many old, dualistic-based paradigms. It would help to review the past and, as Buddy the horse noted, not repeat past mistakes. Look to various time periods and see that limiting the expression of ideas and thought (even the written word itself, such as when printing presses were outlawed, or in ancient civilizations when possessing knowledge of counting or reading was considered an infraction of some human law) merely served to keep you in control and ignorance.

There are many religions that incorporate power and control issues. I am not here to argue theology, but I would encourage all of you to look to the basic patterns operating underneath many of your religious stories and beliefs. The notion of God and Devil sets you up in a dualistic game. For example, did I offend you when I said God was a murderer? Is murder always the Devil's work? Is everything "bad" always a result of the "other" in your life? If so, then you are playing with dualism.

As one opens to the Oneness-in-All paradigm, one finds a flow of harmony and a sense of humor underlying the old notions that separate and categorize. Remember, too, that categorizing the "holy" is just as much a limiting concept as categorizing evil as the Devil's work.

On the road to Unity, one begins to make peace with the "other" in one's life, be it holy or evil. The murderer, thief, rapist, abuser, bum, and drunk are all disowned aspects of the collective psyche. So too are the saint, virgin, healer, and all forms of the divine priest/priestess.

As one opens in understanding, one opens to the neglected, dark, shadow content of one's being. Why? Because it is a part of who you are. Often, there is so much emotion tied up in these "others" that humans cannot tolerate the idea of considering them human. This is how the Devil came into being. He was a group consciousness "other" designed to embody and hold all the shadow aspects that humans could not. In the same way, God was to embody all the aspects that humans did not believe they were worthy of embodying.

As one opens more, therefore, one embraces not just the God aspects, but the Devil aspects as well. One begins to see that they are All One. That is the nature of All That Is.

Let us return to stories for a moment. Can you conceive the sum total of human time on earth as a vast story? One in which you are actor, writer, producer, and even publicity manager? As the story of earth unfolds, you move from not knowing you are a part of the story to uncovering various roles to understanding that you are the story itself. The story is about becoming, about remembering your divine plan and place in being the story.

Consider all the parts you humans have agreed to play: scientist and scholar, magician and dictator, friend and foe. All are myriad aspects of One—ever flowing, interweaving plots and subplots, roles changing, genders shifting, on all levels you transforming, as the story gets told.

Now is the time to re-member your parts, all of them. There is much in the human social sciences about discovering your inner artist, patriarch, matriarch, jester, wild man or woman. But now what? As you reclaim more of your shadow selves, your lost inner children, what will you do with this cast of characters? Where will it lead? If you are reading this book and considering talking with animals, at some point you may wonder, well, where does this take me?

All roads lead to you. In recognizing yourself as divine playwright, you realize that all characters sprang from you and are, therefore, you. Begin to join one with the other, scientist with scholar, lost child with wise woman in the forest, murderer with saint. They have much information to share—indeed, many stories to tell.

Now is the time to retell all the stories. As you see past the words, read between the lines, and glance through time, you begin to see who these characters are who have brought you to this place in being where there is, at last, an opening, a revealing, a recalling, a remembering. They are you. The "other" is always you.

The story is different now, alive in a more conscious way. You are at the end of the story, about to grasp how you have created this multilevel dream that now awakens you. You meditate on the dream and see how all the parts are beautifully interwoven, one element upon the other in an exquisite way, and that remembering moves you, shifts you, brings you into an ever-deepening understanding at precisely the right instant in time and space so that the gestalt of synchronicities can fall upon you, enveloping you, uplifting you, opening you so that you finally remember who you really are.

Welcome home.

Weaving

Spiders ~ Dawn Brunke

We are the weavers of the universal patterns. Peoples from old knew this and fashioned stories about us.

We have been with you since the beginning of this book, helping you to pull together various threads of knowledge, idea, exposition, and texture of thought that are beneficial to readers and humanity in general.

We are often expressed as an old female (Grandmother Spider). This reflects the tone of our presence throughout this world. We are of the old, female energy. We are one and have always been one, but in the spirit of exploration and creation, we have unraveled our existence. We recreate patterns of unity and interdimensionality via webs of all sorts. With webs you can catch ideas and fleeting thoughts (such as through nets); with webs you can connect, one to the other (the computer web and web of life); and with webs you can move faster and quicker through the gamut of creational possibilities [here the spider shows me webbed feet as a metaphor].

We are a key symbol of connection and movement. We come as you begin to tie up loose threads. As a web, everything in this work will be connected, though several threads will also remain unspun, so to speak. In this manner others may pick up where you leave off. It is our intention that *this* be the new model of creation—not a work in and of itself, but many works interconnected, all part of a much larger work.

As humanity awakens, you will be asked to view the larger picture, the further-reaching, expansive ideas that connect us all. Many key words that have arisen in the last year—trust, vulnerability, openness—are necessary to understand so that you and all those who are reading this may open to a larger perception of our mutual place and holding in the universal energetic pattern.

We are the weavers. We weave time, ideas, thoughts, perceptions, and humanity together with All That Is.

We bless this work.

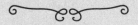

3 Q

Closet Doors
and Spirit Dust

As a child, I was afraid of the dark—especially the dark that lurked beyond my closet door. Every night before I went to bed, I would make certain the door was firmly shut. Even so, I would sometimes have nightmares about the scary things in the closet, loud and boisterous and shadowy. If the closet door was shut, the scary things couldn't come out, though sometimes their voices would call to me.

One night, I dreamed that a voice slipped out of the closet and hid in the room before I had a chance to shut the doors. The voice called out, saying that if I would just walk over to the closet, it would show me how to fly. Still in the dream, I pushed back the covers and moved slowly across the room. I was afraid, but I very much wanted to fly. When I reached the closet and did as the voice instructed, I was thrilled to find that I could fly! In the twilight of early morning darkness to the first rays of morning light, I flew around the room as the voice called out directions, teaching me how to turn and soar, go faster and slower, float nearly motionless, dip below the floor and rise above the ceiling. The voice, I was to discover, belonged to a teacher whom I would meet in future dreams.

Being seven years old at the time, I wondered if I really could fly. That morning, I tried making the same movements my dreambody had learned. Though it didn't work, I *knew* something magical had happened. I knew that things had changed.

Though my fear of the dark subsided, I still dreamed about what existed beyond the closet door. As I grew older and studied dreams and the patterns of the unconscious, I came to understand that the closet door was the image my dreamwriters used to convey the portent of a threshold, that place of transitional crossing from ordinary to nonordinary realities. For myself, an emotional mixture of fear and exhilaration was often present at such crossings.

While at college, I dreamed of loud noises coming from the closet. Still in the dream, I got out of bed and saw a bright light shining through the cracks of the louvered door. Though I felt the old childhood fear, curiosity was greater. I cracked open the door.

I saw, then, that the light was coming from above a shelf. Finding a ladder in the closet, I climbed to an opening in the ceiling and stepped into an enormous room. It was bright and clean, though still in the process of being built. All around me, workers were working. Cheerily shouting to one another were plasterers and sanders, painters and electricians, all very busy and happily working on this room. They went about their business joyfully, smiling at me as I stood in wonderment.

As with the flying dream, I woke from this dream with profound elation. The large bright room was a place of creativity, alive with beauty. I knew the place was part of me and that finding it signaled an opening to growth and new creations. However, in order to get there, I first had to summon up my courage. I had to open the closet door.

Time and again, we are brought back to face our fears. Perhaps the reason that experiences of all sorts come to us, in the varied incredible ways in which they do, is because we are nearing readiness to open up our next closet door.

For myself, this book has revealed a number of closet doors I never knew existed. I have been both challenged and changed by the experience. I have come to appreciate the kindness, the wisdom and, perhaps most of all, the humor of animals. I am continually grateful for and amazed by the beautiful, mysterious, amusing, and heart-filled ways in which relationships of all kinds unfold.

A number of people have asked me what I have learned from all of this.

I have learned that quite often listening is more productive than talking. I have learned that experiences come to us for very good reasons and what we choose to do with these experiences—forget about them, deny their truth, modify them to suit our image, or honor and work with them—is up to us. I have learned that there are many answers to our questions, and my answer may not necessarily be yours. I have learned that at a certain point explanations cannot be a substitute for experience, and that allowing yourself to live with a sense of wonder is something you will never regret. I have learned that sometimes words and thinking are a defense for feeling deeply. And yet, I have also learned that sometimes the best way we can express our feelings and the genuineness of who we are, at this particular moment, in this particular world, is through the sharing of our tales.

One summer morning I saw a black and white moth on the other side of my office window. Not only was I drawn to the moth, I felt inexplicably happy, for it seemed the moth was waiting for me. When I asked if it had a message to share or was just enjoying the morning, the moth began a dance of sorts, moving in a circle, right side up to upside down and back again. Then she spoke:

We are carriers of thoughts. We bring energies, new ideas, and inspiration lightly and with subtlety to humans and others. We are constantly interacting with our light bodies.

The moth showed this to me as a steadily changing, fluid movement of yellowish glow around her wings. It moved as if dancing with her, first flaring in one direction, then rounding like a ball of encircling light. I moved to make sure I wasn't seeing a light mirage, but there it was: a transparent golden halo of light throbbing around the moth. Returning to her circular jig, the moth continued,

We are carriers of thought forms that meld light and energy and thought. We are related to our brothers and sisters, the butterflies. They bring beauty into the world and remind humans of the colors that are inherent in other worlds that interact with your own. They are a dimensional bridge to beauty and the interaction of light and other worlds.

Moths bring a slightly heavier energy. We bring transformations. We are often seen as omens, for we bridge the psychic realm to many humans. We can help link you to other modes of perception. Generally, when a moth comes to work with you, as I have come to you, it is for a shift in perception, a gentle encouragement to open and see things in a new way.

Is there something for me to see in a new way?
You already have.

Remember to open to the possibilities that are all around you, and be willing to expand your mind. This does not mean accepting all ideas as true, but finding what works for you. Sometimes what doesn't fit now will fit later, or what fits now will no longer fit at another time or place. This is part of our teaching: that energy is constantly shifting, changing, and the interaction is a dance, a play, a joy to participate in and become one with.

We also teach balance. I am particularly about balance, as I am black and white and gray. I am symmetrical and yet I join my halves in a way in which I am fully one.

Regarding the subject of lightbodies, these are the more subtle energy bodies that all living beings possess. Moths have a particular link to that, going back into our history. We were once very large, as large as humans, and there are many stories about this, not only in human culture. Moths, too, have a mythology.

A mythology! I told the moth I would love to hear a moth myth. And so the moth, being quite agreeable, began.

Once upon a time, as you say, there was a world where huge mothed creatures lived in close proximity to the land. Even though we were quite large, we hovered about the land. We were almost weightless, and could float close to the ground as we tended to it, as a mother to the land. In this time and place, the land was red and like a desert. There was not much vegetation.

The mothed creatures were creators, responsible for bringing sun energy (which is to say the enlightened energy of the universal spirit) down onto the land so as to imbue the creatures and plants with bits of spirit.

There were special moths who traveled to the sun. There, they would swallow pieces of the sun energy and then fly back to the planet. The sun would work its way through their body and emerge as dust upon their wings. As they fluttered around the land, the dust would fall as spirit onto everything, and everything became alive. And that is why, even now, you will still see dust on the wings of moths.

[A pause.] That is a creation story, one of our oldest. It is a myth, you under-stand, and must be held in that light. Just as your race has different stories, we too have a very rich mythology with some wonderful stories to tell.

Is there anything else you'd like to share?

I hope your readers will open to the mysteries all around you, all the time. Wherever you look, there are mysteries and miracles. And if you ever need some help, just ask a moth.

As I thanked her, the moth flew away. But that was not the end.

Guided by sudden intuition, I stood to face the bookshelves. My eyes were lead to an old softcover copy of Carlos Castaneda's *Tales of Power.* Plucking the book from the shelf, I began to laugh. There it was, right on the bookcover: a drawing of a large moth. Surrounding the moth's physical body was a lightbody, shimmering with a yellowish glow. It was the same shape and color I had just seen on the window moth.

Adrift in the flow of synchronicity, I opened the book without plan—to the page where don Juan tells Carlos it is time to talk about moths:

"The moths are heralds or, better yet, the guardians of eternity," don Juan said. . . . "For some reason, or for no reason at all, they are the depositories of the gold dust of eternity."

The metaphor was foreign to me. I asked him to explain it.

"The moths carry a dust on their wings," he said. "A dark gold dust. That dust is the dust of knowledge."

"What does knowledge have to do with the dust on the wings of moths?" I asked after a long pause.

"Knowledge comes floating like specks of gold dust, the same dust that covers the wings of moth. The moths have been the intimate friends and helpers of sorcerers from time immemorial," he said. "I had not touched upon this subject before, because of your lack of preparation."

"But how can the dust on their wings be knowledge?"

"You'll see."[1]

Three days later, the moth came again to my window. She had another myth, she told me. She liked my plans for the last, so she had another to share. And thus she began:

In the beginning, there was a central fire. It burned at the center of the land, where we moths lived. The fire was ever burning. During the day, the fire would connect to the sun, pulling in beams of light energy onto the planet. At night, we would flit around the fire. You could think of it as a campfire, where everyone sits around in a circle, laughing and singing and telling stories. So it was with us. The fire and the circle are ancient symbols, for light and circles are connections to the One.

In the night, under the great black starry sky, we would hover near the fire and dream the stories of our race. The fire (as the land connection to the sun) was the storyholder. The stories were not in the fire, nor were they with us, but in the relationship between us. We had great love for the light, such joy sometimes we could hardly contain ourselves, and that is why some of us flew too close to the fire, thus returning, in a blaze, to the light.

The myth of moths and fire, or light, is part of who we are. I was pleased you found the connections to other stories of our people, our race. We honor your writing. We are scribes as well. Did you know that our personal stories are written on our wings? It is, as you have been learning, all about pattern. We hold our stories in the paintings on our wings, just as you hold your pattern within your cells and DNA.

Before I could ask another question, the moth continued in a flowing river of thought. Listening to her words, I smiled deeply.

We are creatures of light and movement. We bridge the earth to the sun, to light, to universal connection. It is this I want to address: that all communication is about relation. It is good for humans to open to animals, to begin to trust their wisdom, but it is important for you, too, to understand that all communication is about interrelation.

Remember the form I showed to you of energy shifting and changing? That is what I bring to you to express to others. Energy is ever shifting. There is no absolute. Absolute is the static desire to hold and control. Rather, there is the ever shifting, ever changing. In the experience of that, you find relation, a meeting of consciousness, energy, light, form and spirit. That is where you find the truth of who you are.

I bring the message of movement to you. Keep moving, shifting, and expanding. Trust the meetings of the heart, of the soul, wherein you find a melding of thought and mind and dimension. There you find the spiral that leads you to the All.

The myth I have told of moths and fire represents the desire for union. The point is not to burn yourself up in the fire, as some humans mistakenly think. What we bring is the relation of moths to fire, which is to say the relationship of you to the divine nature of who you really are.

The beating of our wings is the beating of your heart. It is all a constant movement, a drumbeat. It can be heard in the stampeding of the elephants, the echoes of the whales, the howling of the coyotes, the songs of birds. All is movement, all is becoming.

You are not going anywhere, for you are already here. The animals are saying you need not go anywhere, just join the dance. To wake up and sing and shout and laugh and flap your wings so that dust of spirit flutters down among all you meet: This is the dance. This is the joy. This is the love.

Appendix
How to Begin

Some humans open unexpectedly to the animal world and begin to learn communication skills through interactions with a specific animal or group of animals. If you find yourself the apprentice to an animal teacher, consider yourself lucky indeed!

Many people learn the basics of animal communication skills from other humans, often by attending workshops or reading books on the subject. By cultivating inner stillness, one learns to quiet the mind and open the heart in order to see, hear, and feel at deeper levels. Many communicators also emphasize the powerful gift of imagination as an aid to rediscovering the connection that is ever present between humans, animals, and all of nature.

For those who would like some advice on getting started, several communicators share beginning exercises and tips below. The information presented here is by no means exhaustive. It is merely a starting off point for those readers who can't wait to open to this wonderful form of fellowship with the animal world. For more information or to contact the communicators in this book, please visit www.animalvoices.net.

THE BASICS

Carole Devereux ~ *Communicating with Your Animal*
If you have ever wondered if you could communicate telepathically with your animal, try following these simple steps.

Sit or stand quietly beside your animal in a peaceful and calm place. Open yourself to listening without judging until the chatter in your mind begins to still. Once you are comfortable in this deep silence (as in a meditative silence), you can become receptive and trusting of your own feelings.

It is important to establish rapport with the animal before plunging into what you want to talk about. Rushing into a discussion sometimes causes an animal to feel it as an attack. Similarly, if you are worried about something, you might transmit that emotion to the animal. You want to be patient, calm, and relaxed. Breathe softly and quietly.

Once you feel rapport is established and there is a calm mental environment surrounding you and the animal, begin by asking a simple question or considerately stating a problem. Be patient if you do not succeed the first time. This takes discipline and one-pointed focus.

An example of good phrasing for a question is, "You are not eating today. Is there something you would like to tell me?" Close your eyes for a moment to "see" if the animal is sending a visual image or message. We often receive communication in symbolic language. Good communication is a marriage of both words and pictures. This works with all species and is at the core of this universal language.

When you send a message, you may also project a mental picture with it which corresponds to what you are saying, thinking, and feeling.

Recognizing that we sometimes "force" our communications onto our animals, either out of frustration or ignorance, is important. It is wiser to smile and cultivate flexibility. Humans are also unrelenting in their efforts to get quick results. We need to learn to be fully present and grounded when learning this new skill.

If you find you cannot hear your animal's message, then ask again. Wait and check yourself for negative thinking, doubt, or insecurities, making certain that you are thinking in positive terms. Let go of any conventional ideas about the human/animal bond. If you get pictures you do not understand, ask for clarification. You will learn to interpret these images as you progress. Allow whatever mode of communication you experience to occur naturally, whether it is a feeling, picture, word, thought, or sensation. We all receive messages differently.

When there is love for an animal and a willingness to learn and accept animals as they are, our ability grows. Even with the most skeptical students, in time and with training, a deeper understanding and communion with animals is possible. (Adapted from *Spirit of the Horse* by Buddy and Carole Devereux)

Chrys Long-Ago ~ The Basics of Animal Communication

The basics of animal communication are simple. As with many things in life, experience is key. For beginners, I recommend performing the following steps often. With practice, you will learn to discern your own inner voice and refine your ability to communicate with animals.

Preparation

1. It is very important to start with a statement of intent. Make the declaration, "I intend to talk with *(animal's name here)*."
2. Take some time to center yourself. Calm and clear your mind. Begin the Mindfulness Meditation (below), allowing any doubts, fears, or anxieties to pass through your mind without judgment.

─ ─

MINDFULNESS MEDITATION

"One just sits."

—CHOGYAM TRUNGPA

The Mindfulness Meditation is more than 2,500 years old. The primary focus is breathing. However, the intent is to sustain a serene awareness, allowing thoughts and feelings to come and go, undistracted. This mindfulness is your true self, your essence.

- Sit comfortably in an erect, respectful posture with your eyes closed and your back fairly straight.
- Let your attention rest on your breathing.
- When thoughts, physical sensations, or external sounds arise, simply acknowledge and accept them, allowing them to pass through without judgment.
- When you notice your mind has wandered, gently bring it back to your breathing and continue.

─ ─

Communication

1. Sending: It is nice to start by introducing yourself. Then, convey your message as a detailed picture along with emotions and words to form a layered package.
2. Receiving: Relax your visualization and remain open to experience what is sent. Sometimes animal communicators are encumbered by their own thoughts and wish to verify a message. To do this, first explain that your apprehension does not translate into "Danger!" but comes from your own performance anxiety. Apologize for interrupting, and humbly ask for the information to be repeated. Reset your relaxed mind. Express gratitude for whatever you receive.
3. Closing: It's aggravating to have someone suddenly disappear from a conversation, so remember to have good manners and say good-bye first. Conclude with a distinct "Thank you" by sending a feeling of appreciation and thanks.

FINE TUNING

Anita Curtis ~ On the Value of Imagination

Many people worry about communications received being "just my imagination." You need an imagination to be able to do this work. If you cannot imagine you can do something, you will not be able to do it! Working with another person offers an opportunity for verification of the information you receive. You will soon learn to trust your abilities. Communicate with as many animals as possible. The more you do, the more you will believe that you are actually hearing them. (From *How to Hear the Animals* by Anita Curtis)

Jane Hallander ~ On Learning to Relax and Meditate

Learn to relax and be one with the animals.

Choose an animal, then "become" that animal in your mind. Feel how it moves, breathes, what its fur, hair, or feathers feel like to it.

Learn to meditate with an empty mind for at least a half hour at a time.

Don't devalue any communication you think you might have received from an animal. Most of the time, you will be correct in your perception.

Marcia Ramsland ~ On Building Self-Confidence

I suggest that you write out both your questions and what you receive as answers. That does a couple of things. First, it gives your left brain something to do (writing) instead of criticizing what you're doing. The logical critical mind will often come up and say, "You can't do this," or "You're crazy," or "Other people can do this, but you can't." That's what most people think who are interested in this: they believe it's possible, but they don't believe they can do it. I know this, because it is exactly where I came from. You have to build up your self-confidence.

Penelope Smith ~ On Admiration and Appreciation

Another way of increasing willingness to communicate and adding new dimensions of loving understanding is to send admiration and appreciation to animals. Simply sit calmly, and admire all the beautiful qualities—physical and spiritual—that you can find about the animal. You can also verbalize your feelings of appreciation and respect on a daily basis. Your mutual trust and affection will grow. That's what we're aiming for. You can't lose. So, practice, practice, practice with as many domestic and wild animals as possible, and have loads of fun! (From *Animal Talk* by Penelope Smith)

Notes

CHAPTER 1: THE JOURNEY HOME

1. J. Allen Boone, *Kinship with All Life* (New York: Harper & Row, 1954), 8.
2. T. S. Eliot, "Little Gidding," in *Collected Poems* (New York: Harcourt Brace Jovanovich, 1970).
3. J. Allen Boone, *Kinship with All Life*, 9.
4. Ibid., 27–28.
5. J. Allen Boone, *Adventures in Kinship with All Life* (Joshua Tree, Calif.: Tree of Life Publications, 1990), 46.

CHAPTER 2: HOW DOES IT WORK?

1. J. Allen Boone, *Kinship with All Life*, 46.
2. Ibid.
3. Ibid., 52.
4. Ibid., 53.

CHAPTER 3: BEGINNING WITH BIRDS

1. Ted Andrews, *Animal-Speak: The Spiritual and Magical Powers of Creatures Great and Small* (St. Paul: Llewellyn Publications, 1993), 141.

CHAPTER 8: VIOLET: ON BEING A CAT AND LIGHT WORKER

1. For more on the Orange Cat Contingent, see Penelope Smith, *Animals . . . Our Return to Wholeness* (Point Reyes, Calif.: Pegasus Publications, 1993), 133–135.

CHAPTER 9: PAST LIVES, FUTURE LIVES, AND LIVING IN THE NOW

1. Penelope Smith, *Animals . . . Our Return to Wholeness*, 246.
2. Anita Curtis, *Animal Wisdom: Communications with Animals* (Gilbertsville, Penn.: Anita Curtis, 1996), 161–162. See 159–166 for full story regarding BB.
3. Ibid., 9.
4. Ibid., 127–128.
5. Stephen Hawking, *A Brief History of Time from the Big Bang to Black Holes* (New York: Bantam Books, 1988), 139.
6. Derived from Burton Watson, *Chuang Tzu: Basic Writings* (New York: Columbia University Press, 1964), 45.

CHAPTER 13: THE INNERNET

1. W. Brugh Joy, *Avalanche: Heretical Reflections on the Dark and the Light* (New York: Ballantine, 1990), 185.
2. Marcia Ramsland, "Jarvi and the Animal Communication Network," in Penelope Smith, *Animals . . . Our Return to Wholeness*, 151. See 145–151 for full story.

CHAPTER 14: BUDDY, ELLIE, AND ANCESTOR HORSE: WELCOME TO KNOWING

1. For more information on the Oxherding pictures, see Philip Kapleau, *The Three Pillars of Zen* (Boston: Beacon Press, 1967) and Katsuki Sekida, *Zen Training* (New York: John Weatherhill, 1975).

CHAPTER 15: MIRACLE AND MANIFESTATION MADE REAL

1. Brooke Medicine Eagle, "It's a Miracle" at www.medicine-eagle.com/6_5.html.
2. As Fools Crow died on the Pine Ridge Reservation in South Dakota in 1989, five years before Miracle was born, he did not know of the white buffalo calf's presence. However, he spoke several times about White Buffalo Calf Woman, or (as he called her) Calf Pipe Woman. Fools Crow related that Calf Pipe Woman had returned many times since her first appearance on earth. Moreover, Fools Crow said the original pipe that Calf Pipe Woman gave to the Sioux had been kept by a succession of caretakers and was currently in the southwest. Fools Crow told Mails that he had seen the pipe and called that day "the crowning event of my life." For more, see Thomas Mails, *Fools Crow* (Lincoln, Nebr.: Reprint by University of Nebraska Press, 1990).

CHAPTER 17: DOLPHINS, WHALES, AND THE MULTIDIMENSIONAL NOW

1. Joan Ocean, *Dolphins into the Future* (Kailua, Hawaii: Dolphin Connection, 1997), 16.
2. Ibid., 67.
3. Ibid., 162.
4. Ibid., 163.

CHAPTER 18: THE CETACEAN NATION

1. For more on the Dogon, see Robert K. G. Temple, *The Sirius Mystery* (Rochester, Vt.: Inner Traditions International, 1987).

CHAPTER 20: PETS

1. All quotes regarding Geisha are from Chrys Long-Ago, "Guinea Pig Seminar," *Alaska Wellness Magazine*, November/December 1997, 8–9.

CHAPTER 21: PESTS

1. J. Allen Boone, *Kinship with All Life*, 124–125.
2. J. Allen Boone, *Adventures in Kinship with All Life*, 111.
3. J. Allen Boone, *Kinship with All Life*, 144. See 129–157 for the full story of Freddie the Fly.
4. Joanne Lauck, *The Voice of the Infinite in the Small: Revisioning the Insect-Human Connection* (Mill Spring, N.C.: Swan-Raven & Company, 1998), 61.
5. Ibid., 60.

CHAPTER 23: ANIMALS EATING ANIMALS:
THE PREDATOR/PREY RELATIONSHIP

1. Joseph Campbell, *The Way of the Animal Powers* (London: Summerfield Press, 1983), 152.

CHAPTER 25: ANIMAL SPIRITS: COYOTE, JAGUAR, AND CROW

1. The web site "Shamanism: Working with Animal Spirits" can be found at www.animalspirits.com.

CHAPTER 27: WHEN ALL THE WORLD IS WISE

1. J. Allen Boone, *Kinship with All Life*, 136.
2. Walt Whitman, "Song of Myself," *Leaves of Grass*, lines 1–3.
3. William Blake, "Auguries of Innocence," *Poems* (original text, Dante Gabriel Rossetti, editor, 1863), lines 1–4.
4. Walt Whitman, "Song of Myself," *Leaves of Grass*, lines 1,334–1,336.

CHAPTER 28: RECALLING THE SONG

1. Michael J. Roads, *Talking with Nature* (Tiburon, Calif.: H. J. Kramer, 1987), 23.
2. Ibid., 98.
3. J. Allen Boone, *Kinship with All Life*, 59.

CHAPTER 30: CLOSET DOORS AND SPIRIT DUST

1. Carlos Casteneda, *Tales of Power* (New York: Simon & Schuster, 1974), 35–36. (The moth "lightbody" drawing can be found on the 1974 softcover version of this book.)

Bibliography

Abbey, Lloyd. *The Last Whales.* New York: Ivy Books/Ballantine, 1989.

Andrews, Ted. *Animal-Speak: The Spiritual and Magical Powers of Creatures Great and Small.* St. Paul: Llewellyn Publications, 1993.

Ayres, Toraya. "Messages from the Animal Kingdom." www.spiritweb.org/Spirit/animal-kingdom-ayres.html, 1997.

Bach, Richard. *Jonathan Livingston Seagull.* New York: Avon Books, 1970.

Bly, Robert. *A Little Book on the Human Shadow.* New York: Harper & Row, 1988.

Boone, J. Allen. *Kinship with All Life.* New York: Harper & Row, 1954.

———. *Adventures in Kinship with All Life.* Joshua Tree, California: Tree of Life Publications, 1990. (Originally published as *The Language of Silence.* New York: Harper & Row, 1970.)

———. *Letters to Strongheart.* Harrington Park, New Jersey: Robert H. Sommer Publisher, 1977.

———. *You Are the Adventure!* Harrington Park, New Jersey: Robert H. Sommer Publisher, 1977.

Braden, Gregg. *Walking between the Worlds: The Science of Compassion.* Bellevue, Washington: Radio Bookstore Press, 1997.

Broomfield, John. *Other Ways of Knowing: Recharting our Future with Ageless Wisdom.* Rochester, Vermont: Inner Traditions International, 1997.

Campbell, Joseph. *The Way of the Animal Powers.* London: Summerfield Press, 1983.

Casteneda, Carlos. *Tales of Power.* New York: Simon & Schuster, 1974.

Connelly, Dianne. *All Sickness Is Home Sickness.* Columbia, Maryland: Centre for Traditional Acupuncture, 1986.

Curtis, Anita. *Animal Wisdom: Communications with Animals.* Gilbertsville, Pennsylvania: Anita Curtis, 1996.

———. *How to Hear the Animals.* Gilbertsville, Pennsylvania: Anita Curtis, 1998.

Devereux, Carole, and Buddy. *Spirit of the Horse.* La Center, Washington: Centaur Publications, 1999.

Dillard, Annie. *Teaching a Stone to Talk*. New York: Harper & Row, 1982.

Eagle, Brooke Medicine. *Buffalo Woman Comes Singing*. New York: Ballantine, 1991.

Eliot, T. S. *Collected Poems*. New York: Harcourt Brace Jovanovich, 1970.

Getten, Mary. *The Orca Pocket Guide*. San Luis Obispo, California: EZ Nature Books, 1996.

Gurney, Carol. *The Language of Animals: Seven Steps to Communicating with Animals*. New York: Bantam-Dell, 2001.

Hiby, Lydia. *Conversations with Animals*. Troutdale, Oregon: New Sage Press, 1998.

Joy, W. Brugh. *Avalanche: Heretical Reflections on the Dark and the Light*. New York: Ballantine, 1990.

Kapleau, Philip. *The Three Pillars of Zen*. Boston: Beacon Press, 1967.

Kharitidi, Olga. *Entering the Circle: Ancient Secrets of Siberian Wisdom Discovered by a Russian Psychiatrist*. San Francisco: Harper, 1997.

Kowalski, Gary. *The Souls of Animals*. Walpole, New Hampshire: Stillpoint Publishing, 1991.

Lauck, Joanne Elizabeth. *The Voice of the Infinite in the Small: Revisioning the Insect-Human Connection*. Mill Spring, North Carolina: Swan Raven & Company, 1998.

Lee, Patrick Jasper. *We Borrow the Earth*. London: Thorsons, 2000.

Mails, Thomas E. *Fools Crow*. Lincoln, Nebraska: Reprint by University of Nebraska Press, 1990. (Originally published New York: Doubleday, 1979.)

McElroy, Susan Chernak. *Animals as Teachers and Healers*. New York: Ballantine, 1997.

——. *Animals as Guides for the Soul*. New York: Ballantine, 1998.

Müller, René K., webmaster, editor of "SpiritWeb," www.spiritweb.org/.

Myers, Arthur. *Communicating with Animals*. Chicago: Contemporary Books, 1997.

Ocean, Joan. *Dolphins Into the Future*. Kailua, Hawaii: Dolphin Connection, 1997.

Pickering, Robert B. *Seeing the White Buffalo*. Denver: Denver Museum of Natural History Press, 1997.

Pogacnik, Marko. *Nature Spirits & Elemental Beings: Working with the Intelligence in Nature*. Forres, Scotland: Findhorn Press, 1996.

Pope, Raphaela, and Elizabeth Morrison. *Wisdom of the Animals: Communication between Animals and the People Who Love Them*. Holbrook, Massachusetts: Adams Media Corporation, 2001.

Quinn, Daniel. *Ishmael*. New York: Bantam, 1992.

Rasmussen, Knud, comp. "Netsilik Eskimo Song," in *Eskimo Songs and Stories: From the Fifth Thule Expedition*. Trans. Edward Field. New York: Delacorte Press, 1973.

Reynolds, Rita M. *Blessing the Bridge: What Animals Teach Us About Death, Dying, and Beyond.* Troutdale, Oregon: New Sage Press, 2001.

Roads, Michael J. *Talking with Nature.* Tiburon, California: H. J. Kramer, 1987.

———. *Journey into Nature.* Tiburon, California: H. J. Kramer, 1990.

———. *Journey into Oneness.* Tiburon, California: H. J. Kramer, 1994.

———. *Into a Timeless Realm.* Tiburon, California: H. J. Kramer, 1995.

Robbins, Dianne. *The Call Goes Out: Messages from the Earth's Cetaceans.* Livermore, California: Oughten House, 1997.

Sams, Jamie, and David Carson. *Medicine Cards: The Discovery of Power through the Ways of Animals.* Santa Fe: Bear & Co., 1988.

Schul, Bill. *Life Song: In Harmony with All Creation.* Walpole, New Hampshire: Stillpoint Publishing, 1994.

Schweitzer, Albert. *Out of My Life and Work.* London: Holt Allen, 1933.

Sekida, Katsuki. *Zen Training.* New York: John Weatherhill, 1975.

Smith, Penelope. *Animal Talk: Interspecies Telepathic Communication.* Point Reyes, California: Pegasus Publications, 1989.

———. *Animals . . . Our Return to Wholeness.* Point Reyes, California: Pegasus Publications, 1993.

St. John, Patricia. *Beyond Words: Unlocking the Secrets to Communicating.* Walpole, New Hampshire: Stillpoint, 1994.

Tobias, Michael, and Kate Solisti-Mattelon, editors. *Kinship with the Animals.* Hillsboro, Oregon: Beyond Words Publishing, 1998.

Turner, Victor. *The Forest of Symbols.* Ithaca, New York: Cornell University Press, 1967.

Van Lippe-Biesterfeld, Irene. *Dialogue with Nature.* Forres, Scotland: Findhorn Press, 1997.

Watson, Burton. *Chuang Tzu: Basic Writings.* New York: Columbia University Press, 1964.

White, E. B. *Charlotte's Web.* New York: Harper & Row, 1952.

Whitman, Walt. *Leaves of Grass.* New York: Viking Press, 1959.

Whitman, Walt. *The Complete Poems.* New York: Penguin Books, 1979.

Wright, Machaelle Small. *Behaving as if the God in All Life Mattered.* Jeffersonton, Virginia: Perelandra Ltd., 1997.

Wyllie, Timothy. *Dolphins, ETs and Angels: Adventures among Spiritual Intelligences.* Santa Fe: Bear & Company, 1992.